SOURCES OF
THE AMERICAN
SOCIAL TRADITION

Volume I

SOURCES OF THE AMERICAN SOCIAL TRADITION

EDITED BY

David J. Rothman

&

Sheila M. Rothman

Basic Books, Inc., Publishers New York

Library of Congress Cataloging in Publication Data

Rothman, David J   comp.
  Sources of the American social tradition,

  Bibliography: p.
  I.   United States—Social conditions—Addresses,
essays, lectures.   I.   Rothman, Sheila M., joint comp.
II.   Title.
HN57.R574   309.1′73   74-78474
ISBN 0-465-08084-7 (v.I)

Printed in the United States of America
DESIGNED BY VINCENT TORRE
10 9 8 7 6

To Matthew
to help him understand that history
is more than the story of great persons

CONTENTS

The New Nation, 1800–1865

IV.   Went to Kansas, 1862
       MIRIAM COLT   147
V.   The San Francisco Vigilance Committee,
       1851   153
VI.   Religion in the United States of America,
       1844
       ROBERT BAIRD   158

Chapter 8 / *The Common School*   163

I.   On the Education of Youth, 1790
       NOAH WEBSTER   165
II.   Report for the Massachusetts Board of
       Education, 1848
       HORACE MANN   169
III.   Reports of the Philadelphia Public Schools,
       1819–1850   172
IV.   School Curriculum and Rules, Cheshire,
       Connecticut, 1826–1827   177
V.   New North American Reader, 1844
       LYMAN COBB   181
VI.   Report of the Pennsylvania Hospital
       for the Insane, 1843   184
VII.   The Mother at Home, 1834
       JOHN ABBOTT   188

Chapter 9 / *The American Art Union*   193

I.   American Art Union Bulletin, 1849   194
II.   Experiences of a Yankee Stonecutter, 1852
       HORATIO GREENOUGH   198
III.   Essay on the American Scenery, 1836
       THOMAS COLE   200
IV.   The Art Idea, 1864
       JAMES JACKSON JARVIS   203
V.   The Letters of Washington Allston,
       1830–1832   206
VI.   The Bunker Hill Monument Association,
       1824   211

Chapter 10 / *Abolitionist Societies*   216

I.   The Philosophy of the Abolition
       Movement, 1853
       WENDELL PHILLIPS   217
II.   Appeal to the Christian Women of the
       South, 1836
       ANGELINA GRIMKÉ   221
III.   Antislavery Manual, 1837
       LAROY SUNDERLAND   226
IV.   Report of the American and Foreign
       Antislavery Society, 1849   230
V.   Narratives of Riots at Alton, 1838
       EDWARD BEECHER   233

SUGGESTIONS FOR FURTHER READING   240

PREFACE

OVER THE PAST several years, teaching and research in American history have undergone a fundamental change. To an unprecedented degree, the discipline has moved from a primary focus on political, diplomatic, and military history to a broader interest in social history. Heretofore, elections, treaties and wars, politicians, ambassadors, and generals tended to dominate the writing and teaching of American history. Now such concerns as social order, social mobility, and ethnicity, the roles of anonymous Americans, women, and immigrants are of major interest. In a sense, the scene has shifted from Washington and the state capitals to the local communities, from legislative halls to families and factories. From all indications, this change is not a passing fancy. Social history has already revised our understanding of the past in such novel and important ways that it is not likely again to be neglected.

It is the aim of this book to bring before students in American history the issues, the questions and answers, that are at the heart of this new perspective. That the book takes the form of a collection of sources reflects several important considerations.

We are well aware of the fact that "documents" have a rather low reputation as teaching tools in history classrooms. But that reputation, we are convinced, is undeserved. Or to put this another way, it reflects the fact that in the past "documents" almost always were political or diplomatic documents. Hence, as a rule, students had already read in texts or in other books about the same document that they then saw in a collection. The Fourteen Points, for example, of Woodrow Wilson were already familiar to them; to read the document itself served only as the occasion to review or to memorize them. Moreover, these types of documents are generally dry and static. To read the legislation we know as the Missouri Compromise tells little about why and how the Compromise was enacted.

Documents in American social history are of a very different quality. First, they are often intrinsically interesting, supplying vivid examples of how persons lived, say, on the frontier, or how they adjusted to life in new immigrant ghettos. Second, and even more important, they enable the students to form ideas of their own, to analyze by themselves the process of change over time. In essence, the sources make the students active, not passive, inviting them to react to materials, not to memorize them.

To these ends, the sources in this book do not approach American history in scattered, hit-or-miss fashion. Rather, we have organized the materials around institutions and around themes that are central to the American experience. The Introduction that follows will present in more detail the intellectual bases for this kind of focus. It suffices to note here that in each chapter, five or six selections will explore in detail the same subject. In this way, students will have the opportunity to put the pieces of the story together, to reach a synthesis of their own. Our hope is that these materials will move the student outward, into the field of American history—that they will open up, not close off, inquiry. Just as the law school case book uses several cases to create an awareness of a general theme, so each of these chapters uses several documents to create an awareness of the crucial elements in the development of American society. We have not attempted to be "complete" in our coverage. We assume that a text or related readings will be used alongside this book. But we have, to facilitate the use of this volume, arranged the materials in chronological fashion; each of the chapters here should fit neatly into the normal sequence of discussion in the American history survey course or in the American social history course. For purposes of clarity and readability, we have modernized spelling and punctuation and have omitted ellipses when we made excerpts from lengthy documents. At no point have we altered the meaning of the original material; our goal throughout has been to make these documents accessible and interesting to the student. At the same time, we have selected for analysis the institution, be it the family or the church or the factory or the department store, at a moment in time when it illuminates a broader trend in American society, or it is itself of such crucial significance as to warrant close attention.

In our own use of these sources in classrooms here and abroad, we have found that they excite and stimulate students. Either in classroom discussions or in smaller section meetings, the sources have encouraged and enabled students to reach for interesting and important themes in the story of America's past. We trust that other teachers will find these selections as useful as we have.

SHEILA M. ROTHMAN
DAVID J. ROTHMAN

New York City

INTRODUCTION

MOST OF US share an instinctive curiosity about the ways that Americans before us lived their lives. We wonder how our predecessors organized their households, how they dressed and ate, how they conducted their friendships, courtships, and marriages, how they reared and educated their children, how they amused themselves, and how they earned their livings. What was it really like for frontier settlers to inhabit the wilderness, for immigrants to walk paved streets in strange cities? What was it like to be an ordinary American at different times in our past? These are simple questions, but they exert a powerful appeal to our imagination.

Despite the inherently interesting character of these inquiries, historians have been notably reluctant to pursue them. Until very recently, the craft of history has focused almost exclusively on great events and exceptional personalities. Presidential elections, diplomatic maneuvers, military contests, Congressional politics—these subjects have dominated, almost monopolized, the writing and teaching of history. This choice is not difficult to understand. History is the story of change, the account of how a society moves from one point in its development to another. In order to pursue this theme, historians have traditionally focused on the top, on the obviously important decision makers, and then looked down to the rest of society for implications of their actions. As a result, the story of the American Revolution becomes essentially a chronicle of the activities and ideas of political elites here and in England; the coming of the Civil War is understood first and foremost in terms of national party structure and leadership. American history becomes the story of George Washington and John Adams, Abraham Lincoln and Stephan Douglas. The lives of ordinary Americans, by comparison, seem unimportant and irrelevant.

Since the most scholarly and professional historians did not bother to satisfy our curiosity about anonymous Americans, the amateurs did. Eager to bring this important information to light, these amateur historians all too often were content to present a haphazard collection of quaint stories. This is how colonial women dressed, this is how their children played, this is what they ate. They reported on charming old customs and offered a string of curiosities. In many ways, our forefathers became our "most unforgettable characters." But this kind of approach, unfortunately, gave us little understanding of why earlier styles of life differed so dramatically from our own. Even more important, it made no effort to link its catalogue of customs to the problem of historical change. In these pages, too, ordinary Americans seemed irrelevant to the major events in our past.

Over the past several years, a growing number of historians have attempted to break out of this mold, to inform us about the bottom as well as the top layers of society and, at the same time, to show us how crucial their contributions have been to historical change. The goals of this new social history are twofold. First, it insists that to understand change one must look beyond the role of the elite, beyond the activities of leaders in business and politics. No shift, for example, was more important to America's history than the change from an agrarian to an industrial economy, from a nation of small farms to one of large factories. It will not do, insist social historians, to analyze this phenomenon exclusively in terms of the robber barons or entrepreneurs who organized the first factories, railroads, and oil combines. Rather, one must look also to the workers who operated the machines or extracted the mineral resources from the ground. Why were they willing to take on these tasks? Where did they come from—native farms or European villages? How did they adjust to the new rhythm of industrial work? How did they struggle with their lot? Did their struggles advance or retard industrial progress? Only by answering these questions can the full story of change be mapped and understood.

Second, social history is determined to expand its focus to encompass all levels of society. Traditional studies of political or economic elites invariably isolated their materials—the realm of politics seems to have little to do with the realm of business. In a sense, these historians constructed a "political man," one who held office or bargained for power in the caucus rooms as if politics were all he knew and all he was—as if the politician was not a member of an ethnic group, an economic class, or a church. The goal of social history is to bring these several considerations together, to integrate rather than to particularize.

To this end, social history focuses on the institutions of society, the organizations that crucially influence and shape individual behavior, that to a large degree determine the way people act and think. Institutions in this sense are the organizations that take individual pieces and shape them into a common mold. Whether it be the school, the family, the church, or the factory, the institution trains its members in common styles of behavior. Social history is not as concerned with the psychological or biological variations among people as it is with the ways that they learn to act together. If biography is mainly interested in the special attributes and contributions of one person, social history is concerned with the special qualities and attributes of the group. The group can be those in school together, those on the assembly line together, or those sitting around the dining-room table together. From this perspective, society is made up of a collection of institutions; the task of social history is to analyze how each of them influences individual behavior and how they operate together to give a unity to people's lives and experiences.

Think for a moment of the impact of institutions on our own lives; it immediately becomes apparent how important institutions must have been to the lives of our predecessors. Think of how much of our ordinary behavior reflects lessons we have learned within the family. Or think of the school, not its instruction in reading or writing, but its transmission of a code of behavior, the rules that will guide us in public conduct. The church, too, is an institution of major importance— it carefully and insistently defines acceptable and unacceptable styles of action. The factory is no less an institution; it instructs workers and managers alike in right and wrong behavior, establishing not only work habits but life habits as well. Hence, if one is to understand the way that people behaved in the past, the best starting point is to examine the institutions that dominated their lives.

Once social history accepts institutions as its cast of characters, many important issues immediately present themselves. In any given era, which institutions exerted the most crucial influences? The hierarchy visible today would offer little guide to the past. We might not list the church as one of the most important institutions now, but surely we could not omit it from an analysis of seventeenth-century society. Once we have a sense of the hierarchy of institutions for a period in our past, we can alert ourselves to the emergence of new institutions, and try to understand the causes and implications of such changes. When did the school begin to rival the family in importance? What difference did it make to the family that the factory became the central workplace, giving out its own special messages? This focus on institutions permits us to analyze the degree of agreement and disagreement among the institutions, offering us a broad view of the entire society.

In fact, this institutional focus allows us to understand better the problems of social order and disorder in American society. A tight bond among citizens is forged when they all follow the rules set down and established for them by institutions. If everyone plays the game by the same rules, the stability of the society is promoted. Common expectations and common practices become preeminent. Hence, an institutional focus in social history allows us to observe the ways by which American society has attempted to achieve consensus among its members. This approach also illuminates the sources of discontent and disorder; conflict is no less central to the story of American history than is consensus. When different institutions transmit fundamentally opposing messages, we have located a source of tension that can reveal both the particular points of conflict and the more general issue of social cohesion. When a religious institution tells its members to give alms to the poor and tries to moderate the thrust for profits by instilling a sense of obligation to others, and at the same time marketplace institutions urge people to be thrifty in order to invest and to make as handsome a profit as possible, we have a dynamic that surely will be relevant to political factionalism, economic conflict, and religious dissension. This example comes right out of early Massachusetts history, as we shall see when we read the will of a Puritan merchant, Robert Keayne.

Ultimately, social history is concerned with such things as the nature of courtship patterns, education, and church going, not simply because they are intrinsically interesting, but because of the light they shed on the larger questions of social order and social change. The details are both revelatory and significant. The selections that follow reflect this judgment. The documents are interesting in themselves, and therefore one's curiosity about life on the frontier or life in a factory will be satisfied. But the larger implications of these bits of information should emerge as well. The materials are organized by institutions, and they are designed to illuminate the workings of the major institutions that have shaped American society. From the Puritan church in the colonial period, to the factory and plantation in the antebellum period, to the department store and immigrant ghetto in the late nineteenth century, to the family in the 1920s, and to the relief office in the 1930s, down to the black ghetto and counterculture commune of our own day, the history of America's institutions may inspire an ongoing fascination with the nature and substance of American social history.

American Colonial Society, 1607–1800

THE PROPER PLANTATION

THE PURITAN CHURCH

THE COLONIAL FAMILY

THE REVOLUTIONARY CROWD

INTRODUCTION

THE FIRST English settlers in the New World confidently expected to transplant their own particular institutions intact into their new environment. The adventurers in Virginia in 1607 wished to establish trading enterprises resembling those that had succeeded so well in other parts of the world, especially Ireland and India. Puritan newcomers to Massachusetts, while determined to improve on some English practices, also anticipated duplicating many of the political and social arrangements that were typical of England in the seventeenth century. But in fact no simple transfer of institutions took place. Time and again, New World conditions modified European customs. The wilderness did not prove to be hospitable soil for Old World programs.

American social history in the colonial period is in many ways the story of traditional European institutions undergoing change, of surprising and unanticipated results from the most carefully calculated plans. This theme emerges vividly in the experience of the Virginia settlement. The Virginia Company had a very clear idea of how it would profit from New World wealth: the *proper plantation*, a fortified trading post, would enable the company men to skim off the riches of the wilderness. But reality did not follow expectation. An outpost quickly became a colony; a military organization became a complex society. And with that story, American social history properly begins.

The Puritans also carried across the ocean an elaborate design for the new commonwealth, but invariably the New World experience upset their plans. Their goal was nothing less than to show their Anglican brethren the error of their religious ways. But here the *Puritan church* had to confront a series of unexpected challenges. In the end, this church was one of the most important institutions in the community, influencing the behavior of members and nonmembers alike. To understand the nature of public order in Massachusetts, one must analyze the workings of the church. For all its power, this institution was a hybrid whose exact shape and structure came as a surprise to its originators.

Another institution of major significance in ordering seventeenth- and eighteenth-century American communities was the *family*. But again, the organization of the family in the New World differed in many ways from its European counterpart. The family's role in main-

3

taining public order expanded, perhaps because many other institutions existed here in only a rudimentary state. To understand the stability of American colonial society, as well as the ways by which New World conditions altered European institutions, the changes in family organization demand close scrutiny.

Finally, the structure of American society emerges vividly in the crisis of the Revolution. This was a time of testing, a period when traditional lines of authority were severed and new ones were established. No institution presented a more dramatic challenge to everyday political life than the *Revolutionary crowd*. The ways it functioned and the ways citizens understood its role reveal just how different American society was from European society by the outbreak of the Revolution.

Chapter I

The Proper Plantation

THE INITIAL SETTLEMENT of the English at Jamestown, Virginia, in 1607, was anything but a glorious adventure. The first encounter with the New World was brutal and debilitating; the mortality rate among the arrivals was high, and those who survived lived dangerously close to savagery. The English were unprepared for what they found and were hard put to deal with it. Their intention had been to reap an easy and quick profit from the resources of the New World. They planned to mine the wealth of America, not to establish a permanent rural society. But their grandoise expectations were soon disappointed. As they tried to adjust they moved, unthinkingly but steadily, to a new design. By 1624, after incredible hardships and disappointments, and to many people's genuine surprise, there was actually an ongoing agricultural settlement in Virginia.

The organizing spirit of the Jamestown enterprise was the Virginia Company, a joint-stock company chartered by the Crown with exclusive rights to the land and minerals of the territory. The capital for the venture came from selling shares to the public; the Crown, while encouraging the enterprise, was unwilling to fund it. Instead, Englishmen eager to accumulate a profit, anxious to see their flag fly over New World territory, or determined to spread the gospel of Christ to the heathens in foreign parts bought the company shares. Here was an enterprise that would bring wealth to its investors, glory to England, and Christianity to the Indians.

The Virginia Company set out to accomplish these goals by establishing a *proper plantation*, that is, a fortified trading post. All comers to Virginia were employees of the Virginia Company and were obliged to labor in its behalf in return for a share of the profits. From this trading post the company workers were to venture forth into the wilderness and gather in the riches of the new land. Remembering how the Spanish explorers had first discovered temples of gold in Mexico and Peru and then enslaved a well-organized band of natives to work

5

the mines, the company hoped to repeat the experience and reap similar rewards. The natives in Virginia would show them to the gold and, where necessary, dig it up.

In the spirit of this plan, the Englishmen decided to make their base at Jamestown. It was a swampy area, with land hardly fit for cultivation. But it was well situated on a river, and therefore easy to defend and ideal for making trading trips into the interior. Obviously, no member of the Virginia Company in 1607 intended to transplant English society here. On the contrary, this was to be a quasi-military adventure. Living on the edge of the New World, they would exploit it.

Unhappily for the company, there were no temples of gold in Virginia, nor any tractable Indian tribes ready to make up labor gangs. And there was no obvious commodity that could be loaded onto ships and sold profitably in England. As a result, the company found it impossible to reap a return on its investment. Moreover, having anticipated immediate wealth and regular commerce between Jamestown and London, the company had made few preparations for self-sustaining agricultural activities. Soon the band at Jamestown was facing the most elementary problems of survival. In 1609, when the company treasury in London was low and supply boats were late in coming, the Virginia adventurers suffered starvation, to the point where instances of cannibalism occurred. Clearly the organization at Jamestown was floundering badly.

Under the pressure of these circumstances, the company changed tactics. Recognizing that the only thing of value the company owned in the New World was the land itself, it began urging English settlers to emigrate. In 1618, for the first time, the company tried to attract families, not adventurers, to the colony. To this end they held out the promise of land ownership, a comparatively rare condition among lower-class Englishmen. Their hope, in return, was to make a profit from the land taxes. A kind of company store, which would sell provisions to the settlers, would also prosper. In this way the company transformed Virginia from a trading post into a colony. Its goal changed from exploitation to settlement. In one sense, the company did succeed; settlers came and the colony started to grow. But the company could not make its profit. Taxes had to be kept very low or else Englishmen could not make the trip to the New World. As subsistence farmers began to raise their own commodities, they had less and less occasion to buy provisions from the company store. And there was still no crop raised in Virginia that could bring handsome profits in England; although some farmers experimented with growing tobacco, no one as yet was very enthusiastic about the crop. By 1624, the company was bankrupt and the Crown took over control of the colony. But if one enterprise was dead another had been born. The colony in Virginia was well rooted and would continue to expand. American society had begun to develop.

I

The several motives of Englishmen in supporting the colonization of the New World emerge clearly in this pamphlet advertising the glories of Virginia. Since the venture had the approval, but not the financial backing, of the Crown, the joint-stock company had to raise money by selling shares to the general public; in pursuing this goal, it tried to appeal to the widest audience. Thus, this tract plays skillfully upon the patriotism of the English, on their Christianity, and on their desire, as investors, for a good profit. In all, the response to this well-drawn argument was generous. And even when the infant colony suffered setbacks, investors continued to put up funds.

NOVA BRITANNIA, 1609

The country itself is large and great assuredly, though as yet, no exact discovery can be made of all. It is also commendable and hopeful every way, the air and climate most sweet and wholesome, and very agreeable to our nature. It is inhabited with wild and savage people, that live and lie up and down in troupes like herds of deer in a forest; they have no law but nature, their apparel, skins of beasts, but most go naked; the better sort have houses, but poor ones; they have no arts nor sciences, yet they live under superior command such as it is; they are generally very loving and gentle, and do entertain and relieve our people with great kindness; the land yieldeth naturally for the sustenance of man, abundance of fish, infinite store of deer, and hares, with many fruits and roots.

There are valleys and plains streaming with sweet springs, there are hills and mountains making a sensible proffer of hidden treasure, never yet searched; the land is full of minerals, plenty of woods; the soil is strong and sends out naturally fruitful vines running upon trees, and shrubs: it yields also resin, turpentine, pitch and tar, sassafras, mulberry trees and silkworms, many skins and rich furs, many sweet woods, and costly dyes; plenty of sturgeon, timber for shipping. But of this that I have said, if bare nature be so amiable in its naked kind, what may be hope, when art and nature both shall join and strive together, to give best content to man and beast? As now in handling the several parts propounded, I shall show in order as they lie.

For the first how it may tend to advance the kingdom of God, by reducing savage people from their blind superstition to the light of religion, when some object, we seek nothing less than the cause of God, being led on by our own private ends, and secondly how we can warrant

Originally entitled "Nova Britannia, Offering Most Excellent Fruits by Planting in Virginia" (London, 1609). Reprinted in *Tracts and Other Papers Relating Principally to the Colonies in North America*, ed. Peter Force (Washington, D.C., 1836–1844), vol. I, pp. 11–17.

a supplantation of those Indians, or an invasion into their right and possessions.

But we must beware that under this pretense that bitter root of greedy gain be not so settled in our hearts, if it fall not out presently to our expectation, we slink away with discontent, and draw our purses from the charge. What must be our direction then, no more but this: if thou do once approve the work, lay thy hand to it cheerfully, and withdraw it not till task be done, for here lies the poison of all good attempts; when as men without hauling and pulling will not be drawn to performance, for by this others are discouraged, the action lies undone, and the first experience is lost. But are we to look for no gain in the adventures? Yes, undoubtedly, there is assured hope of gain but look it be not chief in your thoughts; God that has said by Solomon— Cast thy bread upon the waters, and after many days thou shalt find it—He will give the blessing. And as for supplanting the savages, we have no such intent: Our intrusion into their possessions shall tend to their great good, and no way to their hurt, unless as unbridled beasts, they procure it to themselves. We purpose to proclaim and make it known to them all, by some public interpretation, that our coming hither is to plant ourselves in their country; yet not to supplant and root them out, but to bring them from their base condition to a far better: First, in regard of God the Creator, and of Jesus Christ their Redeemer, if they will believe in Him. And secondly, in respect of earthly blessing, whereof they have now no comfortable use, but in beastly brutish manner, with promise to defend them against all public and private enemies.

We require nothing at their hands, but a quiet residence to us and ours, that by our own labor and toil, we may work this good unto them and recompense our own adventures, costs, and travels in the end; wherein, they shall be most friendly welcome to join their labors with ours, and shall enjoy equal privileges with us, in whatsoever good success, time or means may bring to pass. To which purpose, we may verily believe that God has reserved in this last age of the world, an infinite number of those lost and scattered sheep, to be won and recovered by our means.

But for my second point propounded, the honor of our King, by enlarging his kingdoms, to prove how this may tend to that, no argument of mine can make it so manifest, as the same is clear in itself.

And upon good warrant I speak it here in private, what by these new discoveries into the Western parts, and our hopeful settling in chief places of the East, with our former known trades in other parts of the world, I do not doubt (by the help of God) but I may live to see the days (if merchants have their due encouragement) that the wisdom, Majesty, and Honor of our King shall be spread and enlarged to the ends of the world, our navigations mightily increased, and his Majesty's customs more than trebled.

And as for the general sort that shall go to be planters, be they never so poor, so they be honest, and take pains, the place will make them rich; all kinds of artificers we must first employ, to make it fit all necessaries, for comfort and use of the colony, and for such as are of no trades (if they be industrious) they shall have there employment enough for there is a world of means to set many thousands awork, partly in such things as I mentioned before, and many other profitable works, for no man must live idle there.

And by this employment, we may happily stop the course of those irregular youths of no religion, that daily run from us to Rome and Rhemes for exhibition, which after a little hammering and training there by Parson and his imps, they become pliable for the impression of any villainy whatsoever, as appears by their positions and practices at home and abroad.

And hereby our mariners shall not lie idle, nor our owners sell their ships for want of freight: you know how many good ships are daily sold, and made away to foreign nations; how many men for want of employment, betake themselves to Tunis, Spain, and Florence, and to serve in courses not warrantable, which would better beseem, our own walls and borders to be spread with such branches, than their native country.

The thing to make this plantation is money, to be raised among the adventurers, [stockholders] wherein the sooner and more deeply men engage themselves, their charge will be the shorter, and their gain the greater.

First you shall understand that his Majesty has granted us an enlargement of our charter, with many ample privileges, wherein we have knights and gentlemen of good place, named for the King's Council of Virginia to govern us. As also every planter and adventurer shall be inserted in the patent by name. This ground being laid, we purpose presently to make supply of men, women, and children (so many as we can) to make the plantation. We call those planters that go in their persons to dwell there and those adventurers that adventure their money and go not in person, and both do make the members of one colony. We do account twelve pound ten shillings to be a single share adventured. Every ordinary man or woman, if they will go and dwell there, and every child above ten years that shall be carried thither to remain, shall be allowed for each of their persons a single share, as if they had adventured twelve pound ten shillings in money. Every extraordinary man, as divines, governors, ministers of state and justice, gentlemen, physicians, and such as be men of worth for special services, are all to go as planters, and to execute their several functions in the colony, and are to be maintained at the common charge, and are to receive their dividend (as others do) at seven years end, and they are to be agreed with all before they go, and to be rated by the council, according to the value of their persons, which shall be set down and registered in a book, that it may always appear what people have gone to the plantation, at what time they went, and how their persons were valued. And likewise, if any that go to be planters will lay down money to the treasurer, it shall be also registered and their shares enlarged accordingly, be it for more or less. All charges of settling and maintaining the plantation and of making supplies shall be born in a joint stock of the adventurers for seven years; we supply from here at our own charge all necessary food and apparel, for fortifying and building of houses in a joint stock, so they are also to return from thence the increase and fruits of their labors, for the use and advancement of the same joint stock, till the end of seven years; at which time we purpose (God willing) to make a division by commissioners appointed, of all the lands granted unto us by his Majesty, to every of the colony, according to each man's several adventure, agreeing with our register book, which we doubt not will be for every share of twelve pound ten shillings, five hundred acres at least. And as for the value and little worth now of those grounds in Virginia, we know that in England within these thirty or forty years, the yearly rent of those grounds (in many places) were not worth five shillings, that now go for forty or more.

II

The anticipation among the company leaders that the 1607 expedition would quickly and easily skim off the wealth of the New World is apparent in this list of those first participating in the venture. The occupations of these men, as well as the absence in the list of women and children, make clear that it was to be a trading company operation, not the start of a colony. The second document— a call for new recruits—composed in 1609, represents something of a shift in company thinking. They were now beginning to think more in terms of self-sufficiency among the adventurers. Still, it is clear that trade and not settlement was uppermost in their minds.

THE VIRGINIA COMPANY LIST OF ADVENTURERS, 1607

The names of them that were the first planters, were these following.*

Counselors
Mr. Edward Maria Wingfield
Capt. Bartholomew Gosnoll
Capt. John Smyth
Capt. John Rat[c]liffe
Capt. John Martin
Capt. George Kendall

Gentlemen
Thomas Sands
John Robinson
Ustis Clovill
Kellam Throgmorton
Nathaniel Powell

Robert Behethland
Jeremy Alicock
Thomas Studley
Richard Crofts
Nicholas Houlgrace
Thomas Webbe
John Waler
William Tankard
Francis Snarsbrough
Edward Brookes
Richard Dixon
John Martin
George Martin
Anthony Gosnold

* With diverse others to the number of 105.
In *Narratives of Early Virginia, 1606–1625*, ed. Lyon Gardiner Tyler (New York, 1907), pp. 125–26.

Thomas Wotton
Thomas Gore
Francis Midwinter

Carpenters
William Laxon
Edward Pising
Tho. Emry
Rob. Small

Anas Todkill
John Capper

Gentlemen
Mr. Robert Hunt, *Preacher*
Mr. George Percie
Anthony Gosnoll
Capt. Gabriell Archer
Robert Ford
William Bruster
Dru Pickhouse
John Brookes

James Read, *Blacksmith*
Jonas Profit, *Sailor*
Tho. Couper, *Barber*
John Herd, *Bricklayer*

William Garret, *Bricklayer*
Edward Brinto, *Mason*
William Love, *Tailor*
Nic. Skot, *Drummer*

Laborers
John Laydon
William Cassen
George Cassen
Tho. Cassen
William Rods
William White
Ould Edward
Henry Tavin
George Golding
John Dods
William Johnson
Will. Unger

Will. Wilkinson, *Surgeon*

Boys
Samuell Collier
Nat. Pecock
James Brumfield
Rich. Mutton

THE CALL FOR NEW RECRUITS, 1609

To render a more particular satisfaction and account of our care, in providing to attend the *Right Honourable the Lord de la Warr*, in this concluded and present supply, men of most use and necessity to the *Foundation* of a *Commonwealth*; and to avoid both the scandal and peril of accepting idle and wicked persons; such as shame or fear compels into this action; and such as are the weeds and rankness of

In *The Genesis of the United States*, ed. Alexander Brown (New York, 1890), vol. 1, pp. 352–53.

this land; who being the surfeit of an able, healthy, and composed body must need be the poison of one so tender, feeble, and as yet unformed: and to divulge and declare to all men what kind of persons, as well for their religion and conversations, as faculties, arts, and trades, we propose to accept of—we have thought it convenient to pronounce that for the first provision, we will receive no man that cannot bring or render some good testimony of his religion to God, and civil manners and behavior to his neighbor, with whom he hath lived; and for the second, we have set down in a table annexed, the proportion and number we will entertain in every necessary art, upon proof and assurance, that every man shall be able to perform that which he doth undertake, whereby such as are requisite to us may have knowledge and preparation, to offer themselves, and we shall be ready to give honest entertainment and content, and to recompense with extraordinary reward every fit and industrious person, respectively *to his pains and quality.*

The table of such as are required to *this plantation.*

4.	Honest and learned Ministers	4.	Brickmakers
2.	Surgeons	2.	Tile-makers
2.	Druggists	10.	Fishermen
10.	Iron men for the Furnace and Hammer	6.	Fowlers
2.	Armorers	4.	Sturgeon dressers and preservers of Caviar
2.	Gun-founders	2.	Salt-makers
6.	Blacksmiths	6.	Coopers
10.	Sawyers	2.	Collar-makers for draught
6.	Carpenters	2.	Plowrights
6.	Shipwrights	4.	Rope-makers
6.	Gardeners	6.	Vine-dressers
4.	Turners	2.	Press-makers

2. *Joiners*	2. *Silk-dressers*
2. *Soap-ash men*	2. *Pearl Drillers*
4. *Pitch Boilers*	2. *Bakers*
2. *Mineral men*	2. *Brewers*
2. *Planters of Sugarcane*	2. *Colliers*

III

The daily routine of life in Virginia under company rule was a military one. The men, as employees of the company, did not own any of their own property. Rather, they were housed, fed, and clothed by the company and were expected to obey its every rule. The company's head in Virginia was an officer in charge of the ranks, enjoying vast powers. Below are the rules governing the residents of the Virginia colony in 1610–1611—and they demonstrate with remarkable clarity how far from a rural society the proper plantation was.

ARTICLES, LAWS, AND ORDERS FOR VIRGINIA, 1611

Whereas his Majesty like himself a most zealous Prince hath in his own realms a principal care of true religion and reverence to God, and hath always strictly commanded his generals and governors, with all his forces wheresoever, to let their ways be like his ends, for the glory of God.

And foreasmuch as no good service can be performed, or were well managed, where military discipline is not observed, and military discipline cannot be kept where the rules or chief parts thereof be not certainly set down and generally known, I do now publish them to all persons in the colony, that they may as well take knowledge of the laws themselves, as of the penalty and punishment, which without partiality shall be inflicted upon the breakers of the same.

First, since we owe our highest and supreme duty, our greatest, and all our allegiance to Him from whom all power and authority is derived, we must alone expect our success from Him who is only the blesser of all good attempts, the King of kings. I do strictly command and charge all captains and officers to have a care that the Almighty God be duly and daily served, and that they call upon their people to hear sermons, as that also they diligently frequent morning and evening prayer themselves by their own example and daily life, and duty herein, encouraging others thereunto, and that such, who shall often and will-

Originally entitled "Articles, Laws, and Orders . . . for the Colony in Virginia" (London, 1611). Reprinted in *Tracts and Other Papers Relating Principally to the Colonies in North America* (Washington, D.C., 1836–1844), vol. 3, pp. 9–13, 56–62.

fully absent themselves, be duly punished according to the martial law in that case provided.

That no man speak impiously or maliciously against the holy and blessed Trinity, God the Son, and God the Holy Ghost, or against the known Articles of the Christian faith, upon pain of death.

No man shall use any traitorous words against his Majesty's person, or royal authority upon pain of death.

No man shall speak any word, or do any act, which may tend to the derision of God's holy word upon pain of death.

Every man and woman duly twice a day upon the first tolling of the bell shall upon the working days repair unto the Church, to hear divine service upon pain of losing his or her day's allowance for the first omission, for the second to be whipped, and for the third to be condemned to the galleys for six months. Likewise no man or woman shall dare to violate or break the Sabbath by any gaming, or private abroad, or at home, but duly sanctify and observe the same, both himself and his family, by preparing themselves at home with private prayer, that they may be the better filled for the public.

No manner of person whatsoever shall dare to detract, slander, calumniate, or utter unseemly and unfitting speeches, either against his Majesty or against the committees, assistants unto the counsel, or against the zealous endeavors, and intentions of the whole body of adventurers for this pious and Christian plantation.

No manner of person whatsoever, contrary to the word of God, shall detract, slander, calumniate, murmur, mutiny, resist, disobey, or neglect the commandments, either of the Lord Governor and Captain General, the Lieutenant General, the Marshall, the counsel or any authorized captain, commander, or public officer, upon pain for the first time so offending to be whipped three several times, and upon his knees to acknowledge his offense, for the second time so offending to be condemned to the galley for three years; and for the third time so offending to be punished with death.

No man shall rifle or despoil, by force or violence, take away anything from any Indian coming to trade, or otherwise, upon pain of death.

There shall no captain, master, mariner, sailor, or anyone else of what quality or condition soever, belonging to any ship or ships, at this time remaining, or which shall hereafter arrive within this our river, bargain, buy, truck, or trade with any one member in this colony, man, woman, or child for any tool or instrument of iron, steel, or what else.

Instructions of the Marshall for the Better Enabling of a Private Soldier to the Executing of His Duty in This Present Colony

June 22, 1611.

It is requisite that he who will enter into this function of a soldier, that he dedicate himself wholly for the planting and establishing of true religion, the honor of his Prince, the safety of his country, and to learn the art which he professes, which is in this place to hold war and the service requisite to the subsisting of a colony. There be many men of mean descent, who have this way attained to great dignity, credit, and honor.

Having thus dedicated himself with a constant resolution, he ought to be diligent, careful, vigilant, and obedient, and principally to have the fear of God and his honor in greatest esteem.

He must be careful to serve God privately and publicly; for all professions are there unto tied, that carry hope with them to prosper, and none more highly than the soldier, for he is ever in the mouth of death, and certainly he that is thus religiously armed, fights more confidently and with greater courage.

He must not set his mind overgreedily upon his belly and continual feeding, but rest himself contented with such provisions as may be conveniently provided, by his own labor purchase, or his means reach unto; above all things he must eschew that detestable vice of drunkenness.

He must be true-hearted to his captain and obey him and the rest of the officers of the camp, town, or fort with great respect, for by the very oath which he takes he does bind himself and promises to serve his Prince, and obey his officers: for the true order of war is fitly resembled to true religion ordained of God, which binds the soldier to observe justice, loyalty, faith, constance, patience, silence, and, above all, obedience, through the which is easily obtained the perfection in arms.

He shall continue at his work until the drum beats and that his captain, his officer, or overseers of the work, gives order unto a cessation for the time, and for the same purpose attends to lead him in, whom he shall orderly and comely follow into the camp, town, or fort, by his said captain, officer, or overseer him meeting, to be conducted unto the

church to hear divine service, after which he may repay to his house
or lodging to prepare for his dinner, and to repose him until the drum
shall call him forth again in the afternoon, when so (as before) he
shall accompany his chief officer unto the field, or where else the work
lies, and there to follow his easy task until again the drum beats to
return home; at which time according as in the forenoon, he shall
follow his chief officer unto the church to hear divine service and after
dispose of himself as he shall best please, and as his own business shall
require.

IV

*By 1618, the company realized that its original goals could not be
fulfilled and they therefore moved to encourage permanent settlement. They instituted a headright system, guaranteeing fifty acres
of land to any Englishman who paid his own way over to the New
World, and an additional fifty acres for every person he brought
with him. They also tried to make conditions as attractive as
possible, to enhance the likelihood of settlement. Among other
things, they founded a House of Burgesses, so that traditional
English political practices would take hold here. As the letter from
the company to Virginia's officials makes clear, a vitally important
shift had occurred in the relationship between the company and
its constituents. In 1609–1610, when exploitation of Virginia's
wealth had been the primary goal, military discipline was encouraged. Now that settlement was the goal, no concession was too
great to make conditions more attractive for would-be emigrants.
For the first time, women and marriage play a role in the story.*

LETTER TO THE GOVERNOR IN VIRGINIA, 1622

There come now over in this ship, and are immediately to follow in
some others many hundreds of people, to whom as we here think
ourselves bound to give the best encouragement for their going, there is
no way left to increase the plantation, but by abundance of private
undertakers; so we think you obliged to give all possible furtherance
and assistance, for the good entertaining and well settling of them, that
they may both thrive and prosper and others by their welfare be drawn
after them. This is the way that we conceive most effectual for the
engaging of this state, and securing of Virginia, for in the multitude of
people is the strength of a kingdom. The allotting out of the settling
of private persons, we leave unto your wisdom and judgment; not doubt-

Originally entitled "Letter to the Governor and Council in Virginia," August
12, 1622, by the Treasurer and Council for the Virginia Company. In *Records
of the Virginia Company of London*, ed. S. M. Kingsbury (Washington, D.C.,
1933), vol. 3, pp. 492–94.

ing but you will find out some course as shall give content to reasonable minds; not suffering any to plant or set down anywhere but with so sufficient a number of able men and well provided, as may, not in their own, but in your judgments (who shall be therefore accountable), defend themselves from any assaults of the Indians. In which regard, as also for their better civil government, we think it fit that the houses and buildings be so contrived together as may make if not handsome towns yet compact and orderly villages; that this is the most proper and successful manner of proceeding in new plantations.

We send you in this ship one widow and eleven maids for wives for the people in Virginia: there hath been especial care had in the choice of them; for there hath not any one of them been received but upon good commendations. We pray you all therefore in general to take them into your care; and more especially we recommend that at their first landing they may be housed, lodged, and provided for of diet till they be married; for such was the haste of sending them away, as that straightened with time we had no means to put provisions aboard. And in case they cannot be presently married we desire they may be put to several households that have wives till they can be provided of husbands. There are nearly fifty more which are shortly to come, are sent by certain worthy gentlemen, who taking into their consideration that the plantation can never flourish till families be planted, and the respect of wives and children fix the people on the soil. Therefore have given this fair beginning: for the reimbursing of whose charges it is ordered that every man that marries them give 120 weight of the best leaf tobacco for each of them, and in case any of them die, that proportion must be advanced to it upon those that survive. That marriage be free according to the law of nature, yet would we not have these maids deceived and married to servants, but only to such free men or tenants as have means to maintain them. We pray you therefore to be fathers to them in this business, not enforcing them to marry against their wills; neither send we them to be servants, save in case of extremity, for we would have their condition so much bettered as multitudes may be allured thereby to come unto you. And you may assure such men as marry those women that the first servants sent over by the company shall be consigned to them; it being our intent to preserve families, and to prefer married men before single persons.

V

The persistent inability of the company to return a profit to its investors bred bad feeling among its more influential investors. In the early 1620s, investigating committees went over to Virginia to discover who was to blame for the poor financial condition. Charges promoted countercharges, and company officials busily defended themselves. In 1622, there occurred the proverbial straw that broke the company's back: an Indian massacre of many of its settlers. An

uproar immediately broke out. Why had the company been unable
to prevent this or to protect itself? Officials, in the document below,
tried to respond, but they were clearly on the defensive. (Compare
the tone of this reply to that of the 1609 document, Nova Britannia.*)*
Within two years, the company was bankrupt and disbanded; but
the settlers in Virginia remained, and the colony's roots were firmly
established.

THE STATE OF THE COLONY IN VIRGINIA, 1622

That all men may see the impartial ingenuity of this discourse, we freely confess, that the country is not so good, as the natives are bad, whose barbarous selves need more cultivation then the ground itself, being more overspread with incivility and treachery, than that with briars. For the land, being tilled and used well by us, deceive not our expectation but rather exceeded it far, being so thankful as to return a hundred for one. But the savages, though never a nation used so kindly upon so small desert, have instead of that harvest which our pains merited, returned nothing but briars and thorns, pricking even to death many of their benefactors. Yet doubt we not, but that as all wickedness is crafty to undo itself, so these also have more wounded themselves than us, God Almighty making way for severity there, where a fair gentleness would not take place. The occasion whereof thus I relate from thence.

The last May there came a letter from Sir Francis Wiat Governor in Virginia, which did advertise that when in November last he arrived in Virginia and entered upon his government, he found the country settled in a peace (as all men there thought), sure and unviolable, not only because it was solemnly ratified and sworn, but as being advantageous to both parts; to the savages as the weaker, under which they were safely sheltered and defended; to us, as being the easiest way then thought to pursue and advance our projects of buildings, plantings, and effecting their conversion by peaceable and fair means. And such was the conceit of firm peace and amity as that there was seldom or never a sword worn, by which assurance of security. The plantations of particular adventurers and planters were placed scatteringly and stragglingly as a choice vein of rich ground invited them, and the further from neighbors held the better. The houses generally set open to the savages, who were always friendly entertained at the tables of the English, and commonly lodged in their bedchambers. The old planters (as they thought now come to reap the benefit of their long travels) placed with wonderful content upon their private lands, and their familiarity with the natives, seeming to open a fair gate for their conversion to Christianity.

The country being in this estate, an occasion was ministered of sending to Opachankano, the King of these savages, about the middle of March last, what time the messenger returned back with these words

Originally entitled "A Declaration of the State of the Colonie and Affairs in Virginia" (London, 1622). Reprinted in *Records of the Virginia Company of London* (Washington, D.C., 1933), vol. 3, pp. 549–51, 555–57.

from him, that he held the peace concluded so firm as the sky should sooner fall than it dissolve. Yea, such was the treacherous dissimulation of that people who then had contrived our destruction, that even two days before the massacre, some of our men were guided through the woods by them in safety. Yea, they borrowed our own boats to convey themselves across the river (on the banks of both sides whereof all our plantations were) to consult of the devilish murder that ensued, and of our utter extirpation, which God of His mercy (by the means of themselves converted to Christianity) prevented. And as well on the Friday morning (the fatal day) the twenty-second of March, as also in the evening, as on other days before, they came unarmed into our houses, without bows or arrows, or other weapons, with deer, turkey, fish, fur, and other provisions to sell and trade with us for glass, beads, and other trifles. Yet in some places, they sat down at breakfast with our people at their tables, whom immediately with their own tools and weapons either laid down, or standing in their houses, they basely and barbarously murdered, not sparing either age or sex, man, woman, or child, so sudden in their cruel execution that few or none discerned the weapon or blow that brought them to destruction. In which manner they also slew many of our people then at their several work and husbandries in the fields, and without their houses, some in planting corn and tobacco, some in gardening, some in making brick, building, sawing, and other kinds of husbandry, they well knowing in what places and quarters each of our men were, in regard of their daily familiarity and resort to us for trading and other negotiations, which the more willingly was by us continued and cherished for the desire we had of effecting that great masterpiece of works, their conversion. And by this means that fatal Friday morning, there fell under the bloody and barbarous hands of that perfidious and inhuman people, contrary to all laws of God and men, of nature and nations, three hundred forty seven men, women, and children, most by their own weapons. And not being content with taking away life alone, they fell after again upon the dead, making as well as they could, a fresh murder, defacing, dragging, and mangling the dead carcasses into many pieces, and carrying some parts away in derision, with base and brutish triumph. That the slaughter had been universal, if God had not put it into the heart of an Indian belonging to one Perry to disclose it, who living in the house of one Pace, was urged by another Indian his brother (who came the night before and lay with him) to kill Pace. Telling further that by such an hour in the morning a number would come from different places to finish the execution, who failed not at the time, Perry's Indian rose out of his bed and revealed it to Pace, that used him as a son. And thus the rest of the colony that had warning given them by this means was saved. Such was (God be thanked for it) the good fruit of an infidel converted to Christianity. For though three hundred and more of ours died by many of these pagan infidels, yet thousands of ours were saved by the means of one of them alone which was made a Christian. Blessed be God forever, whose mercy endureth forever.

Thus have you seen the particulars of this massacre, wherein treachery and cruelty have done their worst to us, or rather to themselves; for whose understanding is so shallow, as not to perceive that this must needs be for the good of the plantation after, and the loss of this blood to make the body more healthful, as by these reasons may be manifest.

First, because betraying innocence never rests unpunished.

Secondly, because our hands, which before were tied with gentleness and fair usage, are now set at liberty by the treacherous violence of the savages, not untying the knot, but cutting it. So that we, who hitherto have had possession of no more ground than their waste, and our purchase at a valuable consideration to their own contentment gained, may now, by right of war and law of nations, invade the country, and destroy them who sought to destroy us. Whereby we shall enjoy their cultivated places, possessing the fruits of others' labors. Now their cleared grounds in all their villages (which are situated in the fruitfulest places of the land) shall be inhabited by us, whereas heretofore the grubbing of woods was the greatest labor.

Thirdly, because those commodities which the Indians enjoyed as much or rather more than we, shall now also be entirely possessed by us. The deer and other beasts will be in safety, and infinitely increase, which heretofore not only in the general huntings of the King, but by each particular Indian were destroyed at all times of the year, without any difference of male, dame, or young.

There will be also a great increase of wild turkeys, and other weighty fowl, for the Indians never put difference of destroying the hen, but kill them whether in season or not, whether in breeding time, or sitting on their eggs, or having new hatched, it is all one to them.

Fourthly, because the way of conquering them is much more easy than of civilizing them by fair means, for they are a rude, barbarous, and naked people, scattered in small companies, which are helps to victory, but hindrance to civility. Besides that, a conquest may be of many, and at once; but civility is in particular and slow, the effect of long time, and great industry. Moreover, victory of them may be gained many ways: by force, by surprise, by famine in burning their corn, by destroying and burning their boats, canoes, and houses, by breaking their fishing wares, by assailing them in their huntings, whereby they get the greatest part of their sustenance in winter, by pursuing and chasing them with our horses and bloodhounds to draw after them, and mastiffs to tear them.

Chapter 2

The Puritan Church

IN 1630, under the direction of John Winthrop, the Puritans established their commonwealth in the New World. This was no ordinary
settlement, nor did it seek ordinary goals. The Puritans wished to
establish a community where they could worship in their own particular
manner. But they had not left England to undertake the rigors of the
wilderness for that alone; they also sought to improve their financial
condition. Nevertheless, economic motives were not at the heart of
the movement. Rather, their ultimate purpose in this venture was, in
Winthrop's words, to found "a city upon a hill," to establish a godly
commonwealth, and thereby to set an example for mankind in general
—and the English in particular—of how to conduct themselves in this
world. Their venture was nothing less than utopian. Massachusetts was
to mark a new divide in the history of mankind. In this setting
religious truths, as well as social and political ones, would emerge.
Church organization would follow God's word and by its success promote
emulation. Social relationships among Christians would achieve a new
quality, with men treating one another as brothers. This was a mission
into the wilderness—inspired by the hope of sparking a general reform.

No institution had greater significance in this grandoise plan than
the Congregational church. This church differed in several doctrinal
ways from its Anglican counterpart in England. First, no church
hierarchy ruled over the individual churches. The authority of these
hierarchical bodies, Puritans believed, was an unfortunate outgrowth
of papal practices and had no place in proper church structure. Secondly,
the Congregational church simplified ritual. The elaborate practices of
Catholic churches that had corrupted Protestant procedures had to be
eliminated. Finally, church membership was to become more exclusive,
in order to bring about a closer correspondence between the invisible
church (that heavenly church made up only of the truly saved) and
the visible church (the church on earth). Before gaining membership
and receiving the sacraments, one had to experience, and describe fully

to the congregation, saving grace, that moment of illumination wherein one felt the full majesty of God.

These beliefs reflected something even more fundamental in Puritanism: the covenant theology. Catholicism, they believed, had become far too mechanical a religion, and contemporary Anglicanism lacked any mystery of God. Puritans were determined to realize God as omnipotent without robbing human initiative of all meaning. Hence, according to covenant theology, if men did right, they probably were among the elect, the chosen of God. But there was no predicting with full confidence the workings of the Divine. The tree was known by its fruits; good works were a likely sign of salvation. Nevertheless, no one could be absolutely certain that he was in fact among the chosen of God. Consequently, there was a necessary tension about one's life. Deeply religious Puritans, like Michael Wadsworth, vacillated between moments of confidence and those of acute self-doubt and self-denigration.

The secular functions of the church were almost as significant as its religious ones. The responsibility for maintaining the good order of the community and the proper behavior of its members rested in large part with the church. Each Christian had to assume responsibility for the moral well-being of his neighbor. If, to a modern eye, such a doctrine violated the right of privacy and encouraged snooping, to the seventeenth-century Puritan, mutual responsibility was an obvious and vital part of Christian brotherhood. Thus, offenders against society faced not only sanctions from a civil court, but from the church as well. The judges fined and whipped, the church censured, admonished, and expeled. The line between political and religious crimes was drawn only faintly. To attack the doctrines of the church was to attack the stability of society, and hence both secular and religious institutions responded quickly and punitively. Roger Williams and Anne Hutchinson felt the arm of both church and state for departing from theological doctrines, and their fates are only famous examples of an ongoing discipline.

In the first generation of settlement, 1630 to 1660, the church came close to fulfilling its grandiose expectations, exerting unprecedented influence over men's attitudes and actions. The deviations that did occur were taken so seriously that they testify to the institution's strength. The prosecution of Robert Keayne for selling his nails at too high a price reflected the power of church and state over all aspects of its members' lives. But the hegemony of the church did not stand up well to conditions in the New World. Throughout the seventeenth century its discipline gradually weakened. To be sure, the principles of church authority were slow to change. Men still judged themselves by the rigorous standards of the first generation. But, in fact, citizens were steadily abandoning the ideal of establishing the city on a hill for the more mundane pleasures of life in a growing town.

I

No document better exemplifies the spirit behind the Puritan migration to the New World than John Winthrop's A Modell of Christian Charity. *Delivered as a sermon on board the* Arbella *as the band of Puritans were making their way across the Atlantic,* The Modell *expressed in eloquent and moving terms the hopes and fears of the mission. Winthrop himself, about to become the first governor of the Massachusetts Bay Colony, personified the curious Puritan blend of someone eager for worldly success yet equally concerned with otherworld salvation. He effectively summarized the goals of the first American Puritans.*

A MODELL OF CHRISTIAN CHARITY, 1630

JOHN WINTHROP

Written on Board the Arbella, *on the Atlantic Ocean*

God almighty in His most holy and wise providence hath so disposed of the condition of mankind, as in all times some must be rich, some poor, some high and eminent in power and dignity, others mean and in subjection.

Reason: First, to hold conformity with the rest of His works, being delighted to show forth the glory of His wisdom in the variety and difference of the creatures and the glory of His power, in ordering all these differences for the preservation and good of the whole.

Reason: Secondly, that He might have the more occasion to manifest the work of His spirit. First, upon the wicked in moderating and restraining them, so that the rich and mighty should not eat up the poor, nor the poor and despised rise up against their superiors and shake off their yoke. Secondly, in the regenerate in exercising His graces in them, as in the great ones, their love, mercy, gentleness, temperance, etc., in the poor and inferior sort, their faith, patience, obedience, etc.

Reason: Thirdly, that every man might have need of other, and from hence they might be all knit more nearly together in the bond of brotherly affection. From hence it appears plainly that no man is made more honorable than another, or more wealthy, etc., out of any particular and singular respect to himself, but for the glory of his creator and the common good of the creature, man.

Thus stands the cause between God and us. We are entered into covenant with Him for this work, we have taken out a commission, the Lord hath given us leave to draw our own articles, we have professed to enterprise these actions upon these and these ends, we have hereupon besought Him of favor and blessing. Now if the Lord shall please

In *The American Puritans*, ed. Perry Miller (New York, 1956), pp. 79–83.

to hear us, and bring us in peace to the place we desire, then hath He ratified this covenant and sealed our commission, [and] will expect a strict performance of the articles contained in it, but if we shall neglect the observations of these articles which are the ends we have propounded, and dissembling with our God, shall fall to embrace this present world and prosecute our carnal intentions seeking great things for ourselves and our posterity, the Lord will surely break out in wrath against us, be revenged of such a perjured people, and make us know the price of the breach of such a covenant.

Now the only way to avoid this shipwreck and to provide for our posterity is to follow the counsel of Micah, to do justly, to love mercy, to walk humbly with our God. For this end we must be knit together in this work as one man, we must entertain each other in brotherly affection, we must be willing to abridge ourselves of our superfluities for the supply of others' necessities, we must uphold a familiar commerce together in all meekness, gentleness, patience, and liberality, we must delight in each other, make others' conditions our own, rejoice together, mourn together, labor and suffer together, always having before our eyes our commission and community in the work, our community as members of the same body. So shall we keep the unity of the spirit in the bond of peace. The Lord will be our God and delight to dwell among us as His own people, and will command a blessing upon us in all our ways, so that we shall see much more of His wisdom, power, goodness, and truth than formerly we have been acquainted with. We shall find that the God of Israel is among us, when ten of us shall be able to resist a thousand of our enemies, when He shall make us a praise and glory, that men shall say of succeeding plantations, the Lord make it like that of New England. For we must consider that we shall be as a city upon a hill, the eyes of all people are upon us. So that if we shall deal falsely with our God in this work we have undertaken and so cause Him to withdraw His present help from us, we shall be made a story and a byword through the world, we shall open the mouths of enemies to speak evil of the ways of God and all professors for God's sake, we shall shame the faces of many of God's worthy servants, and cause their prayers to be turned into curses upon us till we be consumed out of the good land whither we are going. And to shut up this discourse with that exhortation of Moses, that faithful servant of the Lord in His last farewell to Israel, Deut. 30., Beloved, there is now set before us life and good, death and evil, in that we are commanded this day to love the Lord our God, and to love one another, to walk in His ways and to keep His commandments and His ordinance, and His laws, and the articles of our covenant with Him that we may live and be multiplied, and that the Lord our God may bless us in the land whither we go to possess it. But if our hearts shall turn away so that we will not obey, but shall be seduced and worship other Gods, our pleasures, our profits, and serve them, it is propounded unto us this day we shall surely perish out of the good land whither we pass over this vast sea to possess it. Therefore let us choose life, that we, and our seed, may live, and by obeying His voice, and cleaving to Him, for He is our life, and our prosperity.

II

The Cambridge Platform of 1648 defined the essentials of Puritan church organization. At the request of the General Court, the governing body of the Massachusetts Bay Colony, a Synod, made up of ministers and laymen, gathered at Cambridge, first in 1646, and then again in 1647 and 1648. These meetings hammered out the form that church government was to take in the new colony, an issue that was of pressing importance to the Puritan mission. The 1648 session was the most productive. It started in a curiously symbolic way. A snake (the personification of the devil) crept into the pulpit at the opening sermon, and an elder, "a man of great faith," killed it immediately. Thereafter, all seemed to go well. The Platform has been called "one of the greatest creations of the founding fathers," and its principles remained foremost in Bay Colony churches throughout the colonial period.

THE CAMBRIDGE PLATFORM, 1648

Of the Form of Church Government; and That It Is One, Immutable, and Prescribed in the Word

Ecclesiastical Polity, or Church Government or Discipline, is nothing else but that form and order that is to be observed in the Church of Christ upon Earth, both for the constitution of it and all the administrations that therein are to be performed.

Of the Nature of the Catholic Church in General, and in Special of a Particular Visible Church

The Catholic Church is the whole company of those that are elected, redeemed, and in time effectually called from the state of sin and death, unto a state of grace and salvation in Jesus Christ.

This Church is either triumphant or militant. Triumphant, the number of them who are glorified in Heaven: Militant, the number of them who are conflicting with their enemies upon Earth.

Of the Officers of the Church, and Especially of Pastors and Teachers

A Church being a company of people combined together by covenant for the worship of God, it appeareth thereby, there may be the essence and being of a church without any officers.

Nevertheless, though officers be not absolutely necessary to the simple being of churches, when they be called, yet ordinarily to their

In *American Christianity*, ed. Robert T. Handy and Lefferts A. Loetschen (New York, 1960), vol. 1, pp. 129–40.

calling they are, and to their well-being; and therefore the Lord Jesus, out of His tender compassion, hath appointed and ordained officers, which He would not have done, if they had not been useful and needful for the Church.

Of Elders, (who are also in Scripture called Bishops) some attend chiefly to the ministry of the word, as the Pastors and Teachers; others attend especially unto rule, who are therefore called Ruling Elders.

The Office of Pastor and Teacher appears to be distinct. The Pastors special work is to attend to exhortation, and therein to administer a word of wisdom. The Teacher is to attend to doctrine, and therein to administer a word of knowledge.

Of the Election of Church Officers

A Church being free, cannot become subject to any, but by a free election; yet when such a people do choose any to be over them in the Lord, then do they become subject, and most willingly submit to their Ministry in the Lord, whom they have so chosen.

And if the Church have power to choose their officers and ministers, then in case of manifest unworthiness and delinquency, they have power also to depose them: For, to open and shut, to choose and refuse, to constitute in office, and remove from office, are acts belonging to the same power.

Of the Admission of Members into the Church

The Doors of the Churches of Christ upon Earth do not by God's appointment stand so wide open, that all sorts of people, good or bad, may freely enter therein at their pleasure, but such as are admitted thereto, as members, ought to be examined and tried first, whether they be fit and meet to be received into church society, or not. The officers are charged with the keeping of the Doors of the Church. Twelve angels are set at the Gates of the Temple, lest such as were ceremonially unclean should enter thereinto.

The things which are requisite to be found in all church members are repentance from sin, and faith in Jesus Christ.

The weakest measure of faith is to be accepted in those that desire to be admitted into the Church, because weak Christians, if sincere, have the substance of that faith, repentance, and holiness which is required in church members; and such have most need of the ordinances for their confirmation and growth in grace.

Of Church Members, Their Removal from One Church to Another, and of Recommendation and Dismission

Church members may not remove or depart from the Church, and so one from another as they please, nor without just and weighty cause, but ought to live and dwell together, forasmuch as they are commanded not to forsake the assembling of themselves together.

It is therefore the duty of church members in such times and places where counsel may be had, to consult with the Church whereof they are members about their removal, that accordingly they having their approbation, may be encouraged, or otherwise desist. They who are joined with consent, should not depart without consent, except forced thereunto.

Order requires that a member thus removing have letters testimonial, and of dismission from the Church whereof he yet is, unto the Church whereunto he desireth to be joined, lest the Church should be deluded; that the Church may receive him in faith, and not be corrupted by receiving deceivers, and false brethren. Until the person dismissed be received into another Church, he ceaseth not by his letters of dismission, to be a member of the Church whereof he was. The Church cannot make a member no member, but by excommunication.

Of Excommunication, and Other Censures

The censures of the Church are appointed by Christ for the preventing, removing, and healing of offences in the Church; for the reclaiming and gaining of offending brethren, for the deterring others from the like offences.

In dealing with an offender, great care is to be taken that we be neither over strict or rigorous, nor too indulgent or remiss; our proceeding herein ought to be with a spirit of meekness, considering ourselves, lest we also be tempted; and that the best of us have need of much forgiveness from the Lord. On some have compassion, others save with fear.

Excommunication being a spiritual punishment, it doth not prejudice the excommunicate in, nor deprive him of his civil rights, and therefore toucheth not princes, nor other magistrates in point of their civil dignity or authority.

Of the Civil Magistrates Power in Matters Ecclesiastical

It is lawful, profitable, and necessary for Christians to gather themselves together into church estate, and therein to exercise all the ordinances of Christ, according unto the word, although the consent of the magistrate could not be had thereunto; because the Apostles and Christians in their time did frequently thus practise, when the magistrates all of them being Jewish or pagan, and most persecuting enemies, would give no countenance or consent to such matters.

Church government stands in no opposition to civil government of commonwealths, nor any way intrencheth upon the authority of civil magistrates in their jurisdiction.

It is not in the power of magistrates to compel their subjects to become church members, and to partake at the Lord's table.

As it is unlawful for church officers to meddle with the sword of the magistrate, so it is unlawful for the magistrate to meddle with the work proper to church officers.

Idolatry, blasphemy, heresy, venting corrupt and pernicious opinions that destroy the foundation, open contempt of the word preached, profanation of the Lord's day, disturbing the peaceable administration and exercise of the worship and holy things of God, and the like, are to be restrained and punished by civil authority.

If any Church one or more, shall grow schismatical, rending itself from the communion of other Churches, or shall walk incorrigibly or obstinately in any corrupt way of their own, contrary to the rule of the word; in such a case, the magistrate is to put forth his coercive power, as the matter shall require.

III

The day-to-day discipline exercised by the Puritan church emerges vividly in the records of the First Church at Dorchester, an outlying section of Boston. The authority of the church extended first and foremost to members; they could be flogged for religious offenses, and excommunicated for major sins. Members' lives were closely watched by fellow congregants; hence the colonists believed that the more the church policed a community, the more well-ordered it would be. The church also had some authority over nonmembers. As many as one-half of the settlers in Massachusetts probably remained outside the church. But attendance at services was compulsory for everybody, and neither the church nor the state would tolerate attacks on doctrine.

RECORDS OF THE DORCHESTER CHURCH, 1659–1779

The thirteenth of September 1659 it was declared unto the church and commended unto them from the general court to have a public day of thanksgiving to be observed by all the churches within this jurisdiction:

In *Records of the First Church at Dorchester in New England, 1636–1734* (Boston, 1891), pp. 32–33, 45–46, 50–51, 58, 70, 75–76, 83, 87.

In humble and thankful acknowledging [of] the mercy of God to New England in the continuation of our peace and for the gracious return of our prayers put up unto Him in the wet spring by giving His people a joint consent to withstand and suppress the blasphemers of His truth and gospel and the day appointed is to be the eighth day of October 1659.

The fifth day of November 1659 it was purposed by our teacher unto the church from some of the elders hereabouts whether it were not convenient that the churches (as many of them as could) should jointly set apart a day of humiliation on the behalf of our native country to which this church did consent.

The Twenty-fifth of January 1660

The day above said, report was made by Mr. Mather unto the congregation, of a sad accident that was fallen out at Hartford, namely of a young man named Abraham Warner, about the age of twenty years (who being left of God and prevailed with by Satan) drowned himself in the water, leaving behind him in his brother's pocket a writing to his father wherein he does advise his father to look to the ways and walkings of the children and families.

The Thirteenth of March 1660

This day Mr. Mather after the evening exercise desired to speak a word or two unto the church the substance thereof was this:

First he desired the church and the members of it to take notice: that children of such as are members of the church are to be looked at as members also though as yet they have not been received to the Lord's Supper.

Secondly his exhortation was unto the brethren and sisters of the church that they would mind it and make conscience of performing that duty of watchfulness and exhortation unto such children as their age and capacity did require or would admit of.

Thirdly his exhortation was unto such children of the church that they would so look at themselves as to expect the benefit and privilege of church watchfulness and that they would so carry themselves as such as must give an account in case of defect according as their age or capacity would permit.

The Twelfth of December 1664

The day above said, after the evening exercise the church was asked to stay, the reason was (as the elder did declare) because there were several young men in the town who would be willing to join to the church if they might have their confession taken in private by writing and declared publicly to the church, they standing forth and owning what was declared, and their engaging themselves in the covenant; upon this there was some debate and some did declare themselves willing that it should be so practiced but one or two of the brethren declared themselves to the contrary. In conclusion the matter was left to a further consideration.

The Second of February 1665

The day above said, it was also proposed to the church the second time whether they would be willing that men as well as women should be received into the church by the private relation being taken in writing and publicly read before the church: after some agitation the conclusion and vote of the church was that it should be left to the elders, namely that they might hear their relations in private and if their voice were so low in private that Mr. Mather could not hear them so as to write it from their mouths, then the party might write it himself and present it to the elders. But if they judged any man able to make a public relation by his own mouth, they should endeavor to persuade him so to do.

The Thirtieth of July 1666

The day above said, the elders made report to the church of some offense that lay upon Mrs. Clark, the wife of Captain Thomas Clark of Boston, about her reproachful and slanderous tongue against the honored governor Mr. Richard Bellengham, and other lying expression against the general court, and for absenting herself from the public ordinances and other miscarriages for which the church thought meet to call her before them to give satisfaction therein; but she not appearing, the church did forbear further proceeding till another time to see if she would personally appear to make answer thereunto.

The Fourteenth of August 1666

The day above said, Mrs. Clark, the wife of Captain Thomas Clark of Boston, was called before the church (she being yet a member of this church) for some offense committed for slanderous and lying expressions of her tongue; but she, manifesting no repentance for the same, was solemnly admonished before the church.

This being sacrament day, Robert Spur was called forth before the church to make his acknowledgment of the offense which he lay under in giving entertainment in his house of loose and vain persons, especially Joseph Belcher, his frequent coming to his daughter contrary to the admonition of the court which was greatly to the offense of the said Belcher's nearest relations and divers others.

Dorchester's Covenant for Reformation

The Fourth of March 1677

Upon serious search into our own hearts and ways in this day of divine rebuke, finding ourselves guilty of many heinous violations of our holy covenant by omissions of duty and commissions of iniquity, we do judge and condemn ourselves of the same, and do jointly and severally renew our said holy covenant with God and one with another.

First, to reform our own hearts, by endeavoring to recover the spirit like and power of Godliness with our first love, faith, zeal, and integrity.

Secondly, to reform our families, engaging ourselves to a conscientious care to set up and maintain the worship of God in them and to walk in our houses with perfect hearts in a faithful discharge of all domestic duties: educating, instructing, and charging our children and our households to keep the ways of the Lord: restraining them, as much as us, from all evil and especially the sins of the times and watching over them in the Lord.

Thirdly, to reform (according to our place and power) the general growing evil of this time; as pride appearing in gaudy apparel or otherwise and profanenesses, and profanation of God's holy Sabbath, taking God's holy name in vain, all irreverence in the ordinances and worship of God, disobedience to superiors, in family, town, church, or commonwealth, drunkenness, idleness, vain company keeping, unrighteous dealing between man and man, lasciviousness, uncleanliness, false speaking, slandering, coveting, with all other violations of God's holy law.

Fourthly, to reform our church to lay aside all envy, wrath, evil, surmises, jealousies, disrespect of persons, undue designings, sidings, contentions, and whatever is contrary to sound love and charity; to own and obey them that are over us in the Lord. To uphold, maintain, encourage, cleave to, and stand by a godly, able, painful, faithful, powerful ministry in this church and congregation; and to our power to encourage, cleave to, and stand by one another, in times of prosecution, to labor to recover the vigorous, studious, and impartial administration of discipline, to uphold the due administration of all God's holy ordinances, to be very serious and solemn in our preparations unto and attendance upon God in all divine worship and sabbaths, fasts, sacraments, that we may obtain the saving good of them.

Fifthly, to reform our defects and neglects of duty toward the children of the covenant, humbly and from our hearts acknowledging and bewailing our sin herein, beseeching and waiting upon God in our Lord Jesus for pardon and healing by His name.

Unto the performance of these things, we do, in the name of our Lord Jesus Christ, engage ourselves unto God, taking this holy covenant by a renewed act of confederation upon ourselves solemnly, with full purpose of heart in the strength of Christ to stand to it in all the parts of it.

June 6, 1671

John Merrifield (though not in full communion) was called forth before the church to answer for his sin of drunkenness and also for contempt and slighting the power of Christ in his church in not appearing formerly, though often called upon and sent unto: but he made some excuse for his drunkenness in that being not well at Boston, he took a little strong water, and coming out in the air distempered him, and for the other offense he did acknowledge his fault therein.

December 19, 1678

Church met again and Samuel Rigbe was called forth again, and he gave so much satisfaction that his censure of admonition was ordered to be respected for a while, and this on his good demeanor: if it did appear for some time then the censure [is] to be taken off. The same time Robert Spursen was called on to give satisfaction but he was not up to full satisfaction; therefore it was voted that he should be admonished. Also Nathan Wiett, John Spur, Daniel Ellen, and Joshua George, for their contempt of and neglecting and refusing to come to give an account of their knowledge to the elders or church, were therefore voted to be excommunicated.

August 28, 1679

Samuel Blake, the son of William Blake, now of the church at Melton, was called before the church to make confession of his sin of fornication before marriage; with time he did own the fact and made some kind of acknowledgment, but his voice was so low that scarcely any heard the little which he spoke except a few which stood close by him.

September 2, 1679

Samuel Rigbe was excommunicated for those sins for which he was formerly admonished and for contempt in not appearing before the church, being called thereunto.

IV

Although it is not likely that many other Puritans felt the anguish of their existence with as keen and acute a sensibility as Michael Wigglesworth, his attitudes and beliefs reflect one major strand in Puritanism. A minister in the Bay Colony, Wigglesworth wrote the widely read Day of Doom; *this account of the judgment day went through five editions between 1662 and 1701. His diary, parts of which are reprinted below, conveys the religious tension that he experienced. Even if personal, psychological explanations account for some of Wigglesworth's feelings, one must remember that he was still a man of his times.*

THE DIARY OF MICHAEL WIGGLESWORTH, 1653

March 1653

Mr. Mitchel preached twice today and we saw His glory. Now woe is me! That I cannot see Christ's glory, I never find my heart more carnal and my eyes more blind that I cannot behold and feel a present excellency in Christ, than when His glory is displayed before me. My love to Christ is gone and all saviour of His sweetness in a manner so

In *The Diary of Michael Wigglesworth, 1653–1657* (New York, 1946), pp. 10–18, 23–31, 46–49, 52–55.

that I may with trembling fear the vileness of my own heart, when Christ is most to be seen. Vain thoughts break in upon me. My soul can't get over a disconsolate, troubled, devoted frame. Ah Lord let me see thy face that will fill up all my emptiness and the dissatisfaction I find in the creature. I wait and oh, that I could long for thy salvation.

O wretch that I am, my iniquity, like clay and fetters, holds me down that the good I would do I can't; the evil I would not do, that do I. Nay I feel my heart apt secretly to give way to my vain thoughts in holy duties, and glued as it were to my sensuality or love to the creature full of hope since and can't get over sinking and disquietments of spirit; and as for pride, why it overcomes me in holiest duties where there should be most abasement.

March the Twenty-third

I came to New Haven, I preached my first sermon at Pequit. Much difficulty I found in my journey, my back and breast almost shaked in pieces with riding. In my pain and anguish I lift up my heart and voice to the Lord my God, and He helped me through the difficulty, giving me so much strength as enabled me to bear it. We were lost the first day and rode above an hour within evening. God brought us to a house where we had a guide to our desired place. Near Pequit we were lost and passed through craggy, dangerous ways; yet God kept us and all [that] belonged to us and brought us safe, notwithstanding the rumors of the Indian plots.

This Sabbath I found much enlargement in private duties, yet pride thereupon prevailing, which I desired to resist and loath myself for. I find vain thoughts and vile heart ready to give them lodging, slow to see and feel any evil in them. And there is also a carnal heart that cannot savor the things of God, but whorishly departs from Him. What impressions and tastes of Himself God leaves at present are soon gone. This makes me exceedingly afraid of myself and my own spirit of whoredoms. These things open a gap to unbelief; I am ashamed to lift up mine eyes to heaven and call God my gracious father, my only portion, seeing I deal so unworthily with Him. Ah wretched backsliding heart! What evil hast thou found in God that thy love and affection to Him are so quickly cooled? I abhor myself before the Lord for my shameless pride, especially now when God is abasing me. I am ashamed of my apostatizing heart of unbelief in departing from the living God, to whom in my distress I am ever crying, arise and save me.

April 17, 18, 19

I was somewhat dejected with some fears in the forenoon and was not yet clear of them in the evening of the Sabbath, having heard Mr. Davenport preach how and what a winter Christians indeed might go through both in respect of grace and comfort. My daily decays [loss] of love to God and saviour of the things of God, this profane, loose heart that is weary of watchful attending upon God in holy duties fills me with fears of my own estate. Chewing upon such cogitations I thought that if God would not save me at last, yet there was something that pleased me in this, that my Lord should have glory in my damnation.

On the sixth day which was the next day after the fast, God let me see the prevalency of a multitude of abominable sins in me. As 1: Weariness of God's service, in which is great unbelief, though God has said 'tis not a vain thing to seek Him; great unthankfulness for such a gracious opportunity which the damned would prize at a high rate. Great slothfulness that cannot away with taking pains in constant seeking God by spiritual worship. 2: Peevishness and impatience, though God were patient and bore long my dullness, nay averseness to learn of Him, now groundless anger makes me give place to the Devil so that my spot is not the spot of God's children. 3: Affirming that for truth which I doubt or am not certain of; now who is the father of lies? 4: Want of natural affection to my father, in desiring the continuance of his life which God ranks among those sins whereto men were given up of God to a reprobate mind. Lord why hast thou caused me to err from thy ways, or hardened my heart from thy fear? 5: Want of honoring my mother, yea, slighting of her speech; now the eye that despises his mother, the ravens of the valley shall peck it out and the young ravens shall eat it. Lord, I can't stand before thee because of these abominations. Against thee I have committed them, not obeying thy holy rules though thou didst redeem me for thy self to thy service. Nay, sixthly, I find again whorish desertions of my heart from God to the creature. It pleased God to make me earnest in prayer both that evening and the next morning for pardon of them for Jesus' sake and for power against them according to God's covenant to redeem me from all iniquity.

April 27

On the fourth day at lecture I found my vile heart apt to be weary beforehand of the feared length of the public ordinances. And I feel my spirit so leavened with sensuality that I cannot but be hankering in my thoughts after creature comforts as of meat and drink when I should be holy intent to God's worship in religious services, especially if they put me by the other. I took time to look into the evil of this also and much I did see. Now the good Lord looks down at last and hears the groaning of his poor prisoner, and comes and saves me from the tyranny of these enemies of his.

June 26

Tuesday was a private fast. I was very deadhearted in the beginning of the day [and] the night before. In public it pleased the Lord to pour upon me some measure of affection, but now woe is me! How incurable is my wound that while I am confessing and shaming myself before God for my pride and sensuality and security, even then pride of God's gifts (good affections) arise. No marvel then He blasts my endeavors and makes the college and country about me fare the worse for my sake. Though He punish my barrenness with public drought; though He say of this poor society: I have shown such and such favour to one of you, and lo! He loathes me, cares not for me, robs me of my glory, and all this for my love; I'll show you no more mercy, my spirit shall strive with no more of you.

July 9

Saturday at night I was importuned to go preach at Roxbury because the elders were both ill. I did so, and preached out of the same text I had done at Concord, the Lord assisting me more than formerly when I preached the same.

Wednesday

I feel such distractions in holy duties, such deadness of heart at lecture, such pride in divine assistance and in my own notions, even then when I have been taught to have no confidence in the flesh, a pang of worldly desires amidst hearing the word, that I am ashamed to lift up my face to heaven. Father forgive or else I perish. Oh hide not thy face, which is my life, from me.

But above all, my vileness breaks forth again while I am hearing the word. An atheistic irreverent frame seizes upon me; and while God is bidding me see His glory I cannot see it; vile and unworthy conceptions concerning God come into my mind. I cannot desire heaven because 'tis a place where I shall see and wonder at and acknowledge the glory of God forever. But I rather desire a heaven where I might be doing for God than only thinking and gazing on His excellency. Blind mind! Carnal heart! I am afraid, ashamed, heavy laden under such cursed frames of heart as ever and anon beset me. My soul groans, my body faints, Lord, while I pray and cry for pardon and redemption.

V

In the first years of settlement, the Puritan community attempted to regulate all aspects of life. The city on the hill would point the way not only in church organization but in economic conduct as well. To this end, the General Court set price and wage regulations. Profit was allowed, but no usury. If a shortage of goods reflected God's judgment (for example, a shipwreck or a drought), a higher price for the item was allowable. But if a merchant's greed caused the price rise, then the court would act. The most famous instance of a Puritan merchant running afoul of these regulations was Robert Keayne's imbroglio over the price of nails. His accusers claimed he charged an excessive price; Keayne consistently maintained his innocence. The court fined him, and the church admonished him— and Keayne never forgot the incident. His last will and testament gave him the opportunity to reargue the case, to protest his unfair treatment. The intensity of his feelings, as well as the norms of the community, emerge clearly in this document. By 1660, the state could no longer maintain economic control. A shortage of goods and of labor bred conditions that outstripped regulation. But for a moment the commonwealth had tried to enforce a broad kind of Christian brotherhood.

THE APOLOGIA OF ROBERT KEAYNE, 1653

THE LAST WILL AND TESTAMENT OF ME, ROBERT KEAYNE,
ALL OF IT WRITTEN WITH MY OWN HANDS AND BEGAN BY
ME, MO: 6: 1: 1653, COMMONY CALLED AUGUST

I, Robert Keayne, citizen and merchant tailor of London by freedom and by the good providence of God now dwelling at Boston in New England in America, being at this time through the great goodness of my God both in health of body and of able and sufficient memory, do therefore now in my health make, ordain, and declare this to be my last will and testament and to stand and to be as effectual as if I had made it in my sickness or in the day or hour of my death, which is in manner and form following.

Thanks to a Merciful God: His Declaration of Faith

First and before all things, I commend and commit my precious soul into the hands of Almighty God, who not only as a loving creator hath given it unto me when He might have made me a brute beast, but also as a most loving father and merciful saviour hath redeemed it with the precious blood of His own dear son and my sweet Jesus from that gulf of misery and ruin that I by original sin and actual transgressions had plunged it into.

I do further desire from my heart to renounce all confidence or expectation of merit or desert in any of the best duties or services that ever I have, shall, or can be able to perform, acknowledging that all my righteousness, sanctification, and close walking with God, if it were or had been a thousand times more exact that ever let I attained to, is all polluted and corrupt and falls short of commending me to God in point of my justification or helping forward my redemption or salvation.

It may be some on the other side may marvel (especially some who have been acquainted with some expressions or purposes of mine in former wills) that I should give away so much of my estate in private legacies and to private uses which might better have been spared and to give little or nothing to any public use for the general good of the country and commonwealth [except] what I have appropriated to our own town of Boston.

To answer this doubt or objection I must acknowledge that it hath been in my full purpose and resolution ever since God hath given me any comfortable estate to do good withal, not only before I came into New England but often since, to study and endeavor both in my life and at my death to do what I could do to help on any public, profitable, and general good here. . . . My thoughts and intents have been about the castle for public defense, the college and schools for learning, the setting up of a bridewell or workhouse for prisoners, malefactors, and

In *The Apologia of Robert Keayne*, ed. Bernard Bailyn (New York, 1964), pp. 1–2, 48, 52–53, 59–60.

some sort of poor people, stubborn, idle, and undutiful youth, as children and servants, to have been kept at work in either for correction or to get their living, and some other things that I need not mention. In which things, though I could not have done so much as I desired, yet so much I should have done as might have proved an example and encouragement to others of greater estates and willing minds to have done more and to have helped to carry them on to more perfection. For I have held it a great degree of unthankfulness to God that when He hath bestowed many blessings and a large or comfortable outward estate upon a man that he should leave all to his wife and children to advance them only by making them great and rich in the world or to bestow it upon some friends or kindred that it maybe hath no great need of it and to dispose none or very little of it to public charitable or good works such as may tend to His glory and the good of others in way of a thankful acknowledgment to Him for so great favors.

But the truth is that unkindness and ill requital of my former love, both in Old England and here which I have taken to promote the good of this place has been answered by divers [various people] here with unchristian, uncharitable, and unjust reproaches and slanders since I came hither, as if men had the liberty of their tongues to reproach any that were not beneficial to them. [These attacks came] together with that deep and sharp censure that was laid upon me in the country and carried on with so much bitterness and indignation of some, contrary both to law or any foregoing precedent if I mistake not, and, I am sure, contrary or beyond the quality and desert of the complaints that came against me, which indeed were rather shadows of offense, out of a desire of revenge. Yet by some it was carried on with such violence and pretended zeal as if they had had some of the greatest sins in the world to censure. . . . Had it been in their power or could they have carried it they would not have corrected or reformed but utterly have ruined myself and all that I had, as if no punishment had been sufficient to expiate my offense [of] selling a good bridle for 2 s. that now worse are sold without offense for 3 s., 6 d. nails for 7 d., and 8 d. nails for 10 d. per hundred, which since and to this day are frequently sold by many for a great deal more. And so [it was] in all other things proportionably, as selling gold buttons for two shilling nine pence a dozen that cost above 2 in London and yet were never paid for by them that complained.

These were the great matters in which I had offended, when myself have often seen and heard offenses, complaints, and crimes of a high nature against God and men, such as filthy uncleanness, fornications, drunkenness, fearful oaths, quarreling, mutinies, sabbath breakings, thefts, forgeries, and such like, which hath passed with fines or censures so small or easy as hath not been worth the naming or regarding. These [things] I cannot think upon but with sad thoughts of inequality of such proceedings, which hath been the very cause of tying up my heart and hands from doing such general and public good acts as in my heart I both desired and intended.

I did submit to the censure, I paid the fine to the uttermost, which is not nor hath been done by many (nor so earnestly required as mine was) though for certain and not supposed offenses of far higher nature, which I can make good not by hearsay only but in my own knowledge,

yea offenses of the same kind. [My own offense] was so greatly aggra-
vated and with such indignation pursued by some, as if no censure could
be too great or too severe, as if I had not been worthy to have lived
upon the earth. [Such offenses] are not only now common almost in
every shop and warehouse but even then and ever since with a higher
measure of excess, yea even by some of them that were most zealous and
had their hands and tongues deepest in my censure. [At that time] they
were buyers, [but since then] they are turned sellers and peddling
merchants themselves, so that they are become no offenses now nor
worthy questioning nor taking notice of in others.

The oppression lay justly and truly on the buyer's hand rather than
on the seller; but then the country was all buyers and few sellers, though
it would not be seen on that side then. For if the lion will say the lamb
is a fox, it must be so, the lamb must be content to leave it. But now
the country hath got better experience in merchandise, and they have
soundly paid for their experience since, so that it is now and was many
years ago become a common proverb amongst most buyers that knew
those times that my goods and prices were cheap pennyworths in comparison of what hath been taken since and especially [in comparison
with] the prices of these times. Yet I have borne this patiently and without disturbance or troubling the Court with any petitions for remission
or abatement of the fine, though I have been advised by many friends,
yea and some of the same Court, so to do, as if they would be willing to
embrace such an occasion to undo what was then done in a hurry and
in displeasure, or at least would lessen or mitigate it in a great measure.
But I have not been persuaded to it because the more innocently that
I suffer, the more patiently have I borne it, leaving my cause therein
to the Lord.

I did not then nor dare not now go about to justify all my actions.
I know God is righteous and doth all upon just grounds, though men
may mistake in their grounds and proceedings, counsel have erred and
courts may err and a faction may be too hard and outvote the better or
more discerning part. I know the errors of my life. The failings in my
trade and otherwise have been many. Therefore from God [the censure]
was most just. Though it had been much more severe I dare not so open
my mouth against it, nor never did as I remember, [except to] justify
Him. Yet I dare not say nor did I ever think (as far as I can call to
mind) that the censure was just and righteous from men. Was the price
of a bridle, not for taking but only asking, 2 s. for [what] cost here
20 d. such a heinous sin? [Such bridles] have since been commonly sold
and still are for 2 s. 6 d. and 3 s. or more, though worse in kind. Was
it such a heinous sin to sell two or three dozen of great gold buttons for
2 s. 10 d. per dozen that cost 2 s. 2 d. ready money in London, bought
at the best hand, as I showed to many by my invoice (though I could
not find it at the instant when the Court desired to see it) and since
was confirmed by special testimony from London? The buttons [were
not even] paid for when the complaint was made, nor I think not yet;
neither did the complaint come from him that bought and owed them
nor with his knowledge or consent, as he hath since affirmed, but merely
from the spleen and envy of another, whom it did nothing concern. Was
this so great an offense? Indeed, that it might be made so, some out of

their ignorance would needs say they were copper and not worth 9 d. per dozen. But these were weak grounds to pass heavy censures upon.

Yea, and our own church, when they called all those complaints over again that was laid to my charge (as it was meet they should) to see how far there was equity in them and how far I was guilty of all those clamors and rumors that then I lay under, they heard my defense equally and patiently, and after all their exquisite search into them and attention to what others could allege or prove against me, they found no cause but only to give me an admonition. Less they could not do without some offense, considering what had passed in Court before against me. Now if the church had seen or apprehended or could have proved that I had been so justly guilty as others imagined, they could have done no less than to have excommunicated and cast me out of their society and fellowship as an unworthy member.

Chapter 3

The Colonial Family

EIGHTEENTH-CENTURY Americans made the family the most vital institution in the perpetuation of social ideas and the preservation of social order. They endowed the family with so many responsibilities that the lines between it and the community were blurred. In a society where many other institutions were in a rudimentary state or were altogether missing, the family performed innumerable tasks. It was, of course, the place where children were reared and nurtured. But it was also a school, teaching its members how to read and write and offering vocational training, through the system of apprenticeship, to outsiders as well as to its own children. Rather than enter a classroom to learn the skills of a trade, a child in the colonial period went to live with his master, learning the necessary arts directly from him. The family was also a center of employment, using the labor of the household and supplementary labor as necessary. Typically, everybody working on the family farm lived in the homestead. Additionally, the family was in charge of the relief of the aged and care of the young. In the absence of hospitals and almshouses, neighbors cared for neighbors, taking in disabled or decrepit people, and feeding, clothing, and caring for them. Then, too, the family was something of a church—with all the various members of the household coming together several times a day for periods of worship. In essence, the colonial household was not an insular, self-serving institution, dedicated only to the welfare of its own kin; it was a public institution, taking into its midst servants, hapless neighbors, and community children.

The family in this period was somewhat larger than its modern counterpart. Not only were more outsiders boarding with it, but there were more children per family, and the households might hold more distant relatives. Extended families—parents, grandparents, and children living under one roof—were by no means uncommon in the colonies. Modified extended families also existed—clusters of families living one next to the other, not under one roof, but not really separated.

Then too, nuclear families—just the parents and children—could be found, particularly in western areas where sons had gone off to look for new and fertile land. Just about every variant of these types existed, testimony to the great variety of conditions under which colonial families organized themselves.

Social expectations of the colonial family were well defined. The family was to be authoritarian, duplicating within its walls the hierarchical structure of the society outside. The father's power, like that of the colonial governor, was supposed to be unlimited. He ruled his offspring, his wife, and the servants or apprentices who lived with him with a firm hand. Ministers counseled him to wear his authority lightly, to rely upon the love and affection of those around him to win obedience. But they left no doubt that when all else failed, his rule must be paramount. The maxim of Solomon, that he who spares the rod invariably spoils the child, was quoted again and again in well-read pamphlets on child care. The parent had to inculcate obedience in the child, and failure would breed a disruptive, lawless citizen.

Did the colonial family, in fact, live up to this charge? Was the authority of the father so complete? Did he invariably control his children and his wife with a firm hand? Or did conditions in the New World operate to undermine his influence? Did a democratization occur within the household? Some of the conditions in the New World may well have worked to lessen parental authority. Clearly, there was an abundance of land, so that sons in America, unlike their counterparts in England, did not have to stand at the beck and call of their fathers, hoping to get a piece of land through inheritance. Instead, they could pick up stakes, move westward, and set up households of their own. So, too, a shortage of labor gave unusual economic opportunities to the lower classes. Unlike England, where too many laborers competed for too few jobs, unskilled workers were in demand. The master who worked his apprentice too hard might find that his servant had run away, confident that he could find employment elsewhere.

Nevertheless, strong pressures operated to buttress parental discipline. The norms upholding the father's authority may well have offset the effects of land wealth and labor shortages. Furthermore the primitive conditions facing the westward migrant—new soil to be broken and houses to be built—may have intensified reliance on his own family, strengthening mutual interdependence rather than weakening it.

The materials below illuminate the workings and relative strengths of these historical forces. The history of the family does not easily lend itself to fixed and sure conclusions. But the field is both inherently interesting and of major importance to understanding the development of American society.

I

Advice-to-parents books have a long tradition in this country. In every generation there are tracts setting down the norms that parents ought to follow—Dr. Spock is only the latest in a long line of authors. On the whole, these volumes are well worth scrutinizing. They do not, it is true, tell us very much in firsthand fashion about the reality of family life; statements of ideals do not present family life as it was lived. Nevertheless, the advice books reveal in dramatic fashion the goals that a society sets for the family, thereby informing us directly of hopes and fears for social order and stability. Moreover, it is not unreasonable to expect some correspondence between ideals and practices. At least we can know the standards by which families judged themselves, and moreover, we can know what themes to look for as we read in individual diaries and letters about family habits. Furthermore, it is important to note who the authors of the tracts were. In the seventeenth century, clergymen composed them; later, as we shall see, it was doctors and psychiatrists. The sermon below, delivered by Congregational minister Benjamin Wadsworth in 1712, is a typical statement of the colonial view of the family, a view that includes the relationships between husbands and wives, children and parents, and servants and masters.

A WELL-ORDERED FAMILY, 1712

BENJAMIN WADSWORTH

DOCTRINE

Christians should endeavor to please and glorify God, in whatever capacity or relation they sustain.

Under this doctrine, my design is (by God's help) to say something about *relative duties*, particularly in *families*. I shall therefore endeavor to speak as briefly and plainly as I can about: (1) *family prayer*; (2) *the duties of husbands and wives*; (3) *the duties of parents and children*; (4) *the duties of masters and servants*.

About Family Prayer

Family prayer is a duty. A family should pray to God for family mercies which are needed, and praise Him for family benefits which are enjoyed. *The neglect of family prayer* expose one to God's displeasure.

To answer some objections too apt to be made against this duty.

In *A Well-Ordered Family*, 2nd edition, by Benjamin Wadsworth (Boston, 1719), pp. 4–5, 22–59, 99–121.

Objection: I am so busy and taken up with much business, that I have no time to pray with my family.

Answer: It is a shame that you should make this objection. Have you time to eat, drink, sleep, to follow your outward affairs, and yet you can spare no time to pray in? Can you find time to receive God's mercies, and none to pray for them, or to give thanks for them? Possibly you spend as much or more time than what is needed for family prayer at this tavern in idleness, in needless chatting or diversion.

If you cannot find time to serve God, do not think that He will find time to save you.

Your honest, lawful business will not suffer for your taking time for family prayer. You should *pray* as well as work for your daily bread. In all your ways acknowledge Him (that is; God) and He shall direct your paths.

About the Duties of Husbands and Wives

Concerning the duties of this relation we may assert a few things. *It is their duty to dwell together with one another.* Surely they should dwell together; if one house cannot hold them, surely they are not affected to each other as they should be. They should have a very great and tender love and affection to one another. This is plainly commanded by God. This duty of love is mutual; it should be performed by each, to each of them. When, therefore, they quarrel or disagree, then they do the Devil's work; he is pleased at it, glad of it. But such contention provokes God; it dishonors Him; it is a vile example before inferiors in the family; it tends to prevent family prayer.

As to outward things. If the one is sick, troubled or distressed, the other should manifest care, tenderness, pity, and compassion, and afford all possible relief and succor. They should likewise unite their prudent counsels and endeavors, comfortably to maintain themselves and the family under their joint care.

Husband and wife should be patient one toward another. If both are truly pious, yet neither of them is perfectly holy, in such cases a patient, forgiving, forbearing spirit is very needful. You, therefore, that are husbands and wives, do not aggravate every error or mistake, every wrong or hasty word, every wry step as though it were a willfuly designed intolerable crime; for this would soon break all to pieces: but

rather put the best construction on things, and bear with and forgive one another's failings.

The husband's government ought to be gentle and easy, and the wife's obedience ready and cheerful. The husband is called the head of the woman. It belongs to the head to rule and govern. Wives are part of the house and family, and ought to be under the husband's government. Yet his government should not be with rigor, haughtiness, harshness, severity, but with the greatest love, gentleness, kindness, tenderness that may be. Though he governs her, he must not treat her as a servant, but as his own flesh; he must love her as himself.

Those husbands are much to blame who do not carry it lovingly and kindly to their wives. O man, if your wife is not so young, beautiful, healthy, well-tempered, and qualified as you would wish; if she did not bring a large estate to you, or cannot do so much for you, as some other women have done for their husbands; yet she is your wife, and the great God commands you to love her, not be bitter, but kind to her. What can be more plain and expressive than that?

Those wives are much to blame who do not carry it lovingly and obediently to their own husbands. O woman, if your husband is not as young, beautiful, healthy, so well-tempered, and qualified as you could wish; if he has not such abilities, riches, honors, as some others have; yet he is your husband, and the great God commands you to love, honor, and obey him. Yea, though possibly you have greater abilities of mind than he has, was of some high birth, and he of a more common birth, or did bring more estate, yet since he is your husband, God has made him your head, and set him above you, and made it your duty to love and revere him.

Parents should act wisely and prudently in the matching of their children. They should endeavor that they may marry someone who is most proper for them, most likely to bring blessings to them.

About the Duties of Parents and Children

They should love their children, and carefully provide for their outward supply and comfort while unable to provide for themselves. As soon as the mother perceives herself with child, she should be careful not to do anything injurious to herself or to the child God has formed in her. Mothers also, if they are able, should suckle their children; and yet through sloth or niceness neglect to suckle them, it seems very criminal and blameworthy.

Yet by way of caution I might say, let wisdom and prudence sway, more than fond or indulgent fancy, in feeding and clothing your children. Too much niceness and delicateness in these things is not good; it tends not to make them healthy in their bodies, nor serviceable and useful in their generation, but rather the contrary.

Parents should bring up their children to be diligent in some lawful business. It is true, time for lawful recreation now and then is not altogether to be denied them. Yet for them to do little or nothing else but play in the streets, especially when almost able to earn their living, is a great sin and shame. They should by no means be brought up in idleness, or merely to learn fashions, ceremonious compliments, and to dress after the newest mode. Such folly as this ruins many children. Boys and girls should be brought up diligently in such business as they are capable of, and as is proper for them. Christians are bid to be not slothful in business. And if Christians should be thus diligent in business, surely they should be brought up to it while young. Train up a child in the way wherein he should go.

Parents should teach their children good manners. A civil, respectful, courteous behavior is comely and commendable; those who will not put suitable marks of respect and honor on others, especially on superiors, or those in authority, do not imitate the commendable examples of the godly recorded in Scripture.

Parents should instruct their children in the only true religion taught in the Scriptures. You should bring them up in the nurture and admonition of the Lord. You should also teach them to be sober, chaste, and temperate, to be just to all and bountiful to the poor as they have opportunity and ability.

Parents should govern their children well; restrain, reprove, correct them as there is occasion. A Christian householder should rule well his own house. Children should not be left to themselves, to a loose end to do as they please, but should be under tutors and governors, not being fit to govern themselves. Children being bid to obey their parents in all things plainly implies that parents should give suitable precepts to and maintain a wise government over their children, so carry it, as their children may both fear and love them. You should reprove them for their faults. He that spares the rod, hates his son. Yet on the other hand, a father should pity his children. You should by no means carry it ill to them, you should not frown, be harsh, morose, faulting, and blaming them when they do not deserve it, but do behave themselves well. Again, you should never be cruel or barbarous in your corrections; and if milder ones will reform them, more severe ones should never be used. You should not suffer your children needlessly to frequent taverns nor to be abroad unseasonable on nights, lest they are drawn into numberless hazards and mischiefs thereby.

About the Duties of Children to Their Parents

Children should love their parents. If children duly consider, they will find they have abundant cause to love their parents, they are very vile if they neglect it.

Children should fear their parents. Children should fear both, fear to offend, grieve, disobey, or displease either of them. The great God of Heaven bids children fear their parents; if therefore they fear them not, they rebel against God.

Children should patiently bear and grow better by the needful corrections their parents give them. O child, if you are not bettered by the correction of parents, you are in danger of being terribly destroyed. Children should be faithful and obedient to their parents. What their parents give them they should be thankful for, but they should not take what is their parents' without their knowledge and good liking. When children are disobedient to parents, God is often provoked to leave them to those sins which bring them to great shame and misery in this world.

Alas, children, if you once become disobedient to parents, you do not know what vile abominations God may leave you to fall into. When persons have been brought to die at the gallows for their crimes, how often have they confessed that disobedience to parents led them to those crimes?

Children should be very willing and ready to support and maintain their indigent parents. If our parents are poor, aged, weak, sickly, and not able to maintain themselves, we are bound in duty and conscience to do what we can to provide for them, nourish, support, and comfort them.

About the Duties of Masters to Their Servants

Masters should suitably provide for the bodily support and comfort of their servants. Servants are part of their household. Masters should keep their servants diligently employed. Indeed, they should allow them sufficient time to eat, drink, sleep; on proper occassions some short space for relaxation and diversion may be very advisable. To be sure, servants should be allowed time for prayer and Bible reading. But though time should be allowed for these things, yet we may say, in general, servants should be kept diligently employed. Do not let your servants be idle; oversee them carefully.

About the Duty of Servants to Their Masters

Servants should fear their masters. Servants should honor their masters. Servants should obey their masters, be diligent and faithful in their service and to their interest. The word of God is very plain and expressive for this. You that are servants, take your Bibles, frequently read these plain commands of the great God, that out of obedience to His supreme indisputable authority you may be moved and quickened, conscientiously to obey your masters, and to be faithful to their interest. And you that are masters, if your servants are disobedient or unfaithful to you, then read to them these plain commands of the great God, endeavoring to impress upon their consciences a sense of God's authority and their own duty.

II

By their very nature, diaries are highly idiosyncratic and personal records. To generalize from any one such source is a highly dubious affair—indeed, any one diary may reflect the precise character of the individual more than any overriding truth about a society. But diaries can convey much about the temper of a time; and in the case of the family, if we are to have any intimate picture of its functioning, we must examine and study them. One of the most famous and interesting diaries of the period comes from Samuel

Sewall, a noted figure in Boston, an officeholder and leader of the community. At the age of forty Sewall found himself a widower, and set about courting a woman in similar circumstance, Mrs. Winthrop. It was not a successful courtship; but his record of the abortive romance illustrates the quality of personal and family relationships in late seventeenth-century Boston.

THE DIARY OF SAMUEL SEWALL, 1720

September 30 [1720]

Mr. Colman's lecture. Daughter Sewall acquaints Madam Winthrop that if she pleased to be within at 3 P.M., I would wait on her. She answered she would be at home.

October 1. Saturday

I dine at Mr. Stoddard's; from thence I went to Madam Winthrop's just at 3. Spake to her, saying my loving wife died so soon and suddenly, 'twas hardly convenient for me to think of marrying again; however, I came to this resolution, that I would not make my court to any person without first consulting with her. Had a pleasant discourse about 7 (seven) single persons sitting in the foreseat September 29, *viz.* Madam Rebecca Dudley, Katherine Winthrop, Bridget Usher, Deliverance Legg, Rebecca Lloyd, Lydia Colman, Elizabeth Bellingham. She propounded one and another for me; but none would do; said Mrs. Lloyd was about her age.

October 3.

Waited on Madam Winthrop again; 'twas a little while before she came in. Her daughter Noyes being there alone with me, I said I hoped my waiting on her mother would not be disagreeable to her. She answered she should not be against that that might be for her comfort. I saluted her, and told her I perceived I must shortly wish her a good time (her mother had told me she was with child and within a month or two of her time). At last Madam Winthrop came too. After a considerable time I went up to her and said if it might not be inconvenient, I desired to speak with her. She assented. Then I ushered in discourse from the names in the foreseat; at last I prayed that Katherine [Mrs. Winthrop] might be the person assigned for me. She instantly took it up in the way of denial, as if she had catched at an opportunity to do it, saying she could not do it before she was asked. Said that was her mind unless she should change it, which she believed she should not; could not leave her children. I expressed my sorrow that she should do it so speedily, prayed her consideration, and asked her when I should wait on her again. [I] took leave.

In *The American Puritans*, ed. Perry Miller (New York, 1956), pp. 244–47, 251–53.

October 6th.

A little after 6 P.M. I went to Madam Winthrop's. She was not within. After a while Dr. Noyes came in with his mother, and quickly after his wife came in; they sat talking, I think, till eight o'clock. I said I feared I might be some interruption to their business; Dr. Noyes replied pleasantly he feared they might be an interruption to me, and went away. Madam seemed to harp upon the same string. Must take care of her children; could not leave that house and neighborhood where she had dwelt so long. I told her she might do her children as much or more good by bestowing what she laid out in housekeeping, upon them. Said her son would be of age the 7th of August. I said it might be inconvenient for her to dwell with her daughter-in-law, who must be mistress of the house.

October 21. Friday

My son the minister came to me by appointment and we prayed one for another in the old chamber, more especially respecting my courtship. About 6 o'clock I go to Madam Winthrop's. She received me courteously. I asked when our proceedings should be made public; she said they were like to be no more public than they were already. Offered me no wine that I remember. I rose up at 11 o'clock to come away, saying I would put on my coat; she offered not to help me. I prayed her that Juno might light me home; she opened the shutter and said 'twas pretty light abroad, Juno was weary and gone to bed. So I came home by starlight as well as I could.

November 4th. Friday

Went again about 7 o'clock; found there Mr. John Walley and his wife; sat discoursing pleasantly. I showed them Isaac Moses's [an Indian] writing. Madam W. served comfits to us. After a while a table was spread, and supper was set. I urged Mr. Walley to crave a blessing; but he put it upon me. About 9 they went away. I asked Madam what fashioned necklace I should present her with; she said, "None at all." I asked her whereabout we left off last time, mentioned what I had offered to give her, asked her what she would give me; she said she could not change her condition, she had said so from the beginning, could not be so far from her children. If she held in that mind, I must go home and bewail my rashness in making more haste than good speed.

Monday, November 7th

My son prayed in the old chamber. Our time had been taken up by Son and Daughter Cooper's visit, so that I only read the 130th and 143rd Psalm. 'Twas on the account of my courtship. I went to Madam Winthrop; found her rocking her little Katee in the cradle. I excused my coming so late (near eight). She set me an armed chair and cushion; and so the cradle was between her armed chair and mine. Gave her the remnant of my almonds; she did not eat of them as before, but laid them away; I said I came to inquire whether she had altered her mind since Friday, or remained of the same mind still. She said, "Thereabouts."

I told her I loved her, and was so fond as to think that she loved me. She said [she] had a great respect for me. I told her I had made her an offer without asking any advice; she had so many to advise with that 'twas a hindrance. The fire was come to one short brand besides the block, which brand was set up in end; at last it fell to pieces, and no recruit was made. She gave me a glass of wine. I think I repeated again that I would go home and bewail my rashness in making more haste than good speed. I would endeavor to contain myself, and not go on to solicit her to do that which she could not consent to. Took leave of her. As came down the steps she bid me have a care. Treated me courteously. Told her she had entered the 4th year of her widowhood. I had given her the *News-Letter* before. I did not bid her draw off her glove as some-time I had done. Her dress was not so clean as sometime it had been.

Midweek, November 9th

Dine at Brother Stoddard's; were so kind as to inquire of me if they should invite Madam Winthrop; I answered, "No."

III

Until the introduction of demographic techniques into the study of history, a host of myths about the nature of the colonial family flourished. Everyone assumed that colonial families were com-posed of very large numbers, including six or more children living with their parents, grandparents, and assorted relatives all under one roof. These were extended families, ostensibly characteristic of a preindustrial society. With the advent of more sophisticated tech-niques, the picture underwent drastic change. Analyzing hundreds of documents, of which the one below is an example, counting the actual size of the families and the numbers of relatives in the house-hold, demographers came out with a different finding. The colonial family was often composed of only one generation, and it was fre-quently a good deal smaller in size than had been believed.

The following document is the record taken in 1688 of the inhabitants of Bristol, Rhode Island. Even a quick glance at the in-formation reveals many basic characteristics of family size. Clearly, before we can understand very much about what went on inside the family, we must know about who was in the family.

CENSUS OF BRISTOL, 1688

Feb. 11. All the Families in New Bristol and Children and Servants

	WIFE	CHILDREN	SERVANTS
Mr. Saffin	1	0	8
G. Lewis	1	6	0
G. Martin	1	6	0
G. Penfield	1	5	0

	WIFE	CHILDREN	SERVANTS
Jeremiah Finny	I	I	0
Joshua Finney	I	0	0
Robert Dutch	I	3	0
Solomon G.	I	3	I
Robert Taft	I	5	0
Nathaniel Bosworth	I	2	0
Tommy and Edward (grandchildren)		2	0
Bellamy Bosworth	I	2	0
Benjamin Fenner	I	2 (grown)	0
——— Bowman	I	2	0
David Cary	I	I	0
John Cary	I	7	0
Nicholas Mead	I	6	0
Hugh Woodbury	I	5	0
Anthony Fry	I	7	0
Capt. Sam Woodbry	I	2	2
Eliaship Adams	0	0	0
Nathaniel Paine	I	4	2
John Rogers	I	3	I
William Hedge	I	3	0
Widow Wally	0	I	0
Nathaniel Reynolds	I	8	0
Jeremy Osborn	I	I	I
Major Wally	I	5	4
Stephen Bucklin	I	2	I
John Walkley	I	5	2
Jabez Howland	I	4	2
Simon Davis	I	I	I
William Brutton	I	2	0
Thomas Blesgo	I	0	2
Joseph Sardy	I	3	0
Sam Smith	I	2	0
Sam Cobbett	I	0	0
Watching Atherton	I	4	0
Capt. Nathaniel Byfield	I	2	10
			I Black
John Wilson	I	3	0
Capt. Benjamin Church	I	6	3
Timothy Ingraham	I	0	0
Capt. Nathan Hayman	I	6	2
Capt. Timothy Clark	I	5	2
William Hoar	I	3	3
Joseph Bastor	I	I	0
Ben Ingle	I	0	0
James Burrough	I	3	I
Smithmason [Anon.]	I	5	0
Dan Langdon	I	7	0
Thomas Doggett	I	2	2
Sam Gallop	I	I	0
Edmund Ranger	I	4	0
James Buzzell	I	I	0
John Gladwin	I	7	0
Peter Papillion	I	4	0
G. White younger	I	I	3
Thomas Walker	I	2	I

	WIFE	CHILDREN	SERVANTS
John Smith	1	3	0
Uzal Wardel	1	6	0
Jabez Goram	1	4	0
G. Denis	1	3	0
G. White	1	4	0
G. Corpe	1	3	0
G. Brown	0	3	0
Pumpmaker [Anon.]	1	2	0
William Throop	1	5	0
His son-in-law	1	1	1
Joseph Landen	1	0	0
G. Row	1	10	0
G. Hampden	1	4	0

      70 families 421 souls
Jacob Mason 1 more
Zachary Cary 1 more
      423

In *Early Rehoboth*, ed. Richard Bowen (Rehoboth, Mass., 1945), pp. 74–76.

IV

Like the family, the school in colonial society was very much concerned with the proper moral upbringing of children. Indeed, the task of schooling, even more clearly in the seventeenth and eighteenth centuries than now, was self-consciously aimed at preparing children for their moral and public roles. Schoolmasters were perceived as parents, a definition that gave them wide authority over the children in their charge, including the responsibility for ensuring their understanding and compliance with the religious and secular standards of the society. Hence, when it came to teaching the skills of reading, teachers delighted in using lessons that would not only improve reading skills but behavior as well. The selection below comes from The New England Primer, *the most popular reading book for children. It takes little imagination to sense what schooling must have been like—and what family life must have been like—if these were the kind of sentences that students poured over.*

THE NEW ENGLAND PRIMER, 1727

Now the child being entered in his letters and spelling, let him learn these, and such like sentences by heart, whereby he will be both instructed in his duty, and encouraged in his learning.

In *The New England Primer* (1727). Reprint edition, ed. Paul L. Ford (New York, 1897), pp. 69–72, 78–80.

THE DUTIFUL CHILD'S PROMISES

I   will fear GOD, and honor the KING.
I will honor my father and mother.
I   will obey my superiors.
I   will submit to my elders.
I   will love my friends.
I   will hate no man.
I   will forgive my enemies, and pray to God for them.
I   will as much as in me lies keep all God's Holy Commandments.
I   will learn my catechism.
I   will keep the Lord's day holy.
I   will reverence God's sanctuary,
    For our GOD is a consuming fire.

AN ALPHABET OF LESSONS FOR YOUTH

A   wise son makes a glad father, but a foolish son
    is the heaviness of his mother.
B   etter is a little with the fear of the
    Lord, than great treasure and trouble therewith.
C   ome unto CHRIST all ye that labor
    and are heavy laden, and He will give you rest.
D   o not the abominable thing which I hate,
    saith the Lord.
E   xcept a man be born again, he cannot
    see the Kingdom of God.
F   oolishness is bound up in the heart of
    a child, but the rod of correction
    shall drive it far from him.
G   rieve not the Holy Spirit.
H   oliness becomes God's house forever.
I   t is good for me to draw near unto God.
K   eep thy heart with all diligence, for
    out of it are the issues of life.
L   iars shall have their part in the lake
    which burns with fire and brimstone.

M   any are the afflictions of the
     righteous, but the Lord delivers them
     out of them all.
N   ow is the accepted time, now is the day of salvation.
O   ut of the abundance of the heart the mouth speaketh.
P   ray to thy Father which is in secret and thy Father
     which sees in secret shall reward thee openly.
R   emember thy Creator in the days of thy youth.
S   alvation belongeth to the Lord.
T   rust in God at all times ye people,
     pour out your hearts before him.
U   pon the wicked God shall rain a horrible
     tempest.
W   oe to the wicked, it shall be ill with him,
     for the reward of his hands shall be given him.
eX   ort one another daily while it is called today,
     lest any of you be hardened through the deceitfulness
     of sin.
Y   oung men ye have overcome the wicked one.
Z   eal hath consumed me, because thy enemies
     have forgotten the words of God.

DUTY OF CHILDREN TOWARD THEIR PARENTS

God hath commanded saying, honor thy father and mother, and who curseth father or mother, let him die the death.

Children obey your parents in the Lord for this is right.

Honor thy father and mother (which is the first Commandment with promise).

That it may be well with thee, and that thou may live long on the Earth.

Children, obey your parents in all things, for that is well pleasing unto the Lord.

My son, help thy father in his age, and grieve him not as long as he lives.

And if his understanding fails, have patience with him, and despise him not when thou art in thy full strength.

Who curseth his father or his mother, his lamp shall be out in obscure darkness.

VERSES

I in the Burying Place may see
    Graves shorter there than I;
From Death's Arrest no age is free,
    Young children too may die;
My God, may such an awful Sight,
    Awakening be to me!
Oh! that by early Grace I might
    For Death prepared be.

AGAIN

First in the Morning when thou dost awake,
To God for his Grace thy Petition make,
Some Heavenly Petition use daily to say,
That the God of heaven may bless thee alway.

V

The stake of the society in the good order of the family is dramatically apparent in the nature of court actions and decisions. The line between a moral offense and an illegal act was not finely drawn in eighteenth-century Massachusetts. To the contrary, the very idea of such a division would have provoked surprise and disapproval from eighteenth-century public officials. In many ways, the court saw itself as acting to strengthen the family's rule—it was as outrageous to disobey one's parent as to disobey a magistrate. The courts, like the schools, devoted an extraordinary amount of attention to enforcing not just a law-abiding life style, but a moral life style as well. The case records below, taken from the Massachusetts court at the end of the seventeenth century, convey the quality of this attention.

RECORDS OF THE SUFFOLK COUNTY COURT, 1671–1680

Division of Lorine Estate

Upon the motion of the administrator of the estate of Thomas Lorine, late of Hull, for a division of said estate, the court orders that the widow have her thirds for her life, the eldest son a double portion and the rest of the children equal portions according to law.

Bragg Sentenced

Peter Bragg, presented by the selectmen of this town for abiding in this town without their leave and having a wife in England. The court sentenced him to depart for England with the first opportunity, on penalty of twenty pounds according to law.

Johnson and Moore Sentenced

Abigail Johnson Senior and Naomi Moore [were] convicted for giving entertainment to persons drinking in their houses at unseasonable times of the night. The court sentenced them to give in twenty pounds bond apiece for the good behavior and pay fees of court. Standing committed till the sentence be performed.

Stiles Presented

Robert Stiles being presented for an idle person, the court admonished him and so dismissed him.

In *Collections*, part 1, 1671–1680, Publications of the Colonial Society of Massachusetts (Boston, 1933), vol. 29, pp. 119, 148, 255, 257, 302, 336, 442–443.

Adams Fined Five Pounds

Jonathan Adams of Medfield being presented for absenting himself from the public worship of God on the sabbath days, he owned in court that he worshipped God but did not frequent the public assembly. The court having considered of his offense sentenced him to pay five pounds in money fine to the county and fees of court.

Robinson's Sentence

James Robinson presented for using wicked expressions, the court disenables the said Robinson from crying anything as a public cryer and, upon his first attempt so to do that, he shall be forthwith apprehended by the Constable of Boston and be whipped with fifteen stripes severely laid on and to pay fee of court.

Scott Sentenced

Sarah Scott presented for reviling and striking her mother. Upon due hearing of the case, the court sentenced her to stand upon a block or stool two foot high in the marketplace in Boston upon a Thursday immediately after lecture with an inscription upon her breast in a fair character for undutiful, abusive, and reviling speeches and carriages to her natural mother and to give bond for her good behavior till the next court of this county, ten pounds herself and five pounds apiece, and to pay fee of court; said Sarah Scott as principal in ten pounds and Nathan Greenwood and Thomas Bill as sureties in five pounds apiece acknowledged themselves respectively bound to the treasury of Suffolk on condition that the said Sarah Scott should be of good behavior till the next court of this county and should then appear.

Smith's Sentence

Joseph Smith bound over to this court to answer for his being found by the watch in the house of Abigail King in Boston amongst others at an unreasonable time of the night, where they had been drinking, of which he was convicted in court. The court having considered of his offense herein and his night walking sentenced him to be sent to the house of correction or to pay twenty shillings in money.

Buckminster Sentenced

Sarah Buckminster, widow, being sent for to appear before the court to answer for her committing of fornication and having a bastard child. She owned in court that her husband had been dead about three years and that she had a child of about six weeks old. The court sentenced her to be whipped with ten stripes and ordered the selectmen of Boston to dispose of her into some good family where she may be under government.

Bedwell's Sentence

Mary Bedwell bound over to answer for her keeping company and being too familiar with Walter Hickson, of which she was convicted in court. The court sentenced her to sit in the stocks two hours and to be whipped with fifteen stripes or to pay forty shillings in money as a fine to the county and fees of court standing committed until the sentence be performed and if at any time hereafter she be taken in company of the said Walter Hickson without other company to be forthwith apprehended by the Constable and to be whipped with ten stripes.

Thorn Fined Five Pounds

Mary Thorn bound over to this court to answer for her selling strong beer and ale without license, she owned in court that she did sell strong beer upon a trading day. The court sentenced her to pay five pounds in money as a fine to the county according to law and fees of court standing committed until she performed this sentence.

Wheeler and Peirce Admonished

Elizabeth Wheeler and Joanna Peirce being summoned to appear before the court to answer for their disorderly carriage in the house of Thomas Watts, being married women and found sitting in other men's laps with their arms about their necks. The court upon their acknowledgement of their fault and promise to avoid such offenses for time to come admonished them, ordered them to pay fees of court, and so discharged them.

Chapter 4

The Revolutionary Crowd

THE YEARS 1763 to 1776 were especially turbulent ones for the American colonists. The period that culminated in the outbreak of the American Revolution witnessed an unprecedented number of riots and disorders. In fact, outbreaks were so numerous that the issue of public disorder inevitably became linked with the Revolution itself. To some contemporaries, as well as to later historians, the origins of the Revolution rested with the internal dissension among the colonists. The issue of home rule (the colonists versus the British) became tied to the issue of who should rule at home (the colonists versus the colonists).

There can be no doubt that there was widespread disorder. Immediately following the passage of the Stamp Act riots broke out in Boston, New York, and Newport. Mob actions forced stamp-tax collectors to resign; the homes and furniture of these representatives of British officialdom were put to fire; and in one case, at least, the crowds ran free for several days without the slightest check from public officials. The great moments in the story of the coming of the Revolution were often violent moments; the Tea Act and the Boston Massacre certainly belong to this tradition. Moreover, other incidents of violence broke out during these same years. In North Carolina frontiersmen protested conditions by taking up arms; and although the militia put down the uprising without firing a shot, force—not legal process—ruled the day. In Westchester, New York tenants of the large estates along the Hudson participated in rent strikes; again, it was the militia and not the courts that settled the issue in favor of the landowners.

It is not surprising that historians attempting to understand the roots of the American Revolution have focused on these riots. Many of them contend that the British efforts to tax the colonists or to extend the power of British administrators were necessary—and not especially harmful—acts, which were altogether within the rights of Parliament. And yet the colonists greeted every measure with frantic protests. Why was it that Americans so violently fought the stamp tax

when their rate of taxation was so low? Why did they see in every British act a menace to their liberty? The answer seemed to rest with the tumult at home. According to this interpretation, they were fighting the British because of internal differences. Fundamental class divisions separated the colonists—upper-class property holders in New York, Massachusetts, and Virginia, be they merchants or planters, had very different interests than the lower-class artisans and the propertyless. The riots reflected these differences, and in a sense the British were trapped in the middle. Tumult from below turned against the British, and hence the Revolution.

But social historians consider this explanation inadequate in many respects, and the image of a class-divided, class-warring society in the colonies appears inaccurate. The economic differences among the citizens seem much less striking than their basic similarities. The spread of property throughout colonial society was by no means equal; in fact, increasing differences did emerge, especially in the cities. Yes, there were some large merchants and planters. But an image of the property-less versus the propertied hardly does justice to the vast numbers of citizen freeholders who owned their tools and land, and gave a middle-class character to the social structure.

The materials that follow focus on the famous riots of the Revolutionary era and offer insights into the basic quality of colonial society. As you read them, question whether these riots seem at root to be moments when the unpropertied attacked the propertied. Or do they point to something quite different: an alliance of the propertied and unpropertied, a harmony of interests, or perhaps even a control of the crowd by the propertied? Does the crowd's behavior seem focused and specific, aimed directly at British actions, or do the mobs seem more free floating in character, expressing a general hostility that those in power might well wish to control? The answers to these questions will illuminate not only the basic nature of American society on the eve of the Revolution but will also offer insights into the origins of the Revolution itself.

I

The first of the great riots in the pre-Revolutionary period took place in protest against the Stamp Act. This was the first time the colonists in number and in concert had so vigorously protested an act of Parliament. Understandably, interest in the riots ran high, both at home and abroad. Not only the colonists but British officials as well wondered what these outbursts meant for the future of the imperial links. Cadwallader Colden, New York's lieutenant governor, wrote to his superiors in England a full account of the New York Stamp Act riot, trying to place the events in the context of the colony's social composition. His description helps to clarify the nature of the relationship between public riots and social harmony in the Revolutionary era.

AN ACCOUNT OF THE STAMP ACT RIOT, 1765

CADWALLADER COLDEN

State of the Province of New York
(Sent to the Secretary of State and Board of Trade.)

The people of New York are properly distinguished in different ranks.

1. The proprietors of the large tracts of land, who include within their claims from one hundred thousand of acres to above one million of acres under one grant.
2. The gentlemen of the law make the second class in which properly are included both the bench and the bar. Both of them act on the same principles and are of the most distinguished rank in the policy of the province.
3. The merchants make the third class. Many of them have rose suddenly from the lowest rank of the people to considerable fortunes, and chiefly by illicit trade in the last war. They abhor every limitations of trade and duty on it, and therefore gladly go into every measure whereby they hope to have trade free.
4. In the last rank may be placed the farmers and mechanics [artisans]. Though the farmers hold their lands in fee simple, they are as to condition of life in no way superior to the common farmers in England; and the mechanics such only as are necessary in domestic life. This last rank comprehends the bulk of the people, and in them consists the strength of the province. They are the most useful and the most moral, but always made the dupes of the former; and often are ignorantly made their tools for the worst purposes.

The gentlemen of the law, both the judges and principal practitioners at the bar, are either owners, heirs, or strongly connected in

Originally entitled "The Account of the Lieutenant Governor of New York, Cadwallader Colden, of the Stamp Act Riot, Sent to the Secretary of State and the Board of Trade in England." In *Collections of the New York Historical Society for the Year 1877* (New York, 1878), vol. 2, pp. 68–71, 74–77.

family interest with the proprietors. In general, all the lawyers unite in promoting contention, prolonging suits, and increasing the expense of obtaining justice. Every artifice and chicanery in the law has been so much connived at, or rather encouraged, that honest men who are not of affluent fortunes are deterred from defending their rights or seeking justice.

People in general complain of these things and lament the state of justice, but yet the power of the lawyers is such that every man is afraid of offending them and is deterred from making any public opposition to their power and the daily increase of it.

The gentlemen of the law some years since entered into an association with intention, among other things, to assume the direction of government by the influence they had in the assembly, gained by their family connections and by the profession of the law, whereby they are unavoidably in the secrets of many families—many court their friendship, and all dread their hatred. By these means, though few of them are members, they rule the House of Assembly in all matters of importance. The greatest number of the assembly, being common farmers who know little either of men or things, are easily deluded and seduced.

By this association, united in interest and family connections with the proprietors of the great tracts of land, a domination of lawyers was formed in this province which for some years past has been too strong for the executive powers of government. A domination founded on the same principles and carried on by the same wicked artifices that the domination of priests formerly was in the times of ignorance in the papish countries. Every man's character who dares to discover his sentiments in opposition to theirs is loaded with infamy by every falsehood which malice can invent, and thereby exposed to the brutal rage of the mob. Nothing is too wicked for them to attempt which serves their purposes—the press is to them what the pulpit was in times of popery.

When the king's order in his private council of the twenty-sixth of July arrived in September last, it revived all the rage of the profession

of the law and, taking advantage of the spirit of sedition which was raised in all the colonies against the act of Parliament for laying a stamp duty in the colonies, they turned the rage of the mob against the person of the lieutenant governor, after all other methods which their malice had invented for that purpose had failed.

In the night of the first of November, a great mob came up to the fort gate with two images carried on a scaffold: one representing their gray-haired governor, the other the devil whispering him in the ear. After continuing thus at the gate, with all the insulting ribaldry that malice could invent, they broke open the lieutenant governor's coach house which was without the walls of the fort, carried his chariot round the streets of the town in triumph with the images, returned a second time to the fort gate, and, in an open place near the fort, finished their insult with all the indignities that the malice of their leaders could invent. Their view certainly was to provoke the garrison, then placed on the ramparts, to some act which might be called a commencement of hostilities, in which case it cannot be said what was further intended. Being disappointed in this, the mob expended their rage by destroying everything they found in the house of Major James of the Royal Artillery, for which no reason can be assigned other than his putting the fort in a proper state of defense as his duty in his department required of him.

While the lieutenant governor was in the country as usual during the heat of summer, he received a letter from General Gage informing him that the public papers were crammed with treason. The minds of the people [were] disturbed, excited, and encouraged to revolt against the government to subvert the constitution and trample on the laws.

When the lieutenant governor came to town he found the general had ordered Major James to carry in such artillery and military stores as he thought necessary for the defense of the fort; and two companies of artillery having opportunely arrived at that time from England, they had likewise been ordered into the fort to strengthen the garrison. Mr. James is certainly a benevolent, humane man and had distinguished himself on several occasions in the late war. No objection could be made to him, but his daring to put the king's fort in a state of defense, against the sovereign lords—the people, as they styled themselves—for which offense they resolved to make him an example of their displeasure.

Before these additional defenses were made and while the garrison consisted only of forty-four privates and two subaltern officers, the fort could not have been defended against a hundred resolute men, in which case the governor must have submitted to every shameful condition which the insolence of the leaders of the mob should think proper to impose upon him. They certainly had this in view while the fort remained in its defenseless state. But after it was put in that state of offense as well as defense, in which it was put after the first of November by the engineers of the army, the style of the leaders of the mob was changed from threatening to deprecating, and they only wanted some color [reason] for desisting from their designs to save their credit with the deluded people. It became evident that the fort could not be carried by assault and that in the attempt the town would be exposed to desolation. In the state the fort then was, it was the opinion of the

gentlemen of the army that one regiment in the city would have been sufficient to have subdued the seditious spirit which then prevailed.

The authors of the sedition place their security in the number of offenders and that no jury in the colonies will convict any of them. Were it possible that these men could succeed in their hope of independence of a British Parliament, many judicious persons think (though they dare not declare what they think) we shall become a most unhappy people, the obligation of oaths daringly profaned, and every bond of society dissolved. The liberty and property of individuals will become subject to the avarice and ambition of wicked men who have art enough to keep the colony in perpetual factions by deluding an ignorant mob, and the colonies must become thereby useless to Great Britain.

II

It is surprising how quickly the colonists integrated the fact of political riots into an overview of the nature of the relationship between the mother country and the colony. After all, to the colonists, who were raised in the English tradition, the rule of the mob was hardly a *phenomenon that should cheer or please them. And yet, the post-1765 riots did not spark fundamental and grave fears for the safety of social order. Instead, the more prevalent response was to urge caution, while at the same time to defend the legitimacy of the riot. One of the most notable examples of this spirit appeared in the writings of John Dickinson. Soon after the Stamp Act was passed, he addressed the following argument to his countrymen.*

LETTER FROM A FARMER IN PENNSYLVANIA, 1768

JOHN DICKINSON

My dear Countrymen,

Could you look into my heart you would instantly perceive a zealous attachment to your interests, and a lively resentment of every insult and injury offered to you, to be the motives that have engaged me to address you.

I am no further concerned in anything affecting *American*, than any one of you; and when liberty leaves it, I can quit it much more conveniently than most of you. But while Divine Providence, that gave men existence in a land of freedom, permits my head to think, my lips to speak, and my hand to move, I shall so highly and gratefully value the blessing received as to take care that my silence and inactivity shall not give my implied assent to any act, degrading my brethren and myself from the birthright, wherewith heaven itself *"hath made us free."*

Sorry I am to learn that there are some few persons who shake their heads with solemn motion, and pretend to wonder, what can be the meaning of these letters. *"Great Britain,"* they say, *"is too powerful to contend with; she is determined to oppress us; it is in vain to speak of right on one side, when there is power on the other; when we are strong enough to resist we shall attempt it; but now we are not strong enough, and therefore we had better be quiet, and if we should get into riots and tumults about the late act, it will only draw down heavier displeasure upon us."*

Are these men ignorant that usurpations, which might have been successfully opposed at first, acquire strength by continuance, and thus become irresistible? Do they condemn the conduct of these colonies, concerning the *Stamp Act*? Or have they forgot its successful issue? Should the colonies at that time, instead of acting as they did, have trusted for relief to the fortuitous events of futurity? If it is needless *"to speak of rights"* now, it was as needless then. If the behavior of the colonies was prudent and glorious then, and successful too, it will be equally prudent and glorious to act in the same manner now, if our rights *are* equally invaded, and may be as successful.

As to *"riots and tumults,"* the gentlemen who are so apprehensive

In *Letters from a Farmer in Pennsylvania*, by John Dickinson (1768). Reprint edition (New York, 1962), pp. 15–20.

of them are much mistaken if they think that grievances cannot be redressed without such assistance.

I will now tell the gentlemen what is "the meaning of these letters." The meaning of them is to convince the people of these colonies that they are at this moment exposed to the most imminent dangers, and to persuade them immediately, vigorously, and unanimously, to exert themselves in the most firm, but most peaceable, manner, for obtaining relief.

The cause of *liberty* is a cause of too much dignity to be sullied by turbulence and tumult. It ought to be maintained in a manner suitable to her nature. Those who engage in it should breathe a sedate yet fervent spirit, animating them to actions of prudence, justice, modesty, bravery, humanity, and magnanimity.

I hope, my dear countrymen, that you will, in every colony, be upon your guard against those who may at any time endeavor to stir you up, under pretenses of patriotism, to any measures disrespectful to our Sovereign, and our mother country. Hot, rash, disorderly proceedings injure the reputation of the people as to wisdom, valor, and virtue, without procuring them the least benefit. I pray God that he may be pleased to inspire you and your posterity, to the latest ages, with a spirit of which I have an idea, that I find a difficulty to express. To express it in the best manner I can, I mean a spirit that shall so guide you that it will be impossible to determine whether an *American's* character is most distinguishable for his loyalty to his Sovereign, his duty to his mother country, his love of freedom, or his affection for his native soil.

Every government at some time or other falls into wrong measures. These may proceed from mistake or passion. But every such measure does not dissolve the obligation between the governors and the governed. The mistake may be corrected; the passion may subside. It is the duty of the governed to endeavor to rectify the mistake, and to appease the passion. They have not at first any other right, than to represent their grievances, and to pray for redress, unless an emergency is so pressing as not to allow time for receiving an answer to their applications, which rarely happens. If their applications are disregarded, then that kind of *opposition* becomes justifiable which can be made without breaking the laws or disturbing the public peace. This conflicts in the *prevention of the oppressors reaping advantage from their oppressions*, and not in their punishment. For experience may teach them what reason did not; and harsh methods cannot be proper until milder ones have failed.

If at length it becomes *undoubted* that an inveterate resolution is formed to annihilate the liberties of the governed, the *English* history affords frequent examples of resistance by force. What particular circumstances will in any future case justify such resistance can never be ascertained till they happen. Perhaps it may be allowable to say generally that it never can be justifiable until the people are *fully convinced* that any further submission will be destructive to their happiness.

When the appeal is made to the sword, highly probable is it that the punishment will exceed the offense; and the calamities attending on war outweigh those preceding it. These considerations of justice and prudence will always have great influence with good and wise men.

We cannot act with too much caution in our disputes. Anger produces anger; and differences, that might be accommodated by kind and respectful behavior, may, by imprudence, be enlarged to an incurable rage. In quarrels between countries, as well as in those between individuals, when they have risen to a certain height, the first cause of dissension is no longer remembered, the minds of the parties being wholly engaged in recollecting and resenting the mutual expressions of their dislike. When feuds have reached that fatal point, all considerations of reason and equity vanish; and a blind fury governs, or rather confounds all things. A people no longer regards their interest, but the gratification of their wrath.

The constitutional modes of obtaining relief are those which I wish to see pursued on the present occasion; that is, by petitions of our assemblies, or where they are not permitted to meet, of the people, to the powers that can afford us relief.

We have an excellent Prince, in whose good dispositions toward us we may confide. We have a generous, sensible, and humane nation, to whom we may apply. They may be deceived. They may, by artful men, be provoked to anger against us. I cannot believe they will be cruel and unjust; or that their anger will be implacable. Let us behave like dutiful children who have received unmerited blows from a beloved parent. Let us complain to our parent; but let our complaints speak at the same time the language of affliction and veneration.

If, however, it shall happen, by an unfortunate course of affairs, that our applications to his Majesty and the Parliament for redress, prove ineffectual, let us then take *another step*, by withholding from *Great Britain* all the advantages she has been used to receive from us. Then let us try, if our ingenuity, industry, and frugality will not give weight to our remonstrances. Let us all be united with one spirit, in one cause. Let us invent—let us work—let us save—let us, continually, keep up our claim, and incessantly repeat our complaints—but, above all, let us implore the protection of that infinitely good and gracious being, "by whom kings reign, and princes decree justice."

Nil desperandum.

Nothing is to be despaired of.
                    A Farmer

III

Few of the colonial riots inspired as many charges and countercharges as the Boston Massacre. For some observers it represented nothing more than an instance of the riffraff of the city, particularly its sailors, needlessly provoking the British soldier; for others, it was the very culmination of their worst fears—British soldiers, quartered in Boston against the wishes of the colonists, had murdered in senseless fashion a well-ordered, albeit protesting, crowd. Below are two reports on the event. They offer the reader the opportunity to play historical detective. Which of the reports seems the more genuine and accurate? More important, the two accounts reveal just how far apart the views of the colonists were from those of the British officials.

CAPTAIN PRESTON'S ACCOUNT OF THE BOSTON MASSACRE, 1770

THOMAS PRESTON

It is [a] matter of too great notoriety to need any proofs that the arrival of his Majesty's troops in Boston was extremely obnoxious to its inhabitants. They have ever used all means in their power to weaken the regiments, and to bring them into contempt by promoting and aiding desertions. On the arrival of the sixthy-fourth and sixty-fifth their ardor seemingly began to abate; it being too expensive to buy off so many, and attempts of that kind rendered too dangerous from the numbers. But the same spirit revived immediately on its being known that those regiments were ordered for Halifax, and has ever since their departure been breaking out with greater violence after their embarkation. One of their justices, most thoroughly acquainted with the people and their intentions, openly and publicly in the hearing of great numbers of people and from the seat of justice, declared "that the soldiers must now take care of themselves, *nor trust too much their arms*, for they were but a handful; that the inhabitants carried weapons concealed under their clothes, and would destroy them in a moment, *if they pleased.*" This, considering the malicious temper of the people, was an alarming circumstance to the soldiery. Since which several disputes have happened between the townspeople and the soldiers of both regiments, the former being encouraged thereto by the countenance of even some of the magistrates, and by the protection of all the party against government. In general such disputes have been kept too secret from the officers. On the second of March, two of the twenty-ninth going through one Gray's ropewalk, the ropemakers insultingly asked them if they would empty a vault [outhouse]. This had the desired effect by provoking the soldiers, and from words they went to blows. Both parties suffered in this affray, and finally the soldiers retired to their quarters. The insolence as well as utter hatred of the inhabitants to the troops increased daily, insomuch that Monday and Tuesday, the fifth and sixth instant, were privately agreed on for a general engagement, in consequence of which several of the militia came from the country armed to join their friends, menacing to destroy any who should oppose them. This plan has since been discovered.

On Monday night about 8 o'clock two soldiers were attacked and beaten. But the party of the townspeople in order to carry matters to the utmost length, broke into two meetinghouses and rang the alarm bells, which I supposed was for fire as usual, but was soon undeceived.

In *English Historical Documents*, vol. 9, *American Colonial Documents to 1776*, ed. Merrill Jensen (London, 1964), pp. 750–53.

About 9 some of the guard came to and informed me the town inhabitants were assembling to attack the troops, and that the bells were ringing as the signal for that purpose and not for fire, and the beacon intended to be fired to bring in the distant people of the country. This, as I was captain of the day, occasioned my repairing immediately to the main guard. In my way there I saw the people in great commotion, and heard them use the most cruel and horrid threats against the troops. In a few minutes after I reached the guard, about one hundred people passed it and went toward the customhouse where the King's money is lodged. They immediately surrounded the sentry posted there, and with clubs and other weapons threatened to execute their vengeance on him. I was soon informed by a townsman their intention was to carry off the soldier from his post and probably murder him.

This I feared might be a prelude to their plundering the King's chest. I immediately sent a noncommissioned officer and twelve men to protect the sentry and the King's money, and very soon followed myself to prevent, if possible, all disorder, fearing lest the officer and soldiers, by the insults and provocations of the rioters, should be thrown off their guard and commit some rash act. They soon rushed through the people, and by charging their bayonets in half-circles, kept them at a little distance. Nay, so far was I from intending the death of any person that I suffered the troops to go to the spot where the unhappy affair took place without any loading in their pieces; nor did I ever give orders for loading them. This remiss conduct in me perhaps merits censure; yet it is evidence, resulting from the nature of things, which is the best and surest that can be offered, that my intention was not to act offensively, but the contrary part, and that not without compulsion. The mob still increased and were more outrageous, striking their clubs or budgeons one against another, and calling out, come on you rascals, you bloody backs, you lobster scoundrels, fire if you dare, God damn you, fire and be damned, we know you dare not, and much more such language was used. At this time I was between the soldiers and the mob, parleying with, and endeavoring all in my power to persuade them to retire peaceably, but to no purpose. They advanced to the points of the bayonets, struck some of them. On which some well behaved persons asked me if the guns were charged. I replied yes. They then asked me if I intended to order the men to fire. I answered no, by no means, observing to them that I was advanced before the muzzles of the men's pieces, and must fall a sacrifice if they fired; that the soldiers were upon the half cock and charged bayonets, and my giving the word fire under those circumstances would prove me to be no officer. While I was thus speaking, one of the soldiers having received a severe blow with a stick, stepped a little on one side and instantly fired, on which turning to and asking him why he fired without orders, I was struck with a club on my arm, which for some time deprived me of the use of it, which blow had it been placed on my head, most probably would have destroyed me. On this a general attack was made on the men by a great number of heavy clubs and snowballs being thrown at them, by which all our lives were in imminent danger, some persons at the same time from behind calling out, damn your bloods—why don't you fire. Instantly three or four of the soldiers fired, one after another, and directly after three more in the same confusion and hurry. The mob then ran away, except three unhappy men who instantly expired, one more is since dead, three others are dangerously, and four slightly wounded. The whole of this melancholy affair was transacted in almost twenty minutes. On my asking the soldiers why they fired without orders, they said they heard the word fire and supposed it came from me. This might be the case as many of the mob called out fire, fire, but I assured the men that I gave no such order; that my words were, don't fire, stop your firing. In short, it was scarcely possible for the soldiers to know who said fire, or don't fire, or stop your firing.

A Council was immediately called, on the breaking up of which three justices met and issued a warrant to apprehend me and eight soldiers. On hearing of this procedure I instantly went to the sheriff and surrendered myself, though for the space of four hours I had it in my power to have made my escape, which I most undoubtedly should have attempted and could easily executed, had I been the least conscious of any guilt. Five or six more are to swear I gave the word to fire. So bitter and inveterate are many of the malcontents here that they are industriously using every method to fish out evidence to prove it was a concerted scheme to murder the inhabitants. Others are infusing the utmost malice and revenge into the minds of the people who are to be my jurors by false publications, votes of towns, and all other artifices. That so from a settled rancor against the officers and troops in general, the suddenness of my trial after the affair while the people's minds are all greatly inflamed, I am, though perfectly innocent under most unhappy circumstances, having nothing in reason to expect but the loss of life in a very ignominious manner, without the interposition of his Majesty's royal goodness.

THE HORRID MASSACRE IN BOSTON, 1770

PERPETRATED IN THE EVENING OF THE FIFTH DAY OF MARCH 1770, BY SOLDIERS OF THE TWENTY-NINTH REGIMENT, WHICH WITH THE FOURTEENTH REGIMENT WERE THEN QUARTERED THERE; WITH SOME OBSERVATIONS ON THE STATE OF THINGS PRIOR TO THAT CATASTROPHE. GATHERED AND PRINTED BY THE TOWN OF BOSTON, 1770.

It may be a proper introduction to this narrative briefly to represent the state of things for some time previous to the said massacre; and this seems necessary in order to the forming a just idea of the causes of it.

At the end of the late war, in which this province bore so distinguished a part, a happy union subsisted between Great Britain and the colonies. This was unfortunately interrupted by the Stamp Act; but it was in some measure restored by the repeal of it. It was again

In *A Short Narrative of the Horrid Massacre in Boston* (Boston, 1770). Reprint edition (New York, 1849), pp. 13–19, 21–22, 28–30.

interrupted by other acts of Parliament for taxing America; and by the appointment of a Board of Commissioners, in pursuance of an act, which by the face of it was made for the relief and encouragement of commerce, but which in its operation, it was apprehended, would have, and it has in fact had, a contrary effect. By the said act the said Commissioners were "to be resident in some convenient part of his Majesty's dominions in America." This must be understood to be in some part convenient for the whole. Judging by the act, it may seem this town was intended to be favored, by the Commissioners being appointed to reside here; and that the consequence of that residence would be relief and encouragement of commerce; but the reverse has been the constant and uniform effect of it; so that the commerce of the town, from the embarrassments in which it has been lately involved, is greatly reduced.

The residence of the Commissioners here has been detrimental, not only to the commerce, but to the political interest of the town and province; and not only so, but we can trace from it the causes of the late horrid massacre. Soon after their arrival here in November 1767, instead of confining themselves to the proper business of their office, they became partisans of Governor Bernard in his political schemes; and had the weakness and temerity to infringe upon one of the most essential rights of the house of commons of this province—that of giving their votes with freedom, and not being accountable therefore but to their constituents. One of the members of that house, Captain Timothy Folgier, having voted in some affair contrary to the mind of said Commissioners, was for so doing dismissed from the office he held under them.

These proceedings of theirs, the difficulty of access to them on office business, and a supercilious behavior, rendered them disgustful to people in general, who in consequence thereof treated them with neglect. This probably stimulated them to resent it; and to make their resentment felt, they and their coadjutor, Governor Bernard, made such representations to his Majesty's ministers as they thought best calculated to bring the displeasure of the nation upon the town and province; and in order that those representations might have the more weight, they are said to have contrived and executed plans for exciting disturbances and tumults, which otherwise would probably never have existed; and, when excited, to have transmitted to the ministry the most exaggerated accounts of them.

Unfortunately for us, they have been to successful in their said representations, which, in conjunction with Governor Bernard's, have occasioned his Majesty's faithful subjects of this town and province to be treated as enemies and rebels, by an invasion of the town by sea and land. While the town was surrounded by a considerable number of his Majesty's ships of war, two regiments landed and took possession of it; and to support these, two other regiments arrived some time after from Ireland; one of which landed at Castle Island, and the other in the town.

Thus were we, in aggravation of our other embarrassments, embarrassed with troops, forced upon us contrary to our inclination, contrary to the very letter of the Bill of Rights, in which it is declared that the raising or keeping of a standing army within the kingdom in time of peace, unless it be with the consent of Parliament, is against law, and without the desire of the civil magistrates, to aid whom was the pretense for sending the troops hither; who were quartered in the town in direct violation of an act of Parliament for quartering troops in America.

As they were the procuring cause of troops being sent hither, they must therefore be the remote and blameable cause of all the disturbances and bloodshed that have taken place in consequence of that measure.

We shall next attend to the conduct of the troops, and to some circumstances relative to them.

The challenging [of] the inhabitants by sentinels posted in all parts of the town before the lodgings of officers, which (for about six months, while it lasted), occasioned many quarrels and uneasiness.

Captain Wilson, of the fifty-ninth, exciting the Negroes of the town to take away their masters' lives and property, and repair to the army for protection, which was fully proved against him. The attack of a party of soldiers on some of the magistrates of the town—the repeated rescues of soldiers from peace officers—the firing of a loaded musket in a public street, to the endangering a great number of peaceable inhabitants—the frequent wounding of persons by their bayonets and cutlasses, and the numerous instances of bad behavior in the soldiery, made us early sensible that the troops were not sent here for any benefit to the town or province, and that we had no good to expect from such conservators of the peace.

It was not expected, however, that such an outrage and massacre, as happened here on the evening of the fifth instant, would have been perpetrated. There were then killed and wounded, by a discharge of musketry, eleven of his Majesty's subjects, viz.:

> Mr. Samuel Gray, killed on the spot by a ball entering his head.
> Crispus Attucks, a mulatto, killed on the spot, two balls entering his breast.
> Mr. James Caldwell, killed on the spot, by two balls entering his back.
> Mr. Samuel Maverick, a youth of seventeen years of age, mortally wounded; he died the next morning.
> Mr. Patrick Carr mortally wounded; he died the fourteenth instant.
> Christopher Monk and John Clark, youths about seventeen years of age, dangerously wounded. It is apprehended they will die.
> Mr. Edward Payne, merchant, standing at his door; wounded.
> Messrs. John Green, Robert Patterson, and David Parker; all dangerously wounded.

The actors in this dreadful tragedy were a party of soldiers commanded by Captain Preston of the twenty-ninth regiment. This party, including the Captain, consisted of eight, who are all committed to jail.

What gave occasion to the melancholy event of that evening seems to have been this. A difference having happened near Mr. Gray's ropewalk, between a soldier and a man belonging to it, the soldier challenged the ropemakers to a boxing match. The challenge was accepted by one of them, and the soldier worsted. He ran to the barrack in the neighborhood, and returned with several of his companions. The fray was renewed, and the soldiers were driven off. This happened several times till at length a considerable body of soldiers was collected, and they also were driven off, the ropemakers having been joined by their brethren of the contiguous ropewalks. By this time Mr. Gray being alarmed interposed, and with the assistance of some gentlemen prevented any further disturbance. To satisfy the soldiers and punish the man who had been the occasion of the first difference, and as an example to the rest, he turned him out of his service; and waited on Colonel Dalrymple, the commanding officer of the troops, and with him concerted measures for preventing further mischief. Though this affair ended thus, it made a strong impression on the minds of the soldiers in general, who thought the honor of the regiment concerned to revenge those repeated repulses. For this purpose they seem to have formed a combination to commit some outrage upon the inhabitants of the town indiscriminately; and this was to be done on the evening of the fifth instant or soon after.

Samuel Drowne [a witness] declares that, about nine o'clock of the evening of the fifth of March current, standing at his own door in Cornhill, he saw about fourteen or fifteen soldiers of the twenty-ninth regiment, who came from Murray's barracks, armed with naked cutlasses, swords, etc., and came upon the inhabitants of the town, then standing or walking in Cornhill, and abused some, and violently assaulted others as they met them; most of them were without so much as a stick in their hand to defend themselves, as he very clearly could discern, it being moonlight, and himself being one of the assaulted persons. All or most of the said soldiers he saw go into King Street (some of them through Royal Exchange Lane), and there followed them, and soon discovered them to be quarreling and fighting with the people whom they saw there, which he thinks were not more than a dozen, when the soldiers came first, armed as aforesaid. Of those dozen people, the most of them were gentlemen, standing together a little below the Town House, upon the Exchange. At the appearance of those soldiers so armed, the most of the twelve persons went off, some of them being first assaulted.

The violent proceedings of this party, and their going into King Street "quarreling and fighting with the people whom they saw there" (mentioned in Mr. Drowne's deposition), was immediately introductory to the grand catastrophe.

These assailants, who issued from Murray's barracks (so-called), after attacking and wounding divers persons in Cornhill, as abovementioned, being armed, proceeded (most of them) up the Royal Exchange Lane into King Street; where, making a short stop, and after assaulting and driving away the few they met there, they brandished their arms and cried out, "Where are the boogers! Where are the cowards!" At this time there were very few persons in the street beside themselves. This party in proceeding from Exchange Lane into King Street, must pass the sentry posted at the westerly corner of the Custom House, which butts on that lane and fronts on that street. This is needful to be mentioned, as near that spot and in that street the bloody tragedy was acted, and the street actors in it were stationed: their station being but a few feet from the front side of the said Custom House. The out-

rageous behavior and the threats of the said party occasioned the ringing
of the meetinghouse bell near the head of King Street, which bell ringing quick, as for fire, it presently brought out a number of the inhabitants, who being soon sensible of the occasion of it, were naturally
led to King Street, where the said party had made a stop but a little
while before, and where their stopping had drawn together a number
of boys, round the sentry at the Custom House. Whether the boys mis-
took the sentry for one of the said party, and thence took occasion to
differ with him, or whether he first affronted them, which is affirmed in
several depositions—however that may be, there was much foul
language between them, and some of them, in consequence of his push-
ing at them with his bayonet, threw snowballs at him, which occasioned him to knock hastily at the door of the Custom House. From
hence two persons thereupon proceeded immediately to the mainguard
which was posted opposite to the State House, at a small distance, near
the head of the said street. The officer on guard was Captain Preston,
who with seven or eight soldiers, with firearms and charged bayonets,
issued from the guardhouse, and in great haste posted himself and his
soldiers in front of the Custom House, near the corner aforesaid. In
passing to this station the soldiers pushed several persons with their
bayonets, driving through the people in so rough a manner that it
appeared they intended to create a disturbance. This occasioned some
snowballs to be thrown at them, which seems to have been the only
provocation that was given. Mr. Knox (between whom and Captain
Preston there was some conversation on the spot) declares that while
he was talking with Captain Preston, the soldiers of his detachment
had attacked the people with their bayonets; and that there was not the
least provocation given to Captain Preston or his party; the backs of
the people being toward them when the people were attacked. He also
declares that Captain Preston seemed to be in great haste and much
agitated, and that, according to his opinion, there were not then present
in King Street above seventy or eighty persons at the extent.

The said party was formed into a half circle; and within a short
time after they had been posted at the Custom House, began to fire
upon the people.

Captain Preston is said to have ordered them to fire, and to have
repeated that order. One gun was fired first; then others in succession,
and with deliberation, till ten or a dozen guns were fired; or till that
number of discharges were made from the guns that were fired. By
which means eleven persons were killed or wounded, as above
represented.

IV

*One result of the Boston Massacre was to inspire a commemorative
meeting and oration every year on March fifteenth. The second
speech in this series was made by Joseph Warren, and he, like*

others, used this occasion to consider British-American problems. His speech offers a good opportunity to evaluate the political implications of mob violence. Compare Warren's views with those in Dickinson's tract. Mob action clearly has become a more legitimate form of political action. There is little indication here of the community being at odds with itself. Rather, to a remarkable degree, Warren's rhetoric points to a confident acceptance of the risks inherent in such violent tactics.

BOSTON MASSACRE ORATION, 1772

JOSEPH WARREN

The ruinous consequences of standing armies to free communities may be seen in the histories of Syracuse, Rome, and many other once flourishing states; some of which have now scarce a name! Their baneful influence is most suddenly felt when they are placed in populous cities; for, by a corruption of morals, the public happiness is immediately affected! And that this is one of the effects of quartering troops in a populous city, is a truth, to which many a mourning parent, many a lost despairing child in this metropolis must bear a very melancholy testimony. Soldiers are also taught to consider arms as the only arbiters by which every dispute is to be decided between contending states; they are instructed implicitly to obey their commanders, without enquiring into the justice of the cause they are engaged to support; hence it is that they are ever to be dreaded as the ready engines of tyranny and oppression. And it is too observable that they are prone to introduce the same mode of decision in the disputes of individuals, and from thence have often arisen great animosities between them and the inhabitants, who, while in a naked, defenseless state, are frequently insulted and abused by an armed soldiery. And this will be more especially the case when the troops are informed that the intention of their being stationed in any city is to overawe the inhabitants. That this was the avowed design of stationing an armed force in this town is sufficiently known; and we, my fellow citizens, have seen, we have felt the tragical effects! *The fatal fifth of March 1770, can never be forgotten.* The horrors of *that dreadful night* are but too deeply impressed on our hearts. Language is too feeble to paint the emotion of our souls, when our streets were stained with the blood of our brethren—when our ears were wounded by the groans of the dying, and our eyes were tormented with the sight of the mangled bodies of the dead.

The immediate actors in the tragedy of that night were surrendered to justice. It is not mine to say how far they were guilty. They have been tried by the country and *acquitted* of murder! And they are not to be again arraigned at an earthly bar; but, surely the men who have promiscuously scattered death amid the innocent inhabitants of a populous city ought to see well to it that they be prepared to stand at

In *English Historical Documents*, vol. 9, *American Colonial Documents to 1776*, ed. Merrill Jensen (London, 1964), pp. 755–59.

the bar of an omniscient judge! And all who contrived or encouraged the stationing troops in this place have reasons of eternal importance to reflect with deep contrition on their base designs, and humbly to repent of their impious machinations.

The infatuation which hath seemed, for a number of years, to prevail in the British councils, with regard to us, is truly astonishing! What can be proposed by the repeated attacks made upon our freedom, I really cannot surmise; even leaving justice and humanity out of question. I do not know one single advantage which can arise to the British nation from our being enslaved. I know not of any gains which can be wrung from us by oppression which they may not obtain from us by our own consent in the smooth channel of commerce. We wish the wealth and prosperity of Britain; we contribute largely to both. Does what we contribute loose all its value because it is done voluntarily?

If we complain, our complaints are treated with contempt; if we assert our rights, that assertion is deemed insolence; if we humbly offer to submit the matter to the impartial decision of reason, the *sword* is judged the most proper argument to silence our murmurs! But this cannot long be the case. Surely the British nation will not suffer the reputation of their justice and their honor to be thus sported away by a capricious ministry; no, they will in a short time open their eyes to their true interest. They nourish in their own breasts a noble love of liberty; they hold her dear, and they know that all who have once possessed her charms had rather die than suffer her to be torn from their embraces.

You have, my friends and countrymen, frustrated the designs of your enemies by your unanimity and fortitude. It was your union and determined spirit which expelled those troops who polluted your streets with innocent blood. You have appointed this anniversary as a standard memorial of the *bloody consequences of placing an armed force in a populous city*, and of your deliverance from the dangers which then seemed to hang over your heads; and I am confident that you never will betray the least want of spirit when called upon to guard your freedom. None but they who set a just value upon the blessings of liberty are worthy to enjoy her. Your illustrious fathers were her zealous votaries. When the blasting frowns of tyranny drove her from public view they clasped her in their arms; they brought her safe over the rough ocean and fixed her seat in this then dreary wilderness; they nursed her infant age with the most tender care; for her sake they patiently bore the severest hardships; for her support they underwent the most rugged toils, in her defense they boldly encountered the most alarming dangers; neither the ravenous beasts that ranged the woods for prey, nor the more furious savages of the wilderness could damp ardor! While with one hand they broke the stubborn glebe, with the other they grasped their weapons, ever ready to protect her from danger. No sacrifice, not even their own blood, was esteemed too rich a libation for her altar!

And as they left you this glorious legacy, they have undoubtedly transmitted to you some portion of their noble spirit, to inspire you with virtue to merit her, and courage to preserve her. You surely cannot, with such examples before your eyes, as every page of the history of this country affords, suffer your liberties to be ravished from you by lawless force, or cajoled away by flattery and fraud. If you, with united zeal and fortitude, oppose the torrent of oppression; if you feel the true fire of patriotism burning in your breasts; if you, from your souls, despise the most gaudy dress that slavery can wear; if you really prefer the lonely cottage (while blessed with liberty) to gilded palaces surrounded with the ensigns of slavery, you may have the fullest assurance that tyranny, with her whole accursed train, will hide their hideous heads in confusion, shame, and despair. If you perform your part, you must have the strongest confidence that the same Almighty Being who protected your pious and venerable forefathers—who enabled them to turn a barren wilderness into a fruitful field, who so often made bare his arm for their salvation, will still be mindful of you, their offspring.

May this Almighty Being graciously preside in all our councils. May He direct us to such measures as He Himself shall approve, and be pleased to bless. May we ever be a people favored of God. May our land be a land of liberty, the seat of virtue, the asylum of the oppressed, a name and a praise in the whole earth, until the last shock of time shall bury the empires of the world in one common undistinguished ruin!

V

To those American colonists who opposed the break with the mother country—Tories—the mob actions represented all that was irrational and mistaken about the move to independence. For the Tories, but not for the Revolutionaries, the unleashing of the mob was to be condemned not only for precipitating the war with England, but for promising to keep this country in turmoil for decades to come. In fact, the differing views on mob action most dramatically separated the Loyalist from the Revolutionary. The Tory analysis presented by Peter Oliver will help the reader to form his own judgments on the impulse and character of mob action in the Revolutionary era.

ORIGIN AND PROGRESS OF THE AMERICAN REBELLION, 1781

PETER OLIVER

Tarring and Feathering

About this time was invented the art of tarring and feathering; and the invention was reserved for the genius of New England. The town of Salem, about twenty miles from Boston, hath the honor of

In *Origin and Progress of the American Rebellion,* by Peter Oliver, ed. Douglas Adair and John Schutz (San Marino, Calif., 1963), pp. 93–96, 98, 100–105, 118–21.

this invention, as well as that of witchcraft in the year 1692, when many innocent persons suffered death by judicial processes.

The following is the recipe for an effectual operation. "First, strip a person naked, then heat the tar until it is thin, and pour it upon the naked flesh, or rub it over with a tar brush. After which, sprinkle decently upon the tar, while it is yet warm, as many feathers as will stick to it. Then hold a lighted candle to the feathers, and try to set it all on fire; if it will burn, so much the better.

I know no other origin of this modern punishment by the rabble of their state criminals than this; namely, that the first book that New England children are taught to read in is called *The New England Primer*. In the front of it is depicted the Pope, stuck around with darts. This is the only clue I can find to lead me to the origin of this invention. In order to keep in memory the soldiers firing on the night of the fifth of March, they instituted an anniversary oration, upon what they called the Massacre. This kept the minds of the rabble in constant irritation, and thus was the fire of contention fed with constant fuel, until the town of Boston was evacuated of the filth of sedition in 1775.

1772

In the winter of this year, the ruling powers seized upon a custom-house officer for execution. They stripped him, tarred, feathered, and haltered him, carried him to the gallows, and whipped him with great barbarity in the presence of thousands, some of them members of the general court. Like the Negro drivers in the West Indies, if you grumbled at so wholesome a discipline, you had iniquity added to transgression, and lash succeeded lash; and there was but one way of escaping, which was to feign yourself dead if you were not already so; for in that case you would be left to yourself to come to life again as well as you could, they being afraid of such dead men lest they themselves should die after them, sooner or later. One customhouse officer they left so for dead, but some persons of humanity stepped into his relief and saved him.

The plague which spread through the great part of Massachusetts, and had overspread the town of Boston was of the confluent sort. It was so contagious that the infection was caught by the neighboring colonies. Rhode Island, some years before in a most riotous manner had rifled the houses and hunted after the lives of several gentlemen who were obnoxious by their attachment to government. In this year, the mob burnt his Majesty's schooner *Gaspee* on the Narragansset Shore, about twenty miles from Newport. This made some noise in England; from a misrepresentation of facts, a commission was sent over, empowering the Governor of Rhode Island, the Chief Justices of Massachusetts, New York, and New Jersies, and the Judge of the Vice Admiralty Court of Massachusetts, to inquire into the facts. The people of that colony were so closely connected, and so disaffected from the nature of their government to British legislation that it was perfectly futile to make an inquiry, and the matter ended without any other effect from the commission than an encouragement to those colonists to play the same game again upon the first opportunity.

Boston Tea Party

Thus things went on until 1773, when the design of the Parliament was announced of sending over the East India Company's tea. The decks were now cleared for an engagement, and all hands were ready. The teas at last arrived in the latter end of autumn, and now committee men and mob men were buzzing about in swarms, like bees, with every one their sting. They applied first to the consignees to compel them to ship the teas back again. The mob collected with their great men in front. They attacked the stores and dwelling houses of the consignees, but they found them too firm to flinch from their duty; the mob insisted that the teas should be sent to England. At last, the rage of the mob, urged on by the smugglers and the heads of the faction, was increased to such a height that the consignees were obliged to fly for protection to the Castle, as the King's ship in the harbor, which was ordered to give them protection, refused it to them. There was no authority to defend any man from injury.

The faction did what was right in their own eyes; they accordingly planned their maneuver and procured some of the inhabitants of the neighboring towns to assist them. The mob had, partly, Indian dresses procured for them, and that the action they were about to perpetrate might be sanctified in a peculiar manner, Adams, Hancock, and the leaders of the faction assembled the rabble in the largest dissenting meetinghouse in the town, where they had frequently assembled to pronounce their annual orations upon their massacre, and to perpetrate their most atrocious acts of treason and rebellion, thus, literally, "turning the house of God into a den of thieves."

Thus assembled on December fourteenth, they whiled away the

time in speechmaking, hissing, and clapping, cursing and swearing until it grew near to darkness; and then the signal was given to act their deeds of darkness. They crowded down to the wharves where the tea ships lay and began to unload. They then burst the chests of tea, when many persons filled their bags and their pockets with it, and made a teapot of the harbor of Boston with the remainder; and it required a large teapot for several hundred chests of tea to be poured into at one time. Had they have been prudent enough to have poured it into fresh water instead of salt water, they and their wives, their children, and their little ones might have regaled upon it, at free cost, for twelve months, but now the fish had the whole regale to themselves. Whether it suited the constitution of a fish is not said; but it is said that some of the inhabitants of Boston would not eat of fish caught in their harbor because they had drank of the East India tea.

After the destruction of the tea, the Massachusetts faction found they had past the Rubicon; it was now neck or nothing. They therefore went upon committees of correspondence and drew up what they called a solemn league and covenant, whereto everyone was to subscribe, not to import from England nor to deal with any that did, and to renounce all connection with those who sold English goods. This was a truly infernal scheme; it was setting the nearest relations and most intimate friends at irreconcilable variance, and it had that most accursed effect of raising a most unnatural enmity between parents and children and husbands and wives.

The dissenting hierarchy lent their aid to sanctify the treason and I knew a clergyman of some note in a country town who went to the meetinghouse where the inhabitants usually assembled upon their civil affairs and took his seat at the communion table, and in the plentitude of priestly power declared to the assembly then convened on the solemn league and covenant that whoever would not subscribe to it was not fit to approach that table to commemorate the death and sufferings of the savior of mankind. This was truly making a league with the Devil and a covenant with hell.

Thus, tarring and feathering, solemn leagues and covenants, and riots reigned uncontrolled. The liberty of the press was restrained by the very men who, for years past, had been halloowing for liberty herself; those printers, who were inclined to support government, were threatened and greatly discouraged. So that the people were deprived of the means of information and the faction had engrossed the press, which now groaned with all the falsities that seditious brains could invent, which were crammed down the credulity of the vulgar.

Lexington and Concord

In the spring of 1775, the war began to redden. General Gage having intelligence that a quantity of warlike stores were collected at Concord, about twenty miles from Boston, judged it most prudent to seize them. Accordingly, just about midnight of the eighteenth of April, he privately dispatched about eight hundred men for that purpose, they executed part of their orders, but to no important effect. This party was attacked by a number who had previous notice of their march. Much stress has been laid upon who fired the first gun. This was immaterial, for as the civil government had been resolved by the Suffolk resolves, the military power had a right to suppress all hostile appearances. But in the present case, the commanding officer ordered the armed rabble to disperse, upon which some of the armed rabble returned an answer from their loaded muskets. The King's troops then returned the fire, the alarm spread, and ten or twelve thousand men, some say more, flanked them and kept in the rear at turns. The battle continued for the whole day. After this first corps had fought, on their return, for many miles, they had expended most of their ammunition, and must have submitted as prisoners had not Lord Percy met them with a fresh brigade, with two pieces of artillery. This fortunate circumstance saved them from total ruin. When united, they still fought, but the cannon checked the progress of the rebels, who kept at a greater distance and chiefly fired from houses and from behind hedges, trees, and stone walls. As the King's troops approached their headquarters, the battle thickened upon them, for every town which they passed through increased the numbers of their enemies, so that they had not less than ten or twelve thousand to combat with in the course of the day.

After the battle of Lexington, there was a general uproar through the neighboring colonies, the echo of which soon extended throughout

the continent. Adams, with his rabble rout and his clergy sounding the
trumpet of rebellion to inspire them, had blown the bellows so long that
the iron was quite hot enough to be hammered. The news of the battle
flew with rapidity; one post met another to tell the doleful tale of the
King's troops burning houses and putting to death the inhabitants of
towns. Industry never labored harder than the faction did in propagat-
ing the most atrocious falsehoods to inspirit the people to the grossest
acts of violence, and they had a great advantage in doing it by engrossing
the tale almost to themselves, and by suppressing the true state of facts.
At last, indeed, General Gage, by great assiduity, found means to
undeceive those who had preserved any coolness of temper. As for the
qui vult decipi decipiatur [those who wish to be deceived, let them be
deceived], he there could make no impression; thus the rupture could
not be closed.

SUGGESTIONS FOR
FURTHER READING

The history of the *Proper Plantation* in Virginia and subsequent developments in the colony are traced in Wesley F. Craven, *The Southern Colonies in the 17th Century, 1607–1689* (Baton Rouge, 1949), and his *White, Red and Black* (Princeton, 1972). An older, but fascinating account of Virginia's social history is to be found in Philip A. Bruce, *The Institutional History of Virginia* (two volumes, New York, 1910).

A brief and readable introduction to *Puritanism* can be found in Edmund Morgan, *The Puritan Dilemma: The Story of John Winthrop* (Boston, 1958). On the decline of the authority of the Puritan Church see Darrett Rutman, *Winthrop's Boston* (Chapel Hill, 1965). An interesting, if erratic, analysis of a major crisis in the Puritan community is Emery Battis's biography of Anne Hutchinson, *Saints and Sectaries* (New Brunswick, N.J., 1962). Indispensable for understanding the Puritan mentality is Perry Miller's *Errand into the Wilderness* (Cambridge, Mass., 1956).

For an intimate picture of the *Colonial Family,* see John Demos, *A Little Commonwealth* (New York, 1970). The ideas that underlay the colonial family are explored in detail by Edmund Morgan's *The Puritan Family* (Boston, 1944). A demographic analysis that relates land ownership to family authority is Philip Grevin, *Four Generations* (Ithaca, New York, 1970).

The actions and motivating ideas of the *Revolutionary Crowd* are explored in Edmund Morgan and Helen Morgan, *The Stamp Act Crisis* (rev. ed., New York, 1963), and in Pauline Maier, *From Resistance to Revolution* (New York, 1972). The ideology of American Revolutionaries, particularly their fears about a British conspiracy against their liberties, is traced superbly by Bernard Bailyn in *The Ideological Origins of American Revolution* (Cambridge, Mass., 1967).

The first representations of the Indians of the New World were highly idealized. Just as the land seemed to be one of milk and honey (see the description in *Nova Britannia*, p. 7), so the Indians seemed to resemble classical Greek figures. The drawings of John White, a member of one of the first expeditions to Virginia, popularized this image: Note how orderly the village arrangement is and how symmetrical the designs are. Surely, no would-be member of the Virginia Company would have to fear such a tribe. *Watercolor of John White, 1591, reproduced from the collection of the Library of Congress.*

By 1624 a far more devil-like image of the Virginia Indians had become popular. Now the scenes were not of peaceable villages but of Indians attacking and being attacked by the English. The engravings that accompanied a 1624 history of John Smith's expedition tried to justify the use of force against the Indians (as did the 1622 account of the Indian massacre, see p. 18). The natives tied and bound Smith, then danced their primitive dance around him; it is John Smith's rifle versus the Indians' bows and arrows. In essence, force had to be met with force. *Engraving of Robert Vaughan, from John Smith, Generall Historie, 1624, reproduced from the collection of the Library of Congress.*

Nothing better illustrates the legitimacy of colonial mob actions than this engraving by Paul Revere of the Boston Massacre. Just as the colonists placed all the blame for the uprising on the British troops, (see *The Horrid Massacre in Boston*, p. 68), so did Revere. The colonists claimed that Captain Preston, with cool calculation, ordered the troops to fire, and Revere has sketched him standing behind his troops, not in front as he insisted; it is not the Custom's House that he is defending but Butcher's Hall. The victims of the fire are all well-dressed Bostonians, not the sailors or youngsters who were actually there. And there is even a gun being fired from the Custom's House itself, another indication of how the British, in calculated fashion, murdered the colonists. Here was a picture sure to inflame colonial sentiments. *Paul Revere, The Boston Massacre, reproduced courtesy of the New-York Historical Society, New York City.*

As one looks at this photograph of the Lowell Mills, it is not difficult to imagine just how different factory work was from agricultural work. The architecture seems to echo the discipline of the machine: ordered, regularized, monotonous. Window follows upon window, row follows upon row. Keep this image in mind when reading the *Lowell Offering* column occasioned by two girls' suicide (p. 98). *Lowell Mills on the Merrimack River, Detroit Publishing Company, 1908, reproduced from the collection of the Library of Congress.*

TO BE SOLD, on board the

Ship *Bance-Island*, on tuesday the 6th of *May* next, at *Afhley-Ferry*; a choice cargo of about 250 fine healthy

NEGROES,

juft arrived from the Windward & Rice Coaft. —The utmoft care has already been taken, and shall be continued, to keep them free from the leaft danger of being infected with the SMALL-POX, no boat having been on board, and all other communication with people from *Charles-Town* prevented.

Auftin, Laurens, & Appleby.

N. B. Full one Half of the above Negroes have had the SMALL-POX in their own Country.

This eighteenth-century poster advertising the forthcoming sale of newly arrived Africans tries to assure would-be buyers of the slaves' physical health. Clearly, it was not a concern for the welfare of the blacks that led the ship's captain to keep them isolated from an epidemic of small-pox; rather, with an eye to profits, he was trying to protect his cargo from disease. Just how significant this dynamic was in the history of slavery is very much in debate (see the Bennet Barrow records, pp. 105). Did the profitability of slave labor place a significant floor on the level of treatment slaves would receive? *Reproduced from the collection of the Library of Congress.*

The isolation of frontier settlers is grimly apparent in this photograph of a Dakota settler. The image of loneliness, of men and women striving to eke out a living against the elements, is all too clear in this setting. Yet one must remember that this family would immediately come to the aid of any neighbor in trouble. Caroline Kirkland might well jibe at neighbor's reliance upon neighbor (see p. 144). But families such as this had little else they could count on in time of crisis. *Dakota Home, 1885, reproduced from the collection of the Library of Congress.*

The order and discipline that the first common schools sought to inculcate is expressed vividly in this lithograph of the children's routine in a New York school. The children march in unison, their arms upraised together. The teacher has all the characteristics of a drill sergeant. And note the clock in the middle of the back wall. Bell-ringing punctuality here, as in the Cheshire schools (see p. 177), was a prime virtue. *First Infant School in Green Street, New York City, lithograph by Imbert after a drawing by A. Robertson, 1828. Reproduced courtesy of the New-York Historical Society, New York City.*

This illustration seems to represent a major state occasion—one in which a major Congressional speech is about to be delivered, for example. But in fact, this is a lithograph of the American Art Union's annual drawing for its lottery prize. Clearly, the Art Union patrons thought of themselves as fulfilling a significant and worthy patriotic duty; they were promoting works of culture to demonstrate American superiority in the arts. Since the lottery scheme was at the heart of the enterprise, (see the American Art Union *Bulletin*, 1849, p. 194), it deserved this kind of celebration. *Lithograph of the American Art Union, Distribution of Prizes, 1847, reproduced courtesy of the New-York Historical Society, New York City.*

Illustrations of the American Anti-Slavery Almanac for 1840.

" Our Peculiar Domestic Institutions."

Northern Hospitality—New-York nine months law. [T...
Slave steps out of the Slave State, and his chains f...
A Free State, with another chain, stands ready to ...
enslave him.]

Burning of McIntosh at St. Louis, in April, 1836.

Showing how slavery improves the condition of the female sex.

The Negro Pew, or "Free" | Mayor of New-Yo...
Seats for black Christians. | fusing a Carman's ...
| to a colored Man.

Servility of the Northern States in arresting and returning fugitive Slaves.

Selling a Mother from her Child.

Hunting Slaves with dogs and guns. A Slave dro...
by the dogs.

" Poor things, ' they can't take care of themselves.' "

Mothers with young Children at work in the field.

A Woman chained to a Girl, and a Man in irons at w...
the field.

Branding Slaves.

Cutting up a Slave in Kentucky.

Paid. | Unpaid.

One of the several techniques used by abolitionist societies to stimulate Northern opposition to slavery was to print and circulate posters portraying the grossest abuses of the system. These societies, in fact, were among the first to use lithographs for organized political ends, and they were proud of it (see Angelina Grimké's comments, p. 225). The images of women being whipped or separated from their children, and of men being branded or hanged, were to dominate people's view of slavery. *Illustrations of the American Anti-Slavery Almanac for 1840, reproduced from the collection of the Library of Congress.*

The New Nation, 1800–1865

THE FACTORY

THE PLANTATION

THE FRONTIER COMMUNITY

THE COMMON SCHOOL

THE AMERICAN ART UNION

ABOLITIONIST SOCIETIES

INTRODUCTION

IN THE DECADES following the Revolution, each of the new nation's three major regions followed a very particular course of development. And in each instance the special character of the region emerged in the rise and spread of one special institution. In the Northeast the first factories sprang up; in the South the plantation took hold; and in the Western territories a new type of frontier community appeared. Certainly similarities did remain among the sections. Small subsistence farms were found throughout the republic, and occasional factories did appear in the South. Nevertheless, the distinctive nature of regional developments is most apparent in these decades, and the differences emerge most clearly in analysis of these three typical institutions.

The first textile mills were organized in New England in the 1820s. Newly created corporations, with sizable aggregates of capital and employing hundreds of laborers, took the nation on its first steps toward industrial development. New kinds of work arrangements and new life styles took hold, demanding adjustment and readjustment on the part of workers. Nowhere was this development more advanced than at Lowell, Massachusetts. The industrial enterprise there became in many ways the test case for industrialism. Americans were understandably nervous about the rise and spread of factories. With images of the horrors of the English mill towns in their minds, citizens honestly questioned the price paid for industry. Would the Lowell experience recapitulate that of Manchester—would factories pauperize and demoralize once honest and independent citizens? Would American laborers even undertake factory work? After all, unlike in England, no group of hungry, landless, and unemployed men roamed the city and the countryside here. Hence, the Lowell enterprise was watched and examined very closely by a wide range of observers. Only slightly exaggerated was the claim that as Lowell went, so would go the course of industrial development in the United States.

No less unusual or important was the character of the plantation. Without question, this institution gave the antebellum South its special character, although subsistence farmers remained in the region, and the number of large-sized plantations was small. For blacks, the slave experience was identical with the plantation experience; and it was the planters who, to an extraordinary degree, dominated the political, eco-

nomic, and social life of the South. If we are to understand the history
of the South in these years, and the experience of both blacks and
whites, the nature of this very peculiar institution must be examined in
detail.

In the West, frontier communities represented a new departure.
Here were communities made up of families on the move, settlers
coming together before there were churches, courts, or other institutions
common to the older Eastern communities. And there was also a notable
paucity of goods and services. Tools were in short supply and so was
labor—and yet somehow the community would have to keep order and
allow citizens to go about the process of dividing and cultivating virgin
soil. The solutions were unpredictable and often ingenious, and highlight the issue of social stability in antebellum America.

Given all these new developments, it is not surprising that Americans in the antebellum period were especially concerned with the
problems of social order. Indeed, one cannot begin to understand the
nature of educational or cultural developments without a sensitivity to
this issue. The Jacksonian period, for example, was a time when various
"reforms" occurred. Most notable among them were new ways of caring
for the insane and the poor, new ways of punishing the criminal, and,
not coincidentally, new ways of educating the populace. The rise of the
common school, the spread of free public education in the new republic,
exemplifies these movements. The question of why common schools
should have developed in these years brings us directly to the issue of
how American society as a whole came to grips with these crucial and
in many ways frightening changes. Indeed, these same concerns had a
vital influence on the development of American culture. The character
of artistic production is as reflective of this concern as the school. And
the founding of one of the most novel institutions to spread artistic
production through the country, the American Art Union, clarifies the
dimensions of this story.

Finally, a focus on the nature of the abolitionist societies unites
these several themes. The outbreak of the Civil War represented the
culmination of both national and regional developments in the years
1800–1860. And one of the very best routes to understanding the causes
of this conflict is through the abolitionist efforts. What was the basis of
their critique of the South? How did the citizenry respond to it? How
was their message spread? An understanding of these issues will clarify
the origins of the most important conflict of nineteenth-century America.

Chapter 5

The Factory

PROBABLY no institution in pre–Civil War America more radically transformed the life styles of those who came under its influence than the factory. Its routine and organization demanded a sharp and dramatic break with traditional rural habits. The first workers who moved from the farm to the factory had to adjust to a new discipline of time and motion, to new relationships among fellow workers and employers. And yet, as dramatic as the shift was, the introduction of the factory into the United States, unlike its introduction into England, was accomplished relatively peaceably and efficiently. Americans took to the machine extraordinarily well.

Two basic measurements highlight the nature of the change that the factory brought to the nation's economy. In 1829, Americans produced 102,000 tons of bituminous coal; by 1859, the figure had leaped to 6,013,000. In 1820, Americans manufactured 54,000 tons of pig iron; by 1859, the amount had swelled to 821,000. These figures point not only to an economic revolution but also to a social one. How did an essentially agrarian nation transform itself into an industrial one? And why did the change proceed smoothly and effectively, with a minimum of protest and a maximum of inventiveness? Indeed, Americans in the 1820s were acutely aware of the blight and misery that factory life had brought to such English cities as Manchester. Whatever benefits they could imagine resulting from industrial production were more than balanced by a nagging fear that the machine would pauperize and demoralize a large number of citizens. Yet they apparently overcame these deep and genuine concerns to accept the factory system. Legislators were eager to incorporate the ventures, and entrepreneurs were prepared to invest in them. And last, but by no means least important, a labor force was ready to enter the mills and work the machines. Rather than attack the power looms of the first textile factories, as some of their counterparts in England had done, American workers, in the

words of one contemporary, "hail with satisfaction all mechanical improvements."

To understand the special nature of this response, the selections that follow focus on one of the first manufacturing enterprises in this country, the Lowell textile mills. In 1822, a group of Boston businessmen established a number of mills at Lowell, some twenty-five miles from Boston. The enterprise grew quickly, so that by 1840 210,000 workers were producing enormous quantities of cotton and woolen goods. But Lowell's importance transcended the size of its factories and their output. Lowell was, in essence, the test case for American industrialism, the experiment that would resolve whether factories here could avoid replicating the English horrors. Accordingly, observers devoted an enormous amount of attention to conditions there. Foreign visitors invariably made Lowell one of their first stops, while state legislators and clergymen frequently visited the site to take its moral temperature.

The founders of Lowell were themselves acutely conscious of the model character of their enterprise. They very self-consciously set out to demonstrate that the factory need not destroy the virtue of the worker or the integrity of the society. In fact, this sense of Lowell as a national experiment coincided with one of the investors' most basic economic concerns. The mills, after all, had to attract a labor force—this at a time when no ready pool of labor was easily available. The agricultural character of the nation's economy meant that nearly all available hands were already occupied on the farm. The solution advanced by the Lowell Associates to this problem was to recruit to their mills the one group that was marginal to the economic life of the farm: the younger daughters of not very well-off New England farmers. But this was not an easy group to attract. Fathers had to be persuaded that the experience would not be ruinous, that their daughters could still marry after leaving the factory, that the girls would not be compromised in any way. So, in a sense, the larger problem of persuading Americans to accept the factory became at Lowell the very specific issue of convincing fathers to let their children come to the mills.

The Lowell system, with its elaborate boardinghouse arrangements, moral policing, and elaborate rules and regulations, was an effort to solve this problem, and it was effective. The success of the Lowell venture went far in proving both the feasibility and desirability of industrial production in the United States.

I

One of the most complete accounts of the Lowell system was written by Henry Miles, a local Protestant clergyman. That as a minister he felt compelled to report on this economic enterprise points to the significance of the moral issues that Lowell posed. That he was prepared to defend the propriety and effectiveness of its arrangements points to the diligence with which the owners sought to assure the nation in general and the parents in particular of the value of their enterprise. Clearly Miles was not an altogether impartial observer; he undoubtedly mingled more with the owners than with the workers. Still, his account may be considered an accurate rendition of the basic organization at Lowell, and it helped assure many of his fellow citizens of the essential legitimacy of factory life.

LOWELL, AS IT WAS AND AS IT IS, 1845

HENRY A. MILES

Lowell has been highly commended by some, as a model community, for its good order, industry, and general freedom from vice. It has been strongly condemned, by others, as a hotbed of corruption, tainting the whole land. We all, in New England, have an interest in knowing what are the exact facts of the case. We are destined to be a great manufacturing people. The influences that go forth from Lowell will go forth from many other manufacturing villages and cities. If these influences are pernicious, we have a great calamity impending over us. Rather than endure it, we should prefer to have every factory destroyed.

If, on the other hand, a system has been introduced, carefully provided with checks and safeguards, and strong moral and conservative influences, it is our duty to see that this system be faithfully carried

In *Lowell, As It Was and As It Is,* by Henry A. Miles (Boston, 1845), pp. 62–63, 66–67, 100–103, 128–35, 140–47.

out, so as to prevent the disastrous results which have developed themselves in the manufacturing towns of other countries. Hence the topics assume the importance of the highest moral questions. The author writes after a nine years' residence in this city, during which he has closely observed the working of the factory system, and has gathered a great amount of statistical facts which have a bearing upon this subject. He believes himself to be unaffected by any partisan views, as he stands wholly aside from the sphere of any interested motives.

A Lowell Boardinghouse

Each of the long blocks of boardinghouses is divided into six or eight tenements, and are generally three stories high. These tenements are finished off in a style much above the common farmhouses of the country, and more nearly resemble the abodes of respectable mechanics in rural villages. These are constantly kept clean, the buildings well painted, and the premises thoroughly whitewashed every spring, at the corporation's expense.

As one important feature in the management of these houses, it deserves to be named that male operatives and female operatives do not board in the same tenement; and the following regulations, printed by one of the companies, and given to each keeper of their houses, are here subjoined, as a simple statement of the rules generally observed by all the corporations.

> Regulations to be observed by persons occupying the boardinghouses belonging to the Merrimack Manufacturing Company.
>
> They must not board any persons not employed by the company, unless by special permission.
>
> No disorderly or improper conduct must be allowed in the houses.
>
> The doors must be closed at ten o'clock in the evening.
>
> Those who keep the houses, when required, must give an account of the number, names, and employment of their boarders; also with regard to their general conduct, and whether they are in the habit of attending public worship.
>
> The buildings, both inside and out, and the yards about them, must be kept clean, and in good order.

The hours of taking meals in these houses are uniform throughout all the corporations in the city. The time allowed for each meal is thirty minutes for breakfast, when that meal is taken after beginning work; for dinner, thirty minutes.

The food that is furnished in these houses is of a substantial and wholesome kind, is neatly served, and in sufficient abundance. Operatives are under no compulsion to board in one tenement rather than another. And then, as to the character of these boardinghouse keepers themselves, on no point is the superintendent more particular than on this. Applications for these situations are very numerous. The rents of the company's houses are purposely low, averaging only from one-third to one-half of what similar houses rent for in the city. There is no intention on the part of the corporation to make any revenue from these houses. They are a great source of annual expense. But the advantages of supervision are more than an equivalent for this.

The influence which this system of boardinghouses has exerted upon the good order and good morals of the place, has been vast and beneficent. To a very great degree the future condition of Lowell is dependent upon a faithful adhesion to this system.

The following table shows the average hours per day of running the mills, throughout the year, on all the corporations in Lowell:

Hours of Labor

	H.	M.		H.	M.
January	11	24	July	12	45
February	12	00	August	12	45
March	11	52	September	12	23
April	13	31	October	12	10
May	12	45	November	11	56
June	12	45	December	11	24

In addition to the above, it should be stated that lamps are never lighted on Saturday evening, and that four holidays are allowed in the year, viz. Fast Day, Fourth of July, Thanksgiving Day, and Christmas Day.

The average daily time of running the mills is twelve hours and ten minutes. Arguments are not needed to prove that toil, if it be continued for this length of time, each day, month after month, and year after year, is excessive, and too much for the tender frames of young women to bear. No one can more sincerely desire than the writer of this book, that they had more leisure time for mental improvement and social enjoyment. It must be remembered, however, that their work is comparatively light. All the hard processes, not conducted by men, are performed by machines, the movements of which female operatives are required merely to oversee and adjust.

Moral Police of the Corporations

The productiveness of these works depends upon one primary and indispensable condition—the existence of an industrious, sober, orderly, and moral class of operatives. Without this, the mills in Lowell would be worthless. Profits would be absorbed by cases of irregularity, carelessness, and neglect; while the existence of any great moral exposure in Lowell would cut off the supply of help from the virtuous homesteads of the country. Public morals and private interests, identical in all places, are here seen to be linked together in an indissoluble connection. Accordingly, the sagacity of self-interest, as well as more disinterested considerations, has led to the adoption of a strict system of moral police.

The female operatives in Lowell do not work, on an average, more than four and a half years in the factories. They then return to their homes, and their places are taken by their sisters, or by other female friends from their neighborhood.

To obtain this constant importation of female hands from the country, it is necessary to secure *the moral protection of their characters while they are resident in Lowell.* This, therefore, is the chief object of that moral police.

No persons are employed on the corporations who are addicted to intemperance, or who are known to be guilty of any immoralities of conduct. As the parent of all other vices, intemperance is most carefully excluded.

In respect to discharged operatives, there is a system observed. Any person wishing to leave a mill is at liberty to do so, at any time, after giving a fortnight's notice. The operative so leaving, if of good character, and having worked a year, is entitled, as a matter of right, to an honorable discharge.

That form is as follows:

Mr. or Miss _____ _____, has been employed by the _____ Manufacturing Company, in a _____ room, _____ years _____ months, and is honorably discharged.

_____ _____, *Superintendent.*

LOWELL, _____ _____

This discharge is a letter of recommendation to any other mill in the city, and not without its influence in procuring employment in any other mill in New England. Those dishonorable have another treatment. The names of all persons dismissed for bad conduct, or who leave the mill irregularly, are also entered in a book, and these names are sent to all the counting rooms of the city. *Such persons obtain no more employment throughout the city.*

Any description of the moral care, studied by the corporations, would be defective if it omitted a reference to the overseers. Every room in every mill has its first and second overseer. At his small desk, near the door, where he can see all who go out or come in, the overseer may generally be found, and he is held responsible for the good order, and attention to business, of the operatives of that room. Hence, this is a post of much importance. It is for this reason that peculiar care is exercised in their appointment. The overseers are almost universally married men, with families; and as a body, numbering about one hundred and eighty in all, are among the most permanent residents, and most trustworthy and valuable citizens of the place. The guiding and salutary influence which they exert over the operatives is one of the most essential parts of the moral machinery of the mills.

It may not be out of place to present here the regulations, which are observed alike on all the corporations, which are given to the operatives when they are first employed, and are posted up conspicuously in all the mills. They are as follows:

Regulations to be observed by all persons employed by the Manufacturing Company, in the factories.

Every overseer is required to be punctual himself, and to see that those employed under him are so.

The overseers may, at their discretion, grant leave of absence to those employed under them, when there are sufficient spare hands in the room to supply their place; but when there are not sufficient spare hands, they are not allowed to grant leave of absence unless in cases of absolute necessity.

All persons are required to observe the regulations of the room in which they are employed. They are not allowed to be absent from their work without the consent of their overseer, except in case of sickness, and then they are required to send him word of the cause of their absence.

All persons are required to board in one of the boardinghouses belonging to the company, and conform to the regulations of the house in which they board.

All persons are required to be constant in attendance on public worship, at one of the regular places of worship in this place.

Persons who do not comply with the above regulations will not be employed by the company.

Persons entering the employment of the company are considered as engaging to work one year.

All persons intending to leave the employment of the company are required to give notice of the same to their overseer, at least two weeks previous to the time of leaving.

Anyone who shall take from the mills, or the yard, any yarn, cloth, or other article belonging to the company will be considered guilty of *stealing*—and prosecuted accordingly.

The above regulations are considered part of the contract with all persons entering the employment of the _____ Manufacturing Company. All persons who shall have complied with them, on leaving the employment of the company, shall be entitled to an honorable discharge, which will serve as a recommendation to any of the factories in Lowell. No one who shall not have complied with them will be entitled to such a discharge.

_____ _____, Agent.

II

The novelty of Lowell emerges vividly in this description by a visiting Englishman, William Scorseby. He made an earnest attempt to discern the root differences between Lowell and its English counterparts. Why was it that Lowell seemed so much less grim, physically and morally, than English mill towns? His answers are but the beginning of a resolution of this issue. They do, however, point the way to a better understanding of the dynamics responsible for the special origins of industrialism in the United States.

AMERICAN FACTORIES AND THEIR FEMALE OPERATIVES, 1845

WILLIAM SCORSEBY

On entering Lowell, a stranger is naturally struck with the contrast presented by that place to an English manufacturing town. Here, in Bradford [England], every building is of stone, or brick, solid, sub-

In *American Factories . . . and Their Female Operatives*, by William Scorseby (Boston: 1845), pp. 11–15, 78–79, 92–95.

stantial, with little of the freshness that might be looked for in so rapidly an increasing town: there, in Lowell, though the mills and boardinghouses are generally of brick, the chief part of the other buildings, houses, hotels, and even churches, are of wood, and nearly the whole as fresh looking as if built within a year. Here, with us, everything, externally, is discolored with smoke; buildings, streets, and causeways alike bearing a sooty covering; the mud of the streets in color and consistency like blackish gray paint, and the air of heaven darkened as by a dense cloud: there, nothing is discolored, neither houses nor mills nor trees—the red brick factories and boardinghouses, and the other edifices of wood painted in light colors, look as fresh as if just finished. Then the trees and plants which, with us, soon become dingy after their foliage bursts out, there, in Lowell, were fresh and flourishing. Hence, as to Lowell, large as it has grown, it is yet rural in its appearance, and, notwithstanding its being a city of factories, is yet fresh and cleanly.

Soon after arriving we were joined by a gentleman, Mr. ——— Lawrence, a principal in a large woolen factory, who had been expecting us—and we had also the assistance of the manager of the cotton mills of one of the principal corporations.

We proceeded, without further delay, to one of the factories, that we might see the factory workers as they came out to their dinners. Several hundreds of young women, but not any children, issued from the mills, altogether very orderly in their manner, and very respectable in their appearance. They were neatly dressed, and clean in their persons; many with their hair nicely arranged. There was not the slightest appearance of boldness or vulgarity; on the contrary, a very becoming propriety and respectability of manner, approaching, with some, to genteel.

When I see the levity of behavior of some of our mill girls as they come out from their work into the street, I cannot but wish that I could show them how their sisters in America conduct themselves, at least the many hundreds whom I saw at Lowell, under the same circumstances. And let me tell you what I consider to be the fact—that no such thing is ever to be seen among the young women of Lowell as *rudeness*, and very rarely indeed, I believe, anything like levity or immodesty of behavior in the streets.

The position in which a majority of these young women are placed— as strangers from the country, separated from their natural protectors and left almost entirely to their own discretion and moral self-depend- ence—is one singularly exposed to risk and temptation. Nor, under ordinary influences, would their being congregated in such considerable numbers together in their sleeping rooms and boardinghouses, by any means tend to their greater security.

But from all the information I could obtain, tested by all available means, and received with all reasonable caution, I have been led to infer that their character and moral conduct are unusually high.

While the case of Lowell will afford us some leading and important suggestions [for British adoption] that case, it will be easily perceived, has its peculiarities; such peculiarities, therefore, must prevent what is done there becoming in all respects a model for us.

One great and striking difference, in the present positions of England and America, is found in the history and rise of our respective manufacturing establishments. In England, for the most part, they consist of enlargements of old, and successions of new manufactories, within a previously existing manufacturing town. But in America, the manufactories consist altogether of new, or at least of very modern erections; and these are not unfrequently planted, as in the case of Lowell, not as grafts upon the stock of a town venerable in age, but as the original occupants of the ground, and as the stock on which the town itself is grafted.

Hence the American manufacturing towns possess, in many cases, the advantage of a peculiar unity of construction—each part, like the mass of machinery in a factory, having an essential relation to, or connection with, the whole. There is no previously existing idle and profligate population to inoculate with its viciousness the incoming country females; nor is there already there any unhappily pauperized population to depress with its burdensomeness the enterprise of the manufacturers. They have not, as with us it commonly happens, to con- tend with preexisting difficulties; but have, or in most cases may have, a clear and unembarrassed field for their manufacturing enterprises—a field wherein they can build on a plan to their liking, adopt the best models, introduce the most perfect and efficient machinery, and then order the principal contingencies, requisite for carrying on their works, on some commodious general plan.

Again, find we a want of analogy in the two countries in several other circumstances, more or less peculiar to the manufactories of the United States, such as, in the high prices they obtain, through their protective tariff and other causes, for their manufactured goods con- sumed at home; in the ample wages which, from the general scarcity of laborers, the operatives may demand, and which the remuneration in high prices enables the manufacturer to pay; in the cheapness of their board and lodging, yielding more clear gain and saving to the prudent operatives; and in the superior and more independent class of persons who, by reason of these latter advantages, are induced to engage in the business of the factories.

III

For all the satisfaction that outsiders took in the progress of the Lowell experiment, the women themselves decidedly did not have an easy time of it. The balance sheet was mixed. The excitement of leaving the confines of the homestead, of accumulating some funds that might go into a dowry, and of being on their own was offset by the experience of coming under a stranger's authority, by the long hours and tedious work, by the exacting routine, and by the women's sense that their work was menial and their status something less than that of respectable women. The redeeming element undoubtedly was that their stay was temporary. For most of them, work at Lowell was a brief interlude, less than four years, between family responsibilities. Lucy Larcom's memoir of what it was like to be a Lowell woman offers the reader a glimpse into the personal nature of the experience.

A NEW ENGLAND GIRLHOOD, 1889

LUCY LARCOM

I went to my first day's work in the mill with a light heart. The novelty of it made it seem easy, and it really was not hard, just to change the bobbins on the spinning-frames every three-quarters of an hour or so, with half a dozen other little girls who were doing the same thing.

And for a little while it was only a new amusement; I liked it better than going to school and "making believe." And there was a great deal of play mixed with it. We were not occupied more than half the time. The intervals were spent frolicking around among the spinning-frames, teasing and talking to the older girls, or entertaining ourselves with games and stories in a corner.

I never cared much for machinery. The buzzing and hissing and whizzing of pulleys and rollers and spindles and flyers around me often grew tiresome. But in a room below us we were sometimes allowed to peer in through a sort of blind door at the great waterwheel that carried the works of the whole mill. It was so huge that we could only watch a few of its spokes at a time, moving with a slow, measured strength

In *A New England Girlhood*, by Lucy Larcom (Boston, 1889), pp. 153–55, 175.

through the darkness that shut it in. It impressed me with something of the awe which comes to us in thinking of the great Power which keeps the mechanism of the universe in motion.

There were compensations for being shut in to daily toil so early. The mill itself had its lessons for us. But it was not, and could not be, the right sort of life for a child, and we were happy in the knowledge that, at the longest, our employment was only to be temporary.

I learned to do a spinner's work, and I obtained permission to tend some frames that stood directly in front of the river windows, with only them and the wall behind me, extending half the length of the mill, and one young woman beside me, at the farther end of the row. She was a sober, mature person, who scarcely thought it worth her while to speak often to a child like me; and I was, when with strangers, rather a reserved girl; so I kept myself occupied with the river, my work, and my thoughts.

The printed regulations forbade us to bring books into the mill. Some of the girls could not believe that the Bible was meant to be counted among forbidden books. The overseer, caring more for law than gospel, confiscated all he found. He had his desk full of Bibles. It sounded oddly to hear him say to the most religious girl in the room, when he took hers away, "I did think you had more conscience than to bring that book here." It was a rigid code of morality under which we lived. Nobody complained of it, however, and we were doubtless better off for its strictness, in the end.

My grandfather came to see my mother once at about this time and visited the mills. When he had entered our room, and looked around for a moment, he took off his hat and made a low bow to the girls, first toward the right, and then toward the left. But we had never seen anybody bow to a room full of mill girls in that polite way, and someone afterward asked him why he did so. He looked a little surprised at the question, but answered promptly and with dignity, "I always take off my hat to ladies."

His courtesy was genuine. Still, we did not call ourselves ladies. We did not forget that we were working-girls, wearing coarse aprons suitable to our work, and that there was some danger of our becoming drudges. I know that sometimes the confinement of the mill became very wearisome to me. In the sweet June weather I would lean far out of the window and try not to hear the unceasing clash of sound inside. Looking away to the hills, my whole stifled being would cry out,

Oh, that I had wings!

Still I was there from choice, and

The prison unto which we doom ourselves,
No prison is.

And I was every day making discoveries about life, and about myself. I loved quietness. The noise of machinery was particularly distasteful to me. I discovered, too, that I could so accustom myself to the noise that it became like a silence to me. And I defied the machinery to make me its slave. Its incessant discords could not drown the music of my thoughts if I would let them fly high enough. Even the long hours, the early rising, and the regularity enforced by the clang of the bell were good discipline for one who was naturally inclined to dally and to dream, and who loved her own personal liberty with a willful rebellion against control. Perhaps I could have brought myself into the limitations of order and method in no other way.

IV

As part of the effort to make Lowell a model community, the mill owners not only supported a library and encouraged its use, but also sponsored a newspaper. The Lowell Offering *was often cited as evidence of the uplifting character of the Lowell enterprise. As one would expect, most of its pages were filled with inconsequential and badly written stories and sentimental poetry. But occasionally something more genuine appeared in its pages. The suicides of two Lowell workers occasioned one such response.*

THE LOWELL OFFERING, 1845

The Suicide

Within a few weeks the papers of the day have announced the deaths of two young female operatives, by their own hands—one in Lowell, the other in an adjacent manufacturing town. With the simple announcement these papers have left the affair to their readers. And how have the community received this intelligence? Apparently with much indifference; but where we hear an expression of opinion it is one of horror. The human being who has dared, herself, to wrench away the barrier which separated her from the Giver of her life, and who will judge her for this rash act, is spoken of as a reckless contemner of His laws, both natural and revealed.

In the first instance, were the causes mental or physical which led to the deed? We believe in this, and indeed in all cases, that both operated upon the individual. Morbid dejection and wounded sensibility have, in these instances, produced that insanity which prompted suicide. Is it not an appropriate question to ask here whether or not there was anything in their mode of life which tended to this dreadful result?

We have been accused of representing unfairly the relative advantages and disadvantages of factory life. We are thought to give the former too great prominence, and the latter too little, in the pictures we have drawn. Are we guilty?

We have not thought it necessary to state, or rather to constantly reiterate, that our life was a toilsome one—for we supposed that would be universally understood, after we had stated how many hours in a

In *The Lowell Offering*, July 1845, p. 154.

day we tended our machines. We have not thought a constant repetition of the fact necessary, that our life was one of confinement, when it was known that we work in one spot of one room. We have not thought it necessary to enlarge upon the fact that there was ignorance and folly among a large population of young females, away from their homes, and indiscriminately collected from all quarters. But, are the operatives here as happy as females in the prime of life, in the constant intercourse of society, in the enjoyment of all necessaries, and many comforts—with money at their own command, and the means of gratifying their peculiar tastes in dress, etc.—are they as happy as they would be, with all this, in some other situations? We sometimes fear they are not.

And was there anything, we ask again, in the situation of these young women which influenced them to this melancholy act? In factory labor it is sometimes an advantage, but also sometimes the contrary, that the mind is sometimes thrown back upon itself—it is forced to depend upon its own resources, for a large proportion of the time of the operative. Excepting by sight, the females hold but little companionship with each other. This is why the young girls rush so furiously together when they are set at liberty. But, when a young woman is naturally of a morbid tone of mind, or when afflictions have created such a state, that employment which forces thoughts back upon an unceasing reminiscence of its own misery, is not the right one.

Last summer, a young woman of this city, who was weary of her monotonous life but saw no hope of redemption, opened her heart to a benevolent lady. "And now," said she, as she concluded her tale of grievances, "what shall I do?" The lady was appalled by a misery for which there was no relief. She could give her kind and soothing words, but these would have no permanent power to reconcile her to her lot. "I can tell you of nothing," she replied, "but *to throw yourself into the canal.*"

There is something better than this—and we are glad so noble a spirit is manifested by our operatives, for there *is* something noble in their general cheerfulness and contentment. "They also serve who only stand and wait." They serve, even more acceptably, who labor patiently and wait.

V

Beginning in the 1840s, and increasing steadily thereafter, a crucial change occurred in Lowell. Where the first factory girls had been recruited exclusively from New England farms, their successors came from the growing numbers of Irish immigrants. The Irish, fleeing from the drastic effects of the potato famine, emigrated to Boston in sizable numbers. One result of this immigration was the creation for the first time of a surplus labor pool in the Northeast. These immigrants, unattached to the farm, were desperate for work, and ready for hire. The mill owners responded predictably—with the success of the Lowell experiment assured, and the availability of labor no longer at issue, they dropped the paternalistic mode of management. In short order, Lowell became less of a model and more of a modern textile town. Wages dropped, hours increased, and the women protested. But the protests had little impact. The Massachusetts legislature did conduct an inquiry into the Lowell factories in 1845, but they found little to criticize. The factory owners were now more or less free to conduct their business in whatever way they wished. There would be few successful challenges to management's authority for the next several generations.

MASSACHUSETTS INVESTIGATION OF LABOR CONDITIONS, 1845

The Special Committee to which was referred sundry petitions relating to the hours of labor, submit the following report:

The first petition which was referred to your committee came from the city of Lowell, and was signed by Mr. John Quincy Adams Thayer, and eight hundred and fifty others, "peaceable, industrious, hard-working men and women of Lowell." The petitioners declare that they are confined "from thirteen to fourteen hours per day in unhealthy apartments," and are thereby "hastening through pain, disease, and privation down to a premature grave." They therefore ask the Legislature "to pass a law providing that ten hours shall constitute a day's work," and that no corporation or private citizen "shall be allowed, except in cases of emergency, to employ one set of hands more than ten hours per day."

On the thirteenth of February, the Committee held a session to hear the petitioners from the city of Lowell.

The first petitioner who testified was Eliza R. Hemmingway. She had worked two years and nine months in the Lowell Factories; two years in the Middlesex; and nine months in the Hamilton Corporations. Her employment is weaving—works by the piece. Her wages average from sixteen to twenty-three dollars a month exclusive of board. She complained of the hours for labor being too many, and the time for meals too limited. In the summer season, the work is commenced at five o'clock A.M., and continued till seven o'clock P.M., with half an hour for breakfast and three-quarters of an hour for dinner. The air in the room she considered not to be wholesome. About one hundred and thirty females, eleven men, and twelve children (between the ages of eleven and fourteen) work in the room with her. The children work but nine months out of twelve. The other three months they must attend school.

Most of the girls are from the country, who work in the Lowell Mills. The average time which they remain there is about three years.

There is always a large number of girls at the gate wishing to get in before the bell rings. On the Middlesex Corporation one-fourth part of the females go into the mill before they are obliged to. They do this to

In *Investigation of Labor Conditions*, Massachusetts House Document, No. 50, March 1845. Reprinted in *A Documentary History of American Industrial Society*, ed. John R. Commons et al. (New York, 1910), vol. 8, pp. 133–51.

make more wages. A large number come to Lowell to make money to aid their parents who are poor. She knew of many cases where married women came to Lowell and worked in the mills to assist their husbands to pay for their farms. The moral character of the operatives is good.

Miss Sarah G. Bagley said she had worked in the Lowell Mills eight years and a half. She is a weaver and works by the piece. She worked in the mills three years before her health began to fail. She is a native of New Hampshire. Last year she was out of the mill a third of the time. She thinks the health of the operatives is not so good as the health of females who do housework. The chief evil, so far as health is concerned, is the shortness of time allowed for meals. The next evil is the length of time employed—not giving them time to cultivate their minds. She spoke of the high moral and intellectual character of the girls. That many were engaged as teachers in the Sunday schools. That many attended the lectures of the Lowell Institute.

Mr. Gilman Gale, a member of the city council, and who keeps a provision store, testified that the short time allowed for meals he thought the greatest evil. He spoke highly of the character of the operatives and of the agents; also of the boardinghouses and the public schools. He had two children in the mills who enjoyed good health.

Mr. Herman Abbott had worked in the Lawrence Corporation thirteen years. Never heard much complaint among the girls about the long hours, never heard the subject spoken of in the mills. Does not think it would be satisfactory to the girls to work only ten hours, if their wages were to be reduced in proportion. Forty-two girls work in the room with him. The girls often get back to the gate before the bell rings.

Mr. John Quincy Adams Thayer has lived in Lowell four years, "works at physical labor in the summer season, and mental labor in the winter." Has worked in the big machine shop twenty-four months, off and on; never worked in a cotton or woolen mill; thinks that the mechanics in the machine shop are not so healthy as in other shops; nor so intelligent as the other classes in Lowell. He drafted the petition. Has heard many complain of the long hours.

On Saturday the first of March, a portion of the Committee went to Lowell to examine the mills, and to observe the general appearance of the operatives therein employed. They first proceeded to the Merrimack Cotton Mills, in which are employed usually 1,200 females and 300 males. They were permitted to visit every part of the works and to make whatever inquiries they pleased of the persons employed. They found every apartment neat and clean, and the girls, so far as personal appearance went, healthy and robust, as girls are in our country towns.

The Committee also visited the Massachusetts and Boott Mills, both of which manufacture cotton goods. The same spirit of thrift and cleanliness, of personal comfort and contentment, prevailed there. The rooms are large and well lighted, the temperature comfortable, and in most of the windowsills were numerous shrubs and plants. These were the pets of the factory girls, and they were to the Committee convincing evidence of the elevated moral tone and refined taste of the operatives. Not only is the interior of the mills kept in the best order, but great regard has been paid by many of the agents to the arrangement of the enclosed grounds. In short, everything in and about the mills, and the boardinghouses appeared, to have for its end, health and comfort. The same remark would apply to the city generally. Your Committee returned fully satisfied that the order, decorum, and general appearance of things in and about the mills could not be improved by any suggestion of theirs, or by any act of the Legislature.

We have come to the conclusion unanimously that legislation is not necessary at the present time, and for the following reasons:

1. That a law limiting the hours of labor, if enacted at all, should be of a general nature. That it should apply to individuals or copartnerships as well as to corporations.

2. Your Committee believes that the factory system, as it is called, is not more injurious to health than other kinds of indoor labor. That a law which would compel all of the factories in Massachusetts to run their machinery but ten hours out of the twenty-four, while those in Maine, New Hampshire, Rhode Island, and other states in the Union were not restricted at all, the effect would be to close the gate of every mill in the State.

3. It would be impossible to legislate to restrict the hours of labor, without affecting very materially the question of wages; and that is a matter which experience has taught us can be much better regulated by the parties themselves than by the Legislature. Labor in Massachusetts is a very different commodity from what it is in foreign countries. Here labor is on an equality with capital, and indeed controls it, and so it ever will be while free education and free constitutions exist. Labor is intelligent enough to make its own bargains, and look out for its own interests without any interference from us.

4. The Committee does not wish to be understood as conveying the impression that there are no abuses in the present system of labor; we think there are abuses; we think that many improvements may be made, and we believe will be made, by which labor will not be so severely tasked as it now is. We think that it would be better if the hours for labor were less, if more time was allowed for meals, if more attention was paid to ventilation and pure air in our manufactories, and workshops, and many other matters. We acknowledge all this, but we say, the remedy is not with us. We look for it in the progressive improvement in art and science, in a higher appreciation of man's destiny, in a less love for money, and a more ardent love for social happiness and intellectual superiority. Your Committee, therefore, while they agree with the petitioners in their desire to lessen the burdens imposed upon labor, differ only as to the means by which these burdens are sought to be removed.

Chapter 6

The Plantation

ALTHOUGH the number of plantations in the antebellum South was not very great, this institution exerted the most profound effect on the lives of both whites and blacks. The plantation determined both the structure of the region's economy and its social organization.

Planters were the minority of a minority. On the eve of the Civil War, when the plantation system was at its height, only some 383,600 families in the entire South owned slaves; and fully one-third of this group only owned one slave. Just 10,658 planters owned over fifty slaves, and a bare 2,292 men owned over one hundred slaves. Altogether, as of 1860 there were probably somewhat less than 4,000 great planters in the South.

Yet it was this group that in the first instance fastened the cotton crop onto the region. In 1820, the Southern states produced 732,000 bales of cotton; by 1840, it was producing some one million bales, and by 1860, an incredible 4,300,000 bales! Not surprisingly, the growth of slavery proceeded apace with the cotton crop. In 1820, there were a little over 1,500,000 slaves in the South. By 1860, the number stood at 4,440,000. For blacks, the plantation was the common experience. Less than 5 percent of all blacks lived on farms where there were less than two slaves; 25 percent of blacks lived on plantations with over fifty slaves. Therefore, if one is to understand the South in the antebellum era, one must look first not to the small family farms which raised crops for subsistence but to the plantations, where slaves in large numbers spent their day planting and harvesting cotton.

Given the size of the region and the vagaries of human nature, a wide variety of styles characterized plantation management. Some units, particularly in the deep South, were probably more determined than others to maximize at all costs the size of the crop. A few especially decent and humanitarian owners devoted more attention to the welfare of their slaves. But one generalization can characterize all plantations: they were economic units designed to produce the cotton crop for a profit. The plantation, at heart, was a factory that turned out raw fibers, not at all unlike those factories in the North that turned the raw fibers into cloth. That the plantation also ordered the relationship between the races is clear. But it was the economic goals of the institution that dictated the behavior of owners and determined the fate of their slaves.

Plantations were, it must be noted, profitable ventures. Planters could ordinarily count on making returns from cotton production that were just about as great as those available to factory owners. To be sure, returns in Virginia, where the land was more exhausted, did not equal those in the Mississippi delta. But on the average, the plantation returned a rather handsome 10 percent profit.

The implications of this fact must be borne in mind as one examines the enormous amount of documentary material that survives from the plantation era. As one reads the planters' records, their correspondence with overseers, the accounts of escaped slaves, or travelers' reports, one must constantly keep the economic realities prominently in mind. Did the planters actually correspond to the image of a cultivated gentleman taking his leisure on a well-appointed veranda? Just how central to his daily routine were the ledger books? What degree of protection did these economic considerations provide for the blacks? Did their productivity in the cotton fields at once insure their continued exploitation by the planters while it set a minimum to the kind of treatment that they would receive? Was the black slave too valuable a commodity to allow owners to overwork or underfeed or excessively punish him? Finally, how did the plantation organize itself to fulfill both economic and social functions? It was at once a factory and a community. It was also a prison. The sources that follow touch on these many facets of the plantation, and permit an assessment of the impact of this institution on the South.

I

The plantation records of Bennet H. Barrow (1811–1854) are remarkably complete. They include not only his diary but also a record of punishments meted out to slaves, the number of slave births and deaths, and the rules and regulations in effect on his plantation. Barrow was typical of his class. He raised cotton on a large scale in Louisiana all the while carrying out the "right" activities, even holding office at the county level, but not above it. There is no reason to think him an especially harsh or particularly benevolent owner. In all, his materials offer an excellent starting point for re-creating a picture of antebellum plantation life.

THE DIARY OF BENNET H. BARROW, 1836–1845

RULES OF HIGHLAND PLANTATION*

No Negro shall leave the place at any time without my permission, or in my absence that of the driver, the driver in that case being responsible for the cause of such absence, which ought never to be omitted to be enquired into.

The driver should never leave the plantation, unless on business of the plantation.

No Negro shall be allowed to marry out of the plantation.

No Negro shall be allowed to sell anything without my express permission. The very security of the plantation requires that a general and uniform control over the people of it should be exercised. Who are to protect the plantation from the intrusions of ill-designed persons when everybody is abroad? Who can tell the moment when a plantation might be threatened with destruction from fire—could the flames be arrested if the Negroes are scattered throughout the neighborhood, seeking their amusement. Are these not duties of great importance, and in which every Negro himself is deeply interested. To render this part of the rule justly applicable, however, it would be necessary that such a settled arrangement should exist on the plantation as to make it unnecessary for a Negro to leave it—or to have a good plea for doing so. You must therefore make him as comfortably at home at possible, affording him what is essentially necessary for his happiness—you must provide for him yourself and by that means create in him a habit of perfect dependence on you. Allow it once to be understood by a Negro that he is to provide for himself, and you that moment give him an undeniable claim on you for a portion of his time to make this provision, and should you from necessity, or any other cause, encroach upon his time—disappointment and discontent are seriously felt. If I employ a laborer to perform a certain quantum of work per day and I agree to pay him a certain amount for the performance of said work when he has accomplished it, I of course have no further claim on him for his time or services—but how different is it with a slave. Who can calculate the exact profit or expense of a slave one year with another. If I furnish my Negro with every necessary of life, without the least care on his part—if I support him in sickness, however long it may be, and pay all his expenses, though he does nothing—if I maintain him in his old age, when he is incapable of rendering either himself or myself any service, am I not entitled to an exclusive right to his time? Good feelings and a sense of propriety would always prevent unnecessary employment on the Sabbath, and policy would check any exaction of excessive labor in common.

* The "Rules" were copied in the Diary on May 1, 1838.
In *Plantation Life in the Florida Parishes of Louisiana, 1836–1846, as Reflected in the Diary of Bennet H. Barrow*, ed. Edwin A. Davis (New York, 1943), pp. 126–36, 406–10, 427–37. Reprinted by permission of the publisher, Columbia University Press.

I never give a Negro a pass to go from home without he first states particularly where he wishes to go, and assigns a cause for his desiring to be absent. If he offers a good reason, I never refuse. Some think that after a Negro has done his work it is an act of oppression to confine him to the plantation, when he might be strolling about the neighborhood for his amusement and recreation—this is certainly a mistaken humanity. Habit is everything. The Negro who is accustomed to remain constantly at home is just as satisfied with the society on the plantation as that which he would find elsewhere, and the very restrictions laid upon him being equally imposed on others, he does not feel them, for society is kept at home for them. No rule that I have stated is of more importance than that relating to Negroes marrying out of the plantation. It seems to me, from what observations I have made, it is utterly impossible to have any method or regularity when the men and women are permitted to take wives and husbands indiscriminately off the plantation. Negroes are very much disposed to pursue a course of this kind, and without being able to assign a good reason, though the motive can be readily perceived, and is a strong one with them, but one that tends not in the least to the benefit of the master, or their ultimate good. The inconveniences that at once strike one as arising out of such a practice are these:

1. In allowing the men to marry out of the plantation, you give them an uncontrollable right to be frequently absent.
2. Wherever their wives live, there they consider their homes, consequently they are indifferent to the interest of the plantation to which they actually belong.
3. It creates a feeling of independence, from being, of right, out of the control of the masters for a time.
4. They are repeatedly exposed to temptation from meeting and associating with Negroes from different directions, and with various habits and vices.
5. Where there are several women on a plantation, they may have husbands from different plantations belonging to different persons. These men possess different habits, are accustomed to different treatment, and have different privileges, so your plantation everyday becomes a rendezvous of a medley of characters. When your Negroes

are at work, and the driver engaged, they either take possession of houses their wives live [in]—and go to sleep or stroll about in perfect idleness—feeling themselves accessible to everything.

6. When a man and his wife belong to different persons, they are liable to be separated from each other, as well as their children, either by caprice of either of the parties, or when there is a sale of property— this keeps up an unsettled state of things, and gives rise to repeated new connections. For to adopt rules merely because they are good in themselves and not to pursue a plan which would make them applicable, would be fallacious. I prefer giving them money of Christmas to their making anything, thereby creating an interest with you and yours. I furnish my Negroes regularly with their full share of allowance weekly: four pounds and five pounds of meat to everything that goes in the field; two pounds over four years; one and a half between fifteen months and four years old; clear good meat. I give them clothes twice a year: two suits, one pair shoes for winter; every third year a blanket—"single Negro—two." I supply them with tobacco. If a Negro is suffered to sell anything he chooses without any inquiry being made, a spirit of trafficking at once is created to carry this on, both means and time are necessary, neither of which is he of right possessed. A Negro would not be content to sell only what he raises or makes or either corn (should he be permitted) or poultry, or the like, but he would sell a part of his allowance also, and would be tempted to commit robberies to obtain things to sell. Besides, he would never go through his work carefully, particularly when other engagements more interesting and pleasing are constantly passing through his mind, but would be apt to slight his work. That the general conduct of master has a very considerable influence on the character and habits of his slave, will be readily admitted. When a master is uniform in his own habits and conduct, his slaves know his wishes, and what they are to expect if they act in opposition to, or conformity with them, therefore, the more order and contentment exist.

A plantation might be considered as a piece of machinery, to operate successfully, all of its parts should be uniform and exact, and the impelling force regular and steady; and the master, if he pretended at all to attend to his business, should be their impelling force. If a master exhibits no extraordinary interest in the proceedings on his plantation, it is hardly to be expected that any other feelings but apathy could exist with his Negroes, and it would be unreasonable for him to expect attention and exaction from those who have no other interest than to avoid the displeasure of their master. In the different departments on the plantation as much distinction and separation are kept up as possible with a view to create responsibility. The driver has a directed charge of everything, but there are subordinate persons who take the more immediate care of the different departments. For instance, I make one person answerable for my stock, horses, cattle, hogs, etc. Another the plantation utensils, etc. One the sick, one the poultry. Another providing for and taking care of the children whose parents are in the field, etc. As good a plan as could be adopted, to establish security and good order on the plantation is that of constituting a watch at night, consisting of two or more men. They are answerable of all trespasses commited during their watch, unless they produce the offender or give immediate alarm. When the protection of a plantation is left to the

Negroes generally, you at once perceive the truth of the maxim that what is everyone's business, is no one's business. But when a regular watch is established, each in turn performs his tour of duty, so that the most careless is at times made to be observant and watchful. The very act of organizing a watch bespeaks a care and attention on the part of a master which has the due influence on the Negro.

Most of the above rules (in fact with the exception of the last) I have adopted since 1833. And with success—get your Negroes once disciplined and planting is a pleasure—a H[ell] without it. Never have an overseer. Every Negro to come up Sunday after their allowance clean and head well combed—it gives pride to everyone, the fact of master feeling proud of them, when clean etc.

Never allow any man to talk to your Negroes, nothing more injurious.

Slave Births: 1836–1839

MOTHER	CHILD	DATE OF BIRTH	COMMENTS
Margaret	Orange	February 1, 1836	
Cealy	Jane Bello	April 22, 1836	
Candis	Isaac	August 1, 1836	
Sidney		July 10, 1836	Born dead.
Maria	Kitty	July 10, 1836	
Harriet	Ned	November 20, 1836	
Patty		December 19, 1836	Died.
Leah	Adeline	March 6, 1837	
Margaret	Edmond	September 21, 1837	Died.
Mary	Rose	January 9, 1838	
Sidney	Robert	February 21, 1838	
Edny		June 7, 1838	[Died].
Fanny		July 4, 1838	Died.
Jane		September 29, 1838	Died.
Candis		October 12, 1838	Died.
Maria	Horace	November 30, 1838	
Harriet	Sally	December 2, 1838	
Leah		December 10, 1838	Died.

Slave Deaths: 1836–1839

NAME	DATE	AGE	COMMENTS
Old Rheuben	1836	60 years	
Old Betty	1836	65 years	Found dead. Crippled five years.
Billy	1836		Died of worms six hours after taken.
Nelly	1837	26 years	Died twenty-four hours after I saw her. Received some injury. In the family way.
Easter	1837	50 years	Died of pleurisy, drinking, etc. Relapse, died very suddenly. Great loss.
William	1837	3 years	Died suddenly. Worms.
Hanover	1837	6 years	Died of worms, suddenly.
Edny's child	1838	1 week	Died of lockjaw, June 13.
Candis' child	1838	1 week	Died of lockjaw, October 19.

NAME	DATE	AGE	COMMENTS
Harriet's Ned	1838		Died suddenly, December 1.
Fanny's child		4 months	Died from carelessness.
Jane's child			Died from disease of mother.
Leah's child	1838	1 week	December 17.

INVENTORY OF THE ESTATE OF BENNET H. BARROW

Succession of Bennet H.   *State of Louisiana*
Barrow, deceased   *Parish of West Feliciana*

Be it remembered that on this the fourteenth day of June in the year of our Lord one thousand eight hundred and fifty-four, I, Bertrand Haralson, Recorder in and for said parish attended this day, at the late residence of Bennet H. Barrow, deceased, for the purpose of making an inventory and appraisement of all the property, real and personal, rights and credits, belonging to Bennet H. Barrow, deceased.

TO WIT

A certain tract of land, with all the buildings and improvements thereon, known as the home place containing about fourteen hundred arpents, which said lands and improvements were valued and appraised at the sum of forty-two thousand dollars.

[*Slave Evaluations*]

Stephen, aged 6 years, valued at two hundred and 50 dollars	250.00
Rodem, aged 5 years, valued at two hundred dollars	200.00
Jack, aged 51 years, valued at eight hundred dollars	800.00
Eliza, aged 44 years, valued at five hundred dollars	500.00
Bazil, aged 20 years, valued at six hundred dollars	600.00
Little Cato, aged 37 years, valued at six hundred dollars	600.00
Hetty, aged 36 years, valued at five hundred dollars	500.00
Amos, an infant, valued at fifty dollars	50.00
Temps, aged 43 years, valued at fifty dollars	50.00
Lindy, aged 23 years, valued at seven hundred dollars	700.00
Virginia, aged 2 years, valued at one hundred and fifty dollars	150.00
Sidney, aged 39 years, valued at six hundred and fifty dollars	650.00
Aggy, aged 20 years, valued at seven hundred and fifty dollars	750.00
Angelle, an infant, valued at fifty dollars	50.00
Cynthis, aged 13 years, valued at four hundred dollars	400.00
Suckey, aged 9 years, valued at three hundred dollars	300.00
Spencer, aged 7 years, valued at three hundred dollars	300.00
Dave, aged 46 years, valued at seven hundred dollars	700.00
Little Jim, aged 24 years, valued at nine hundred dollars	900.00
Maria, aged 19 years, valued at six hundred dollars	600.00
Old Jimmy, aged 59 years, valued at five hundred dollars	500.00
Nat, aged 28 years, valued at eight hundred and fifty dollars	850.00
Levy, aged 39 years, valued at four hundred and fifty dollars	450.00
Grace, aged 29 years, valued at six hundred dollars	600.00
Phil, aged 75 years, valued at one hundred dollars	100.00
Esther, aged 25 years, valued at seven hundred and fifty dollars	750.00
Rilla, aged 3 years, valued at two hundred dollars	200.00

Marshall, aged 9 years, valued at two hundred and fifty dollars   250.00
Ada, aged 23 years, valued at seven hundred and fifty dollars   750.00
Desery, aged 4 years, valued at one hundred and fifty dollars   150.00
Treson, an infant, valued at one hundred dollars   100.00
Louisa, aged 19 years, valued at six hundred and fifty dollars   650.00
Angy, aged 15 years, valued at six hundred and fifty dollars   650.00
Edny, aged 49 years, valued at three hundred dollars   300.00
Lizzy, aged 23 years, valued at six hundred and fifty dollars   650.00
Arie, aged 14 years, valued at five hundred dollars   500.00
Little Phil, aged 26 years, valued at nine hundred and fifty dollars   950.00

Misconduct and Punishments: 1840–1841

Darcas		Left the field today without the consent of the driver. Pretending to be sick.
Anica		Filthiness, in the milk and butter. Her and Darcas alike. December 10, 1840 improved very much.
Peter		Told me several lies Christmas. Drunkard, etc.
Candis		Saw Dennis while runaway.
Jenney		Saw Dennis while runaway.
Patience		Not trashing cotton well. Leaving yellow locks in it, etc.
Julia		Not trashing cotton well.
Bet	X*	Not trashing cotton well.
Luckey	X	Not trashing cotton well.
O. Hannah	X	Not trashing cotton well.
F. Jerry		For going to town with very dirty clothes and keeping himself so, "generally."
Patty		Inattention to work and herself.
Lavenia		Inattention to work and herself.
Mary		For scaring son, Bat. "Stories, etc."
L. Hannah		For taking rails and breaking good ones.
Margaret		With Hannah, but taking none but pieces.
O. Hannah	X	Not trashing cotton enough. Found the gin stopped everytime I've been down at the gin place.
Bet	X	Not trashing cotton enough.
Harriet		Not trashing cotton enough, and dirty clothes.
F. Jerry	X	Up too late and out of his house.
Jerry	X	Up too late and out of his house.
Bet	X	Up after 10 o'clock.
Ben		Up after 10 o'clock.
Wash		Carelessness with his plough, horses, gear, etc.
Dave L.		Neglect in hauling cotton repeatedly.
Wash		Neglect of his horses.
Randall		Up too late, sleeping in chair, etc.
Luce		Neglect of child. Its foot burnt.
Jim		Inattention to work, moving seed, and impudence to driver.
Lize	X	Inattention to work.
Levi	X	Carelessness with his oxen and talking to the workman. Neglect of business.
Bet	XX	Careless in dropping seed, disowning it, etc.
Anica		Meanness to the sick, and hiding from me, etc.
Dennis		Severity to his mules.

° X signifies whipping.

Wade		For lying, and out of his house.
Fanney		Hoeing too careless, and mad.
Oney		Sore back horse.
Oney		Carelessness, ploughing, etc.
Isreal		Impudence to the driver.
Oney	X	Neglect in planting peas, etc.
Julia	X	Neglect in planting peas, etc.
Patience		Bad conduct, impudence to driver, and neglected work.
Patience	X	Did not go in the field till breakfast "late" and told the driver "Alfred" she was sick and had been to the house for a dose of oil, and told me the same, found she had not been and she acknowledged the lie, but told Margaret she would give her some cloth if she would get the earache and tell Patty she had been here after oil, etc. And told me a dozen lies while questioning her. Gave her a very severe whipping.
Maria		For not reporting herself when sick. Remained in the quarter 3 days without my knowledge.
Patty		And all the house ones for general bad conduct. Can't let a peach get ripe, etc.
Jane		The meanest Negro living. Filth in cooking. Saw me coming to the house at 1:20; left the kitchen, etc. Of[f] near two days, foiled her having anything to do with anyone, and chained at nights.
O. Fill	X	Not reporting the plough hands for injuring the cotton, covering up bottom limbs, etc.
Demps		Sound beating with my stick. Impudence of manner.
Atean	X	Covering up cotton limbs with ploughs.
Isreal	X	Covering up cotton limbs with ploughs.

Diary

September 1

Clear, warm—picking above, best picking this year—three sick; gave every cotton picker a light whipping for picking trashy cotton.

2   Clear, wind north—and quite cool—sudden change—hands averaged higher yesterday than they have this year—163—upward of twenty bales out—ten bales behind last year and thirty bales behind 1836—difference in the season.

3   Clear, quite cold. Picking cotton gins place—good picking—started all my gins—don't like the appearance of my crop: most ragged looking crop I ever had, bent and broke down—two sick—three lame, etc.

4   Clear, wind east—cool, picking home (above) since dinner.

5   Cloudy, wind east—best picking today I've had this year—went to Ruffins with family—and went in the swamp killing alligators—after dinner went driving. Started two large bucks in Wades field—stood on the road between Roberts and Ruffins —one came through—Sidney Flower took first shot standing—neither of his *shots* were fatal—ran to me. Missed first fire, second wounded him very badly—ran short distance and stopped, nearly falling.

6   Few clouds, cool mornings. Took Joseph Bell, Fanny Bell, and Grey Luzbourough colts of Lucillas up to train—also Pressure

and Dick Haile—a strong string—O. Jacob cut the end of his right forefinger nearly off—two others slightly cut—with broad ax—average 170 pound cotton yesterday—appearance of rain tonight—sprinkle.

7 Few clouds—wind east—fine picking, averaged 183 yesterday—cotton forty bales out last night—thirty bales behind last year at this time; went down to see John Joor, his cotton has suffered very much for want of rain.

8 Cloudy, warm—hand generally did not pick as well yesterday as day before—fine picking, highest yesterday and this year 260. Atean, small boy Owens, the best boy I ever saw.

9 Clear, pleasant; hands picked finely yesterday; averaged 209.

10 Clear, very cool morning—upward of fifty bales out, thirty odd gined, picking gins, fine picking.

11 Clear, cool morning. Four first rate cotton pickers sick hands picked well yesterday. Atean 300, Dave L. 310, highest this year—sent to town after my bagging and rope, waiting for it three weeks past—knocked the blind teeth out of my gray Luzbourough colt. Little Independence.

12 Clear, cool mornings—five sick, picking above—twenty bales out at gins, pressing home—the best cotton and best picking in upper new corn land cotton I ever saw.

13 Clear, cool morning—weighed cotton in the field—five sick, augue and fever.

14 Cloudy, warm—most of the hands picked well yesterday, highest 325—will have picked off of the new corn land above (fifty acres) twenty-five bales, at least fifty bales to pick—averaged yesterday 209—twenty-five bales pressed last night.

15 Cloudy, *sprinkling* of rain—hands picked higher yesterday than they have done this year—averaged 226—Owens boy thirteen years old picked 200—best boy I ever saw. Very light sprinkle rain this evening.

16 Stormy looking day, great deal of rain last night and still raining—wind from the east. Hands picked well yesterday, highest average this year 234½.

17 Dark and Cloudy—wind south—pressing gins and home—women spinning, men and trash gang trashing cotton and raising house.

18 Cloudy, damp morning—some rain at noon. Picking cotton since breakfast—went driving with James Leak, Dr. Desmont, and Sidney Flower. Started two fawns in my field, ran some time, dogs quit them.

19 Clear pleasant morning—sixty-two bales pressed last night—cotton bend down very much from wind on Sunday—between ninety and one hundred bales out in November—went hunting in my field, started three deer. Killed a young buck—several joined me afterward—went driving on the swamp—started a deer, dogs ran off—in coming out of the drive started a bear. Only one dog—he became too much frightened to do anything.

20 Clear, pleasant—picking P. Rice bottom—hands pick well considering the storm—several sick.

21 Very foggy morning—commenced hauling cotton this morning —first shipment—bales will average 470 pounds upward of 100 out in November. 115 of 400. This time last year had out 125—25 behind last year, owing to the season—cotton more backward in opening—at first picking—never had cotton picked more trashy than yesterday. And today by dinner—some few picked badly—five sick and two children.

22 Considerable rain before breakfast, appearance of a bad day— pressing—four sick—caught Darcas with dirt in cotton bag last night, weighed fifteen pounds—Tom Beauf picked badly yesterday morning. Whipped him, few cuts—left the field some time in the evening without his cotton and have not seen him since—he is in the habit of doing so yearly, except last year. Heavy rains during the day, women spinning—trashing cotton, men and children—Tom B. showed himself—"sick"—cotton picked since the storm looks very bad—cotton market opened this year at 13 and 13¾ cents—bagging and cordage 20 and 24 and 8½ and 9 cents—pork from sixteen to twenty-four dollars a barrel—Never commence hauling cotton that it did not rain—worked the ford at Little Creek in the gins field.

23 Clear, very cool, wind from the north—nine degrees colder than yesterday morning—intend most of the hands to dry and trash cotton today. Frank Kish, Henry, and Isreal pressed bales today, one dollar each—killed a wild cow this morning, as fat as could well be.

24 Clear, quite cold—P. Dohertys gin house burnt down on Friday night last. Light enough at my scaffold yard to read names and figures on the slate—and at least five miles—Mr. Tisdale our trainer came down from Kentucky yesterday—had my cart wheels tired yesterday at Ruffins.

25 Clear, cool—went to town—hauled forty-nine bales to Ratliffs Landing yesterday—twelve to town today—sixty-one in all— went driving yesterday. Killed two fawns—and one young buck in my gins field with the most singular horns I ever heard of or saw—very fat—several sick, most this year.

26 Clear, pleasant weather. Shipped today eighty bales cotton, very fine—six or seven lying up—picked badly for two days past— cotton selling fourteen cents.

27 Clear, pleasant—went hunting in the swamp in company of Dr. Desmont, J. Leake, M. Courtney, W. H. Barrow, Pat Doherty, R. D. Percey, L. Flower, and Mr. Pain from Isle of Madeira— a large wine importer—very large—killed three deer, lost Mr. Pain, stayed until after dark firing guns, etc., the old gentleman found the briar and came up to Ruffins well scratched and bloody—he refused to call Leake by his name—having lost a cargo of wine, vessel springing a *leak*.

28 Cloudy, cool wind from the north—John Joor sent a hand up to exchange with me, yesterday, his hands pick very badly— Dennis and Tom Beauf ran off on Wednesday—Dennis came in yesterday morning after I went hunting. "Sick"—left the sick house this morning—if I can see either of them and have a gun

at the time will let them have the contents of it—Dennis returned to the sick house at dinner.

29 Foggy morning—warm day. A. G. Barrow, Dr. Walker, and
William Munson stayed with me last night, went hunting today.
Munson missed—Emily went to Woodville yesterday—hands
picked better yesterday than they have done since the storm—
averaged 200. Tom B. went to picking, cotton this morning—
didn't bring his cotton to be weighed—came to me after I went
to bed.

30 Clear, pleasant weather—upward of 130 bales out.

II

*By reputation, the cruelest of the plantations were those of the absentee
owners, where the management of affairs was exclusively in the
hands of an overseer. Even during the antebellum period, South-
erners insisted that overseers did not represent the system, while
abolitionists argued to the contrary that they exemplified it. The
correspondence here between an overseer (John Evans) and an
owner (George Jones) offers another vantage point from which to
evaluate plantation conditions. Here, too, the relationship between
economic needs and the fate of the slave emerges vividly, as does
the subtle but not unimportant community pressures that could
limit plantation autocracy.*

THE CORRESPONDENCE OF GEORGE JONES, 1852–1855

John Evans to George Noble Jones

[CHEMOONIE, April 2, 1852]

Mr. Jones, Sir,

I wrote you on the twentieth of March and directed my letter to
Newport, R. I. I will inform you that I am getting on finely now with my
business. I finished planting cotton today at nine o'clock. Now the crop
is all planted. I have cleared up and ditched a nice pond and planted it
in rice. I will be ready to go to ploughing and hoeing corn about the
sixth of this month. The first cotton that I planted is coming up fine.

I have sheared the sheep and altered the lambs but have not spayed
any shoats yet but will next week if it is a good time. The team is a
little thin but will now get fat. Minder had billious colic and I could

In *Florida Plantation Records from the Papers of George Noble Jones*, ed.
U. B. Phillips and J. D. Glunt (St. Louis, 1927), pp. 98, 110–12, 123–24,
150–53. Reprinted by permission of the Missouri Historical Society, St. Louis,
Missouri.

not cure her and I was fearful that she would get worse so I sent for Dr. Randolph and he came one time to see her and she has since recovered. Randolph said that inflammation had taken place was the cause of my not curing her. He said my prescription was right, the rest of the black people are all well except Juner [Juno] and Little Joe. They eat dirt and are bloated up. I think that I have got Joe broken off from eating dirt now and I think I will have Juner curred by another week.

You directed me to send you all of the names of the Negroes on Chemoonie in familes which I will do in my next letter which will be on the fifteenth of this [month]. Jim asked me to let him have Martha for a wife so I have gave them leave to marry. Both of them are very smart and I think they are well matched. Also Lafayette Renty asked for leave to marry Lear, I also gave them leave. Rose, Renty's other wife, says that she don't want to live with Renty on the account of his having so many children and they were always quarreling so I let them seperate. Lear says she is willing to help Renty take care of his children. I will send the load of cotton to Newport on the eighth of this month.

I believe I have written you all of the news from Chemoonie.

John Evans to George Noble Jones

CHEMOONIE, F[L]A. June 15, 1852

Mr. George Jones,

I am glad to hear that your family is all well. I have been enjoying fine health until lately. I am now sick but not confined, I am able to attend to my business.

The black people have not been so well of late either. You will see in the copy of the journal who has been sick. There has been a heap of wet weather in F[l]a. of late which was the cause of the sickness on Chemoonie. I think I notice that most every large plantation in this settlement has got the measles, except your plantations. I am very fearful that they will get here for they are at Billingsleys, close by. I don't allow one of the young hands to leave the plantation, not even to visit El Desteno [a neighboring plantation].

I have the best prospect for a corn crop that I ever have had since I have been managing for you. The cotton crop is not good, it is the smallest cotton that I ever have had for the time of year. I do not like the cotton crop on Chemoonie, there have been too many of those heavy washing rains on this place of late years. The washing rains have carried off a heap of the soil and the soil will have to be replaced by manuring pretty heavily before there can be large crops of cotton made on Chemoonie again.

John Evans to George Noble Jones

Leon Co. F[l]a, Sept. 9, 1854

Mr. George Jones,

Sir, after my best respects to you and family I will state to you that I am well, also the black people with the exception of two light cases of fever on the plantation which will be well by tomorrow.

I am getting on very well with my business and have caught the two boys that ran off and gave them a light flogging and put them to work. The cause of Esau's and Little Dick's running away was this. Jacob and England and Nathan had made a plot to leave if I should attempt to flog them for picking cotton and persuaded those two boys into it. So I gave Jacob and England and Nathan a flogging apiece. They acknowledge they had done wrong so I let them off lightly.

This is the driest and hottest weather in Florida that I have ever experienced. The cotton crop looks bad.

My object in writing to you is principally this—it is not a great while before my term will be up with you. So I think it is always best for both parties to know in due time what we will do another year. I am poor and expect to follow overseeing a few more years, and I think it is to my interest always to know in due time what I am going to do another year, so if we don't agree to live together why it will give us both a chance to look around. We both are pretty well acquainted with each other now and I like the way you have your business managed and I am satisfied to do business for you another year or four more years. I will just leave this with you. I will make this proposition—if you will furnish me plenty of such provisions as the plantation affords, give me six hundred dollars, and allow me the same privileges you have always been giving me, I will live with you four more years if you want me, and you may put just as many hands here as you are a mind to. If you will give me this I never shall ask you to raise my wages anymore. I have been overseeing now eleven years and I think I ought to have as good wages as some of the rest of the overseers in Florida that don't manage any more hands than I do. I have been living with you now eight years nearly, and I can say more than most of the Florida overseers, that I never have had a cross word with my employer. Not flattering of you, I can say with a clear conscience that I have been studying your interest for the last eight years. Please answer this letter soon, and whether you hire me or not you may depend upon my attending to your business promptly until the last hour that I stay with you.

And another thing I forgot to mention is this. Should I take a notion to marry you must give me leave to get a wife. I don't know that I shall ever marry but I merely mention this so we will know what to depend upon. I would not think of getting a wife without your consent. I think if I had a wife I could get along better. I would have someone to help nurse the sick women and so forth.

   John Evans to George Noble Jones

                                    Chemoonie Florida, Oct. 18, 1854
Mr. George Jones,
   Mr. Moxley called on me last week to go to El Desteno and see him whip one of the mill boys, Aberdeen. He said that he went to flog or put Aberdeen's sister in jail and she ran and he caught her and Aberdeen took an ax to him but did not use it, the driver kept him from it. I went down and saw Mr. Moxley give him a genteel flogging which I think he deserved. Aberdeen acknowledged that he did take the ax to Mr. Moxley. There were four of the women run away from him and went to Talla-

hassee and got in jail which cost Moxley about thirteen dollars to get them out and lawyer Davis examined them and reported about town that they were badly whipped, which is not so. I examined their backs myself and I did not see anything that was cruel about them. Also Mr. Blocker and Demilly examined them in jail, so they told me. They say that they were not cruelly flogged. This man Davis is a sort of a queer fellow, so people tell me about town. The cause of those women going to Tallahassee is this—this Negro Tom Blackledge that has Dealier for a wife on El Desteno coaxed them off. This man Davis has Tom hired, and the women went to Tom's house and the jailer heard that they were there and he went and got them and put them in jail. I don't think that Mr. Moxley treats the Negroes on El Desteno cruelly when they don't deserve it. You know that the Negroes on El Desteno have not been at work for the last four years so Moxley has to be pretty strict on them to get anything out of them. I think Moxley is a good planter and would treat the Negroes well if they would behave themselves. There is but one thing I see in Mr. Moxley's management that I don't like and it is this, I think when he flogs he puts it on in too large doses. I think moderate floggings the best. Whenever I see that I have convinced a Negro I always turn him loose. I always punish according to the crime, if it is a large one I give him a genteel flogging with a strap, about seventy-five lashes I think is a good whipping. When picking cotton I never put on more than twenty stripes and very frequently not more than ten or fifteen. I find I get along with this as well as if I was to give them larger whippings. I think if the mill hands was kept steadily at work it would add to the quarters at El Desteno. Mr. Moxley says that the mill hands don't get to work before an hour be sun [after sunrise] some mornings, and Negroes is this disposition, if they see Negroes around them idling why they want to do so too. I merely write this because I think it is my duty when I see anything going on wrong in Florida on your plantations. When you come out you can see for yourself. I think Mr. Moxley is the right kind of man for El Desteno, except the large floggings. Mr. Moxley says if there is not an alteration at El Desteno he won't stay another year. I told him not to get disheartened for he would find you to be the right kind of a man.

George Noble Jones to W. G. M. Davis

El Desteno, Jefferson County, Florida,
January 22, 1855

Dear Sir,

Messrs. Anderson and Houston did me the favor to investigate the conduct of my overseer, Mr. Moxley, in relation to the four women who fled to your house. I regret you could not have been present.

It has always been a source of great anxiety to me to protect my Negroes from unnecessary punishment. I pay the highest wages in hopes of obtaining good overseers. (On large plantations where more than a hundred Negroes are together, it seems necessary to observe a stricter discipline than with a smaller number might be sufficient. That my Negroes have not been seriously injured by the punishment they have received may perhaps be evidenced in their general appearance and in their natural increase which in the last year has been over 10 percent; in a gang of 120, there having been but three deaths of infants and fourteen births and no instance of miscarriage. I should be pleased at any time to see you at my plantation and show you every part of it.)

With many thanks for the interest you have shown in my people I remain etc.

John Evans to George Noble Jones

[Chemoonie, January 10, 1856]

Mr. Jones,

Sir, as we disagreed the other day at your house about the business of the plantation, you appeared to be so much dissatisfied with my management of your business you will not perhaps be much surprised when I inform you that I have come to the conclusion to quit your employment, for you will doubtless recollect perfectly well the fact of my having always told you that I would live with no man who was not satisfied with the manner in which I manage his business. I have always endeavored to do you justice and although I say it no man has ever labored more faithfully for another than I have for you. Your Negroes behave badly behind my back and then run to you and you appear to believe what they say. From circumstances that have happened I am led to believe that I run great risks of my life in the case of Jacob. When I mentioned it to you that my life had been threatened by him you seemed to pay no attention to it whatever. I have always been accustomed to having my friends to see me and the indulgence of it never for a moment caused me to neglect the business committed to my charge and now when I am married and might naturally expect the friends of my wife and self to visit us in a reasonable manner your expression about this matter the other day at your house was enough to let me know that you did not want my friends to come and see me. Taking all these circumstances into due consideration I think I am but acting right when I seek to dissolve the connection that has existed between us for nine years, and in doing so I wish you to believe that I am moved by no unfriendly feelings whatever but solely by a regard for my own interest. You will be pleased to come over early in the morning and let us settle and get your keys. You owe me a little on the taxes I paid for you in 1855.

III

Northern travelers through the South often recorded their impressions of plantation life. Their comments did not always add up to a consistent picture, partly because tourists are not systematic observers, and partly because each visitor brought to the scene his own particular biases and those of his region and class. But this very problem makes these reports all the more valuable today. They not only add to our knowledge about plantation conditions but also illuminate the preconceptions through which Northerners viewed the phenomenon. Nehemiah Adams, a New England minister, spent three months in the South in 1853. The following year he published A Southside View of Slavery.

A SOUTHSIDE VIEW OF SLAVERY, 1860

N E H E M I A H   A D A M S

FAVORABLE APPEARANCES IN SOUTHERN SOCIETY AND IN SLAVERY

Good Order

The streets of Southern cities and towns immediately struck me as being remarkably quiet in the evening and at night.

"What is the cause of so much quiet?" I said to a friend.

"Our colored people are mostly at home. After eight o'clock they cannot be abroad without a written pass, which they must show on being challenged, or go to the guard house. The master must pay fifty cents for a release. White policemen in cities, and in town patrols of white citizens, walk the streets at night."

Here I received my first impression of intereference with the personal liberty of the colored people. The white servants, if there be any, the boys, the apprentices, the few Irish, have liberty; the colored men are under restraint.

From the numbers in the streets, though not great, you would not suspect that the blacks are restricted at night; yet I do not remember one instance of rudeness or unsuitable behavior among them in any place. Around the drinking saloons there were white men and boys whose appearance and behavior reminded me of "liberty and pursuit of happiness" in similar places at the North; but there were no colored men there; the slaves are generally free as to street brawls and open drunkenness. I called to mind a place at the North whose streets every evening, and especially on sabbath evenings, are a nuisance. If that place could enforce a law forbidding certain youths to be in the streets after a certain hour without a pass from their employers, it would do much to raise them to an equality in good manners with their more respectable colored fellowmen at the South.

There have been mournful cases in which the murderer of a Negro has escaped deserved punishments; but it was not because it was a Negro that was killed. The murderers of white people have as frequently obtained impunity.

The laws allow the master great extent in chastising a slave, as a

In *A Southside View of Slavery,* by Nehemiah Adams (Boston, 1860), pp. 24–25, 41, 44, 47–49.

protection to himself and to secure subordination. Here room is given for brutal acts; barbarous modes of inflicting pain, resulting in death, are employed; but it is increasingly the case that vengeance overtakes and punishes such transgressors.

Prevention of Crime

Prevention of crime among the lower class of society is one striking feature of slavery. Day and night every one of them is amenable to a master. If ill disposed, he has his own policeman in his owner. Thus three million of the laboring class of our population are in a condition most favorable to preservation from crimes against society.

A prosecuting officer, who has six or eight counties in his district, told me that during eight years of service, he had made out about two thousand bills of indictment, of which not more than twelve were against colored people. It must follow of necessity that a large amount of crime is prevented by the personal relation of the colored man to a white citizen. It would be a benefit to some of our immigrants at the North, and to society, if government could thus prevent or reach disturbances of the peace through masters, overseers, or guardians. But we cannot rival in our police measures the beneficial system of the South in its distributive agencies to prevent burglaries and arson.

A physician, relating his experience in his rides at night, said that in solitary places the sudden appearance of a white man generally excited some apprehension with regard to personal safety, but the sight of a black man was always cheering, and made him feel safe. Husbands and fathers feel secure on leaving home for several days, even where their houses are surrounded by Negro cabins.

Absence of Mobs

One consequence of the disposal of the colored people as to individual control is the absence of mobs. That fearful element in society, an irresponsible and low class, is diminished at the South. Street brawls and conflicts between two races of laboring people, or the ignorant and more excitable portions of different religious denominations, are mostly unknown within the bounds of slavery.

When the remains of Mr. Calhoun were brought to Charleston, a gentleman from a free state in the procession said to a Southern gentleman, "Where is your underswell?" referring to the motley crowd of men and boys of all nations which gather in most of our large places on public occasions. He was surprised to learn that those respectable, well-dressed, well-behaved colored men and boys on the sidewalks were a substitute for that class of population which he had elsewhere been accustomed to see with repugnant feelings on public occasions.

Absence of Pauperism

Pauperism is prevented by slavery. This idea is absurd, no doubt, in the apprehension of many at the North, who think that slaves are, as a matter of course, paupers. Nothing can be more untrue.

Every slave has an inalienable claim in law upon his owner for support for the whole of life. He cannot be thrust into an almshouse, he cannot become a vagrant, he cannot beg his living, he cannot be wholly neglected when he is old and decrepit.

I saw a white-headed Negro at the door of his cabin on a gentleman's estate, who had done no work for ten years. He enjoys all the privileges of the plantation, garden, and orchard; is clothed and fed as carefully as though he were useful. On asking him his age, he said he thought he "must be nigh a hundred."

Thus the pauper establishment of the free states, the burden and care of immigrants, are almost entirely obviated at the South by the colored population. In laboring for the present and future welfare of immigrants, we are subjected to evils of which we are ashamed to complain, but from which the South is enviably free. To have a neighborhood of a certain description of foreigners about your dwellings; to see a horde of them get possession of a respectable dwelling in a court, and thus force the residents, as they always do, to flee, it being impossible to live with comfort in close connection with them; to have all the senses assailed from their opened doors; to have your sabbath utterly destroyed, is not so agreeable as the presence of a respectable colored population, every individual of which is under the responsible oversight of a master or mistress who restrains and governs him, and has a reputation to maintain in his respectable appearance and comfort, and keeps him from being a burden on the community.

The following case, that came to my knowledge, offers a good illustration of the views which many slaves take of their dependent condition. A colored woman with her children lived in a separate cabin belonging to her master, washing clothes for families in that place. She paid her master a percentage of her earnings, and had laid up more than enough to buy her freedom and that of her children. Why, as she might be made free, does she not use it rather?

She says that if she were to buy her freedom, she would have no one to take care of her for the rest of her life. Now her master is responsible for her support.

REVOLTING FEATURES OF SLAVERY

Homes of the Slaves

The homes of the slaves is a topic of deep interest, bearing in a vital manner upon the system. It can hardly be said in general that slaves have regularly constituted homes. Husbands and wives, in a large proportion of cases, belong to different masters, and reside on separate plantations, the husband sometimes walking several miles, night and morning, to and from his family, and many of them returning home only on Saturday afternoon. In cities, also, husbands and wives most commonly belong to different families. Laboring apart, and having their meals apart, the binds of domestic life are few and weak. A slave, his wife, and their children, around that charmed center, a family table, with its influences of love, instruction, discipline, humble as they necessarily would be, yet such as God had given them, are too seldom seen. To encourage and protect their homes generally would be in effect to put an end to slavery as it is.

It was remarked to me by an eminent and venerable physician at the South that maternal attachments in slave mothers are singularly short-lived. Their pain and grief at the sale of their children, their jealousy, their self-sacrificing efforts for them, are peculiar, but they are easily supplanted.

Everyone can see not only the probability but the cause of this limited parental affection. From the first moment of maternal solicitude, the idea of property on the part of the owner in the offspring is connected with the maternal instinct. It grows side by side with it, becomes a neutralizing element, prevents the inviolable links of natural affection from reaching deep into the heart. We need no slave auctions or separations of families to make us feel the inherent, awful nature of the present system of slavery.

The same day that my friend made his remark to me, I had an accidental confirmation of it in the conversation of an intelligent landlord, who was telling me of the recent lamentable death of an old slave mother who had nursed him and all his brothers and sisters. His mother said to the dying woman, "How do you feel about leaving your children?" for she had several who were still young. "O missis," she said, "you will take care of them; I don't mind them. I don't want to leave you, missis, and your Charley and Ann. What will they do without me, little dears?" Slavery had loosened the natural attachments of this woman to her offspring, and those attachments had sought and found objects to grow upon in the children of another. There must be something essentially wrong in a system which thus interferes with the nature which God has made.

I was in a large colored sabbath school. The superintendent at the close gave the scholars a kind word of exhortation to this effect: "Now, children, I want to repeat what I have said to you so often; you must all try to be good children, wherever you are, remembering that you are never out of God's sight. If you love and obey Him, if your are good children at home, what a comfort you will be to your" (I expected the words *fathers* and *mothers*) "masters and mistresses." I felt as when I have heard the earth fall upon a stranger's coffin; it was all correct, all kind; but the inability to use those names, the perfect naturalness with which other names came in to fill the place of *father* and *mother*, brought to my heart the truth: the slaves generally have no homes. Separated as they necessarily are under the present system, the relations of husbands and wives are not so inviolable as they otherwise would be. Marriage among the slaves is not a civil contract; it is formed and continues by permission of the masters; it has no binding force, except as moral principle preserves it; and it is subject, of course, to the changes of fortune on the part of the owners. This is the theory; but humane and benevolent hearts in every community combine to modify its operation; yet there are cases of hardship over which they are compelled to weep, and very many of them do weep as we should in their places; still the system remains, and now and then asserts its awful power.

Yet the cases of violent separation of husband and wife are not so many as the voluntary and criminal separations by the parties themselves. This, after all, is the chief evil connected with the looseness of domestic ties in slavery. Conjugal love among the slaves is not invariably the poetical thing which amateurs of slaves sometimes picture it; for there are probably no more happy conjugal unions among the slaves than among the whites.

IV

The few accounts of plantation life written by blacks appear in the narratives of those who escaped slavery or were emancipated. These volumes, however, were invariably published in the North with the help of abolitionists, so that one cannot be sure whether the former slave is telling his audience what it wants to hear or whether he is accurately reporting his experiences. Then, too, these slaves may have been atypical, the victims of more brutal treatment, hence their escape, or more benevolent treatment, hence their emancipation. Nevertheless, many of these reports have a ring of authenticity. A close textual analysis may help to reveal the effects of the system upon the slaves. The account below was written by Jacob Stroyer, an emancipated slave who spent his youth on a large plantation in South Carolina. Eventually, Stroyer became a minister in the African Episcopal Church in Salem, Massachusetts.

MY LIFE IN THE SOUTH, 1885

JACOB STROYER

Father

Father had a surname, Stroyer, which he could not use in public, as the surname Stroyer would be against the law; he was known only by the name of William Singleton, because that was his master's name. So the title Stroyer was forbidden him, and could be used only by his children after the emancipation of the slaves.

There were two reasons given by the slaveholders why they did not allow a slave to use his own name, but rather that of the master. The first was that if he ran away, he would not be so easily detected by using his own name as if he used that of his master instead. The second was that to allow him to use his own name would be sharing an honor which was due only to his master, and that would be too much for a Negro, said they, who was nothing more than a servant. So it was held as a crime for the slave to be caught using his own name, which would expose him to severe punishment.

Mother

Mother's name was Chloe. She belonged to Colonel M. R. Singleton too; she was a field hand, and never was sold, but her parents were once.

The family from which mother came, the most of them had trades of some kind; some were carpenters, some blacksmiths, some house servants, and others were made drivers over the other Negroes.

In *My Life in the South,* by Jacob Stroyer (Salem, Mass., 1885), pp. 19–23.

Most of them had trades of some kind; but she had to take her chance in the field with those who had to weather the storm. But my readers are not to think that those having trades were free from punishment, for they were not; some of them had more troubles than the field hands. At times the overseer, who was a white man, would go to the shop of the blacksmith or carpenter, and would pick a quarrel with him, so as to get an opportunity to punish him. He would say to the Negro, "Oh, ye think yourself as good as ye master, ye——." Of course he knew what the overseer was after, so he was afraid to speak; the overseer, hearing no answer, would turn to him and cry out, "Ye so big ye can't speak to me, ye———," and then the conflict would begin, and he would give that man such a punishment as would disable him for two or three months. The merciless overseer would say to him, "Ye think because ye have a trade ye are as good as ye master, ye ———; but I will show ye that ye are nothing but a nigger."

I did not go to the sand-hill, or summer seat, my allotted time, but stopped on the plantation with father, as I said that he used to take care of horses and mules. I was around with him in the barnyard when but a very small boy; of course that gave me an early relish for the occupation of hostler, and I soon made known my preference to Colonel Singleton, who was a sportsman and had fine horses. And, although I was too small to work, the Colonel granted my request; hence I was allowed to be numbered among those who took care of the fine horses, and learned to ride. But I soon found that my new occupation demanded a little more than I cared for.

It was not long after I had entered my new work before they put me upon the back of a horse which threw me to the ground almost as soon as I reached his back. It hurt me a little, but that was not the worst of it, for when I got up there was a man standing near with a switch in hand, and he immediately began to beat me. Although I was a very bad boy, this was the first time I had been whipped by anyone except father and mother, so I cried out in a tone of voice as if I would say, this is the first and last whipping you will give me when father gets hold of you.

When I got away from him I ran to father with all my might, but soon found my expectation blasted, as father very coolly said to me, "Go back to your work and be a good boy, for I cannot do anything for you." But that did not satisfy me, so on I went to mother with my complaint and she came out to the man who whipped me; he was a groom, a white man whom master hired to train his horses, as he was a man of that trade. Mother and he began to talk, then he took a whip and started for her, and she ran from him, talking all the time. I ran back and forth between mother and him until he stopped beating her. After the fight between the groom and mother, he took me back to the stable yard and gave me a severe flogging. And although mother failed to help me at first, still I had faith that when he took me back to the stable yard, and commenced whipping me, that she would come and stop him, but I looked in vain, for she did not come.

Then the idea first came to me that I, with my dear father and mother and the rest of my fellow Negroes, was doomed to cruel treatment through life, and was defenseless. But when I found that father and mother could not save me from punishment, as they themselves had to submit to the same treatment, I concluded to appeal to the sympathy of the groom, who seemed to have had full control over me; but my pitiful cries never touched his sympathy, for things seemed to grow worse rather than better; so I made up my mind to stem the storm the best I could.

One day, about two weeks after Boney Young and mother had the conflict, he called me to him, as though he was in his pleasantest mood; he was singing. I ran to him as if to say by action, I will do anything you bid me willingly. When I got him he said, "Go and bring me a switch, sir." I answered "Yes, sir," and off I went and brought him one; then he said, "Come in here, sir;" I answered, "Yes, sir;" and I went into a horse's stall, but while I was going in a thousand thoughts passed through my mind as to what he wanted me to go into the stall for, but when I got in I soon learned, for he gave me a first-class flogging.

That evening when I went home to father and mother, I said to them, "Mr. Young is whipping me too much now; I shall not stand it, I shall fight him." Father said to me, "You must not do that, because if you do he will say that your mother and I advised you to do it, and it will make it hard for your mother and me, as well as for yourself. You must do as I told you, my son; do your work the best you can, and do not say anything." I said to father, "But I don't know what I have done that he should whip me; he does not tell me what wrong I have done, he simply calls me to him and whips me when he gets ready." Father said, "I can do nothing more than pray to the Lord to hasten the time when these things shall be done away; that is all I can do." When mother stripped me and looked at the wounds that were upon me, she burst into tears, and said, "If he were not so small I would not mind it so much; this will break his constitution; I am going to master about it, because I know he will not allow Mr. Young to treat this child so."

And I thought to myself that had mother gone to master about it, it would have helped me some, for he and she grew up together and he thought a great deal of her. But father said to mother, "You better not go to master, for while he might stop the child from being treated badly, Mr. Young may revenge himself through the overseer, for you know that they are very friendly to each other." So said father to mother, "You would gain nothing in the end; the best thing for us to do is to pray much over it, for I believe that the time will come when this boy with the rest of the children will be free, though we may not live to see it."

V

The most famous, and deadly, slave rebellion in the South was led by Nat Turner in Virginia. Before the revolt was crushed, fifty-seven white planters, women, and children had been killed. The incident gained notoriety from the dimensions of the deed, and also from the document, The Confessions of Nat Turner, *published in 1832 by Thomas Gray, a white Virginian who talked with Turner in his cell before Turner's trial. It is difficult to know how accurately Gray recounted Turner's story. He certainly did make stylistic changes, and possibly he put some of his own sentiments and fears into Turner's mouth. Still, the* Confessions *is worth close scrutiny. It was widely read in the South and helped to increase whites' fear and repression of blacks. Moreover, it offers some insights into Turner's intellectual and emotional character. Ultimately, the* Confessions *not only casts light on the nature of slave life, but may also help to explain why there were not more slave revolts in the South.*

THE CONFESSIONS OF NAT TURNER, 1832

Agreeable to his own appointment, on the evening he was committed to prison, with permission of the jailer, I visited Nat on Tuesday the first of November, when, without being questioned at all, he commenced his narrative in the following words:

Sir,

You have asked me to give a history of the motives which induced me to undertake the late insurrection, as you call it. To do so I must go back to the days of my infancy, and even before I was born. I was thirty-one years of age the second of October last, and born the property of Benjamin Turner, of this county. In my childhood a circumstance occurred which made an indelible impression on my mind, and laid the groundwork of that enthusiasm which has terminated so fatally to many both white and black, and for which I am about to atone at the gallows. It is here necessary to relate this circumstance—trifling as it may seem, it was the commencement of that belief which has grown with time, and even now, sir, in this dungeon, helpless and forsaken as I am, I cannot divest myself of. Being at play with other children, when three or four years old, I was telling them something, which my mother overhearing, said it had happened before I was born. I stuck to my story, however, and related some things which went in her opinion to confirm it. Others being called on were greatly astonished, knowing that these things had happened, and caused them to say in my hearing, I surely would be a prophet, as the Lord had shown me things that had happened before my birth. And my father and mother strengthened me in this my first impression, saying in my presence, I was intended for some great purpose, which they had always thought from certain marks on my head and breast.

My grandmother, who was very religious, and to whom I was much attached—my master, who belonged to the church, and other religious persons who visited the house, and whom I often saw at prayers, noticing the singularity of my manners, I suppose, and my uncommon

In *The Confessions of Nat Turner . . . as Fully and Voluntarily Made to Thomas R. Gray* (Richmond, Va., 1832). Reprint edition (New York: 1964), pp. 5–17.

intelligence for a child, remarked I had too much sense to be raised—
and if I was, I would never be of any service to any one—as a slave.
The manner in which I learned to read and write, not only had great
influence on my own mind, as I acquired it with the most perfect
ease, so much so that I have no recollection whatever of learning the
alphabet—but to the astonishment of the family, one day, when a
book was shown me to keep me from crying, I began spelling the names
of different objects—this was a source of wonder to all in the neighborhood, particularly the blacks—and this learning was constantly improved
at all opportunities. When I got large enough to go to work, while
employed, I was reflecting on many things that would present themselves to my imagination. I was not addicted to stealing in my youth,
nor have never been. Yet such was the confidence of the Negroes in the
neighborhood, even at this early period of my life, in my superior
judgment, that they would often carry me with them when they were
going on any roguery, to plan for them. Growing up among them, with
this confidence in my superior judgment, and when this, in their
opinions, was perfected by divine inspiration, from the circumstances
already alluded to in my infancy, and which belief was ever afterward
zealously inculcated by the austerity of my life and manners, which
became the subject of remark by white and black. By this time, having
arrived to man's estate, and hearing the Scriptures commented on at
meetings, I was struck with that particular passage which says: "Seek
ye the kingdom of Heaven and all things shall be added unto you." I
reflected much on this passage, and prayed daily for light on this subject.
As I was praying one day at my plough, the spirit spoke to me, saying
"Seek ye the kingdom of Heaven and all things shall be added unto you."
Question—What do you mean by the Spirit. *Answer*—The Spirit that
spoke to the prophets in former days—and I was greatly astonished,
and for two years prayed continually, whenever my duty would permit
—and then again I had the same revelation, which fully confirmed me
in the impression that I was ordained for some great purpose in the
hands of the Almighty. Several years rolled round, in which many
events occurred to strengthen me in this my belief. At this time I
reverted in my mind to the remarks made of me in my childhood, and
the things that had been shown me. And as it had been said of me in
my childhood by those whom I had been taught to pray, both white
and black, and in whom I had the greatest confidence, that I had too
much sense to be raised, and if I was I would never be of any use to
anyone as a slave. Now finding I had arrived to man's estate, and was
a slave, and these revelations being made known to me, I began to
direct my attention to this great object, to fulfill the purpose for which,
by this time, I felt assured I was intended. Knowing the influence I
had obtained over the minds of my fellow servants, (not by the means
of conjuring and such like tricks—for to them I always spoke of such
things with contempt) but by the communion of the Spirit whose revelations I often communicated to them, and they believed and said my
wisdom came from God.

And on the twelfth of May 1828, I heard a loud noise in the
heavens, and the Spirit instantly appeared to me and said the Serpent
was loosened, and Christ had laid down the yoke he had borne for the

sins of men, and that I should take it on and fight against the Serpent, for the time was fast approaching, when the first should be last and the last should be first. *Question*—Do you not find yourself mistaken now? *Answer*—Was not Christ crucified? And by signs in the heavens that it would make known to me when I should commence the great work— and until the first sign appeared, I should conceal it from the knowledge of men—and on the appearance of the sign (the eclipse of the sun last February), I should arise and prepare myself, and slay my enemies with their own weapons. And immediately on the sign appearing in the heavens, the seal was removed from my lips, and I communicated the great work laid out for me to do, to four in whom I had the greatest confidence (Henry, Hark, Nelson, and Sam). It was intended by us to have begun the work of death on the fourth of July last. Many were the plans formed and rejected by us, and it affected my mind to such a degree that I fell sick, and the time passed without our coming to any determination how to commence—still forming new schemes and rejecting them when the sign appeared again, which determined me not to wait longer.

Since the commencement of 1830, I had been living with Mr. Joseph Travis, who was to me a kind master, and placed the greatest confidence in me; in fact, I had no cause to complain of his treatment to me. On Saturday evening, the twentieth of August, it was agreed between Henry, Hark, and myself to prepare a dinner the next day for the men we expected, and then to concert a plan, as we had not yet determined on any. Hark on the following morning brought a pig, and Henry brandy, and being joined by Sam, Nelson, Will, and Jack, they prepared in the woods a dinner, where, about three o'clock, I joined them. *Question*—Why were you so backward in joining them? *Answer*—The same reason that had caused me not to mix with them for years before.

I saluted them on coming up, and asked Will how came he there; he answered his life was worth no more than others, and his liberty as dear to him. I asked him if he thought to obtain it? He said he would, or lose his life. This was enough to put him in full confidence. Jack, I knew, was only a tool in the hands of Hark. It was quickly agreed we should commence at home (Mr. J. Travis') on that night, and until we had armed and equipped ourselves, and gathered sufficient force, neither age nor sex was to be spared (which was invariably adhered to). We remained at the feast until about two hours in the night, when we went to the house and found Austin; they all went to the cider press and drank, except myself. On returning to the house, Hark went to the door with an ax, for the purpose of breaking it open, as we knew we were strong enough to murder the family, if they were awakened by the noise; but reflecting that it might create an alarm in the neighborhood, we determined to enter the house secretly, and murder them while sleeping. Hark got a ladder and set it against the chimney, on which I ascended, and hoisting a window, entered and came down stairs, unbarred the door, and removed the guns from their places. It was then observed that I must spill the first blood. On which armed with a hatchet, and accompanied by Will, I entered my master's chamber; it being dark, I could not give a death blow, the hatchet glanced from his head, he sprang from the bed and called his wife, it

was his last word. Will laid him dead, with a blow of his ax, and Mrs.
Travis shared the same fate, as she lay in bed. The murder of this
family, five in number, was the work of a moment, not one of them
awoke; there was a little infant sleeping in a cradle, that was forgotten,
until we had left the house and gone some distance, when Henry and
Will returned and killed it. We got here four guns that would shoot,
and several old muskets, with a pound or two of powder. We remained
some time at the barn, where we paraded; I formed them in a line as
soldiers, and after carrying them through all the maneuvers I was
master of, marched them off to Mr. Salathul Francis', about six hundred
yards distant. Sam and Will went to the door and knocked. Mr. Francis
asked who was there, Sam replied it was him, and he had a letter for
him, on which he got up and came to the door; they immediately seized
him, and dragging him out a little from the door, he was dispatched by
repeated blows on the head; there was no other white person in the
family. We started from there for Mrs. Reese's, maintaining the most
perfect silence on our march, where finding the door unlocked, we
entered, and murdered Mrs. Reese in her bed, while sleeping; her son
awoke, but it was only to sleep the sleep of death, he had only time
to say who is that, and he was no more. From Mrs. Reese's we went to
Mrs. Turner's, a mile distant, which we reached about sunrise on
Monday morning. Henry, Austin, and Sam went to the still, where, finding Mr. Peebles, Austin shot him, and the rest of us went to the house;
as we approached, the family discovered us, and shut the door. Vain
hope! Will, with one stroke of his ax, opened it, and we entered and
found Mrs. Turner and Mrs Newsome in the middle of a room almost
frightened to death. Will immediately killed Mrs. Turner, with one
blow of his ax. I took Mrs. Newsome by the hand, and with the sword
I had when I was apprehended, I struck her several blows over the head,
but not being able to kill her, as the sword was dull. Will turning around
and discovering it, dispatched her also. A general destruction of property and search for money and ammunition always succeeded the
murders. By this time my company amounted to fifteen, and nine men
mounted, who started for Mrs. Whitehead's (the other six were to go
through a byway to Mr. Bryant's and rejoin us at Mrs. Whitehead's),
as we approached the house we discovered Mr. Richard Whitehead
standing in the cotton patch, near the lane fence; we called him over
into the lane, and Will, the executioner, was near at hand with his fatal
ax, to send him to an untimely grave. As we pushed on to the house,
I discovered someone running round the garden, and thinking it was
some of the white family, I pursued them, but finding it was a servant
girl belonging to the house, I returned to commence the work of death,
but they whom I left had not been idle; all the family were already
murdered, but Mrs. Whitehead and her daughter Margaret. As I came
round to the door I saw Will pulling Mrs. Whitehead out of the house,
and at the step he nearly severed her head from her body, with his
broad ax. Miss Margaret, when I discovered her had concealed herself
in the corner, formed by the projection of the cellar cap from the house;
on my approach she fled, but was soon overtaken, and after repeated
blows with a sword, I killed her by a blow on the head with a fence rail.
By this time, the six who had gone by Mr. Bryant's rejoined us, and

informed me they had done the work of death assigned them. We again divided, part going to Mr. Richard Porter's, and from thence to Nathaniel Francis', the others to Mr. Howell Harris', and Mr. T. Doyle's. On my reaching Mr. Porter's, he had escaped with his family. I understood there that the alarm had already spread.

I proceeded to Mr. Levi Waller's, two or three miles distant. I took my station in the rear, and as it was my object to carry terror and devastation wherever we went, I placed fifteen or twenty of the best armed and most to be relied on in front, who generally approached the houses as fast as their horses could run; this was for two purposes, to prevent their escape and strike terror to the inhabitants—on this account I never got to the houses, after leaving Mrs. Whitehead's, until the murders were committed, except in one case. I sometimes got in sight in time to see the work of death completed, viewed the mangled bodies as they lay, in silent satisfaction, and immediately started in quest of other victims. Having murdered Mrs. Waller and ten children, we started for Mr. William Williams'—having killed him and two little boys that were there; while engaged in this, Mrs. Williams fled and got some distance from the house, but she was pursued, overtaken, and compelled to get up behind one of the company, who brought her back, and after showing her the mangled body of her lifeless husband, she was told to get down and lay by his side, where she was shot dead. I then started for Mr. Jacob Wililams', where the family were murdered. Here we found a young man named Drury, who had come on business with Mr. Wililams. He was pursued, overtaken, and shot. Mrs. Vaughan's was the next place we visited—and after murdering the family here, I determined on starting for Jerusalem. Our number amounted now to fifty or sixty, all mounted and armed with guns, axes, swords, and clubs. On reaching Mr. James W. Parker's gate, immediately on the road leading to Jerusalem, and about three miles distant, it was proposed to me to call there, but I objected, as I knew he was gone to Jerusalem, and my object was to reach there as soon as possible; but some of the men having relations at Mr. Parker's it was agreed that they might call and get his people. I remained at the gate on the road, with seven or eight; the others going across the field to the house, about half a mile off. After waiting some time for them, I became impatient, and started to the house for them, and on our return we were met by a party of white men, who had pursued our blood-stained track and who had fired on those at the gate and dispersed them, which I knew nothing of, not having been at that time rejoined by any of them. Immediately on discovering the whites, I ordered my men to halt and form, as they appeared to be alarmed. The white men, eighteen in number, approached us in about one hundred yards, when one of them fired.

I then ordered my men to fire and rush on them; the few remaining stood their ground until we approached within fifty yards, when they fired and retreated. We pursued and overtook some of them who we thought we left dead; after pursuing them about two hundred yards, and rising a little hill, I discovered they were met by another party, and had halted, and were reloading their guns, thinking that those who retreated first, and the party who fired on us at fifty or sixty yards distant, had all only fallen back to meet others with ammunition. As

I saw them reloading their guns, and more coming up than I saw at first, and several of my bravest men being wounded, the others became panic struck and squandered over the field; the white men pursued and fired on us several times. Hark had his horse shot under him, and I caught another for him as it was running by me; five or six of my men were wounded, but none left on the field; finding myself defeated here I instantly determined to go through a private way, and cross the Nottoway River at the Cypress Bridge, three miles below Jerusalem, and attack that place in the rear, as I expected they would look for me on the other road, and I had a great desire to get there to procure arms and ammunition. After going a short distance in this private way, accompanied by about twenty men, I overtook two or three who told me the others were dispersed in every direction. After trying in vain to collect a sufficient force to proceed to Jerusalem, I determined to return, as I was sure they would make back to their old neighborhood, where they would rejoin me, make new recruits, and come down again. On my way back, I called at Mrs. Thomas's, Mrs. Spencer's, and several other places. The white families having fled, we found no more victims to gratify our thirst for blood, we stopped at Major Ridley's quarter for the night, and being joined by four of his men, with the recruits made since my defeat, we mustered now about forty strong. After placing out sentinels, I laid down to sleep, but was quickly roused by a great racket. Starting up, I found some mounted, and others in great confusion; one of the sentinels having given the alarm that we were about to be attacked, I ordered some to ride round and reconnoiter, and on their return the others being more alarmed, not knowing who they were, fled in different ways, so that I was reduced to about twenty again; with this I determined to attempt to recruit, and proceed on to rally in the neighborhood I had left. Dr. Blunt's was the nearest house, which we reached just before day; on riding up the yard, Hark fired a gun. We expected Dr. Blunt and his family were at Major Ridley's, as I knew there was a company of men there; the gun was fired to ascertain if any of the family were at home; we were immediately fired upon and retreated leaving several of my men. I do not know what became of them, as I never saw them afterward. Pursuing our course back, and coming in sight of Captain Harris's, where we had been the day before, we discovered a party of white men at the house, on which all deserted me but two (Jacob and Nat), we concealed ourselves in the woods until near night, when I sent them in search of Henry, Sam, Nelson, and Hark, and directed them to rally all they could at the place we had had our dinner the Sunday before, where they would find me, and I accordingly returned there as soon as it was dark, and remained until Wednesday evening, when discovering white men riding around the place as though they were looking for someone, and none of my men joining me, I concluded Jacob and Nat had been taken, and compelled to betray me. On this I gave up all hope for the present; and on Thursday night, after having supplied myself with provisions from Mr. Travis's, I scratched a hole under a pile of fence rails in a field, where I concealed myself for six weeks, never leaving my hiding place but for a few minutes in the dead of night to get water, which was very near; thinking by this time I could venture out, I began to go about in the night and eavesdrop the houses in the neighborhood; pursuing this course for about a fortnight and gathering little or no intelligence, afraid of speaking to any human being, and returning every morning to my cave before the dawn of day. I know not how long I might have led this life, if accident had not betrayed me, a dog in the neighborhood passing by my hiding place one night while I was out was attracted by some meat I had in my cave, and crawled in and stole it, and was coming out just as I returned. A few nights after, two Negroes having started to go hunting with the same dog, and passed that way, the dog came again to the place, and having just gone out to walk about, discovered me and barked, on which, thinking myself discovered, I spoke to them to beg concealment. On making myself known, they fled from me. Knowing then they would betray me, I immediately left my hiding place, and was pursued almost incessantly until I was taken a fortnight afterward by Mr. Benjamin Phipps, in a little hole I had dug out with my sword, for the purpose of concealment, under the top of a fallen tree. On Mr. Phipps discovering the place of my concealment, he cocked his gun and aimed at me. I requested him not to shoot, and I would give up, upon which he demanded my sword. I delivered it to him, and he brought me to prison. During the time I was pursued, I had many hair breadth escapes, which your time will not permit you to relate. I am here loaded with chains, and willing to suffer the fate that awaits me.

I here proceeded to make some inquiries of him, after assuring him of the certain death that awaited him, and that concealment would only bring destruction on the innocent as well as guilty, of his own color, if he knew of any extensive or concerted plan. His answer was, I do not. When I questioned him as to the insurrection in North Carolina happening about the same time, he denied any knowledge of it.

Chapter 7

The Frontier Community

TO A WIDE RANGE of observers, from European visitors to professional historians, the institution that has exerted the greatest influence on the American character and culture is the frontier. These communities, claimed their most famous historian, Frederick Jackson Turner, established the essential characteristics of American individualism and democratic politics. Pioneers, living on the edge of settlement in a day-to-day encounter with the wilderness, abandoned traditional European habits and adopted uniquely American ones. "This expansion westward," declared Turner, "with its new opportunities, its continuous touch with simplicity of primitive society, furnish the forces dominating the American character. The true point of view in the history of this nation is not the Atlantic coast, it is the Great West."

Neither Turner nor his many followers ever defined the frontier itself very specifically. At some times they seemed to be analyzing a demographic phenomenon; that is, the impact on the community of living in a sparsely settled region. At other times they seemed to be describing a process, how men and women adjusted to wilderness conditions. Nor were they very precise about the period of time during which the frontier flourished—ostensibly its impact on American society was continuous throughout the whole nineteenth century. And they were never very exact about which regions they were analyzing; presumably the experience of the Ohio Valley settlers was duplicated by those in the Mississippi region, and then on the Great Plains, and finally in the Far West. Yet for all the vagueness of the writing, the Turner camp had a compelling breadth of vision. They brought together in a grand design a series of very particular and local developments.

While the spaciousness of this interpretation remains very appealing, one might well wish to question the basic thrust of the argument. That the wilderness or population scarcity influenced both the personality of the settlers and the organization of their communities seems indisputable. What is at issue is the exact nature of that in-

fluence. Did frontier conditions actually stimulate individualism? Or, to the contrary, were Western settlers even more community minded and community dependent than their Eastern counterparts? Did primitive conditions encourage men to go their own way? Should we retain our image of frontiersmen as Daniel Boone types, each with a rifle in hand, striking out further westward as soon as he saw smoke on the horizon? Or were they so reliant on each other as to remind us of seventeenth-century Puritans, knit together in tightly bound communities?

The selections that follow address themselves directly to this question. They are concerned first with the very nature of migration, the way people traveled in early nineteenth-century America. An incredible amount of movement went on during these decades. In 1790, the eastern seaboard states (including Kentucky and Tennessee) accounted for 100 percent of the nation's population. By 1860, only 55 percent of the country resided there. Put another way, some seven million people took up residence in the Midwest, in a territory stretching from Ohio to Wisconsin. How was this shift in population accomplished? Why did settlers move from region to region? Some contemporary accounts of this phenomenon claimed that there was more poetry and fantasy to this movement than there was hard-headed economic calculation. How valid does such an interpretation seem today?

Once on the frontier, how did the settlers arrange their lives? Clearly, they lacked all the customary institutions that functioned in the East—they were without courts or schools or churches or jails. Did they attempt to re-create these familiar institutions or to construct new ones? Did they attempt to copy older forms and in so doing create, albeit unintentionally, some new arrangements? Did these pioneers diligently try to make it on their own, or were they far more comfortable invoking a spirit of cooperation and mutual dependence than we have previously realized?

I

Travelers' accounts of life in the West had a special attraction to Americans in the early nineteenth century, who were eager to read of the customs and manners of their pioneer countrymen. One of the most popular narratives was written by Timothy Flint, a clergyman sent out by the Missionary Society of Connecticut to distribute Bibles and religious tracts and to preach in and around the Mississippi Valley. Although Flint does more than his share of moralizing, he vividly portrays both the motives of frontiersmen and the nature of the communities they organized.

RECOLLECTIONS, 1826

TIMOTHY FLINT

The people in the Atlantic states have not yet recovered from the horror inspired by the term "backwoodsman." When I first visited this country, I had my full share. I heard a thousand stories of gougings and robberies and shooting down with the rifle. I have travelled in these regions thousands of miles under all circumstances of exposure and danger. I never have carried the slightest weapon of defense. I scarcely remember to have experienced anything that resembled insult, or to have felt myself in danger from the people.

When we look round these immense regions, and consider that I have been in settlements three hundred miles from any court of justice, the wonder is that so few outrages and murders occur. It is true there are gamblers and gougers and outlaws; but there are fewer of them, than from the nature of things, we ought to expect. The backwoodsman of the West, as I have seen him, is generally an amiable and virtuous man. His general motive for coming here is to be a freeholder, to have plenty of rich land, and to be able to settle his children about him. It is a most virtuous motive. I fully believe that nine in ten of the emigrants have come here with no other motive. You find, in truth, that he has vices and barbarisms peculiar to his situation. His manners are rough. He wears, it may be, a long beard. He has a great quantity of bear or deer skins wrought into his household establishment, his furniture, and dress. He carries a knife, or a dirk, in his bosom, and when in the woods has a rifle on his back, and a pack of dogs at his heels. An Atlantic stranger, transferred directly from one of our cities to his door, would recoil from an encounter with him. But remember that his rifle and his dogs are among his chief means of support and profit. Remember that all his first days here were passed in dread of the savages. Enter his door, and tell him you are benighted, and wish the shelter of his cabin for the night. The welcome is indeed seemingly ungracious. But this apparent ungraciousness is the harbinger of every kindness that he can bestow, and every comfort that his cabin can afford. Good coffee, corn bread and butter, venison, pork, wild and tame fowls are set before you. You are shown to the best bed which the house can offer. When this kind of hospitality has been afforded you as long as you choose to stay, and when you depart, and speak about your bill, you are most commonly told with some slight mark of resentment that they do

In *Recollections of the Last Ten Years,* by Timothy Flint (Boston, 1826), pp. 74–75, 170–73, 178–83, 198–201, 232–35, 240–43.

not keep tavern. The people here are not yet a reading people. Few good books are brought into the country. The people are too busy, too much occupied in making farms and speculations, to think of literature.

America inherits a taste for puffing. The people are idolaters to the "golden calves." Some favorite man, fashion, or opinion sweep everything before them. This region is the paradise of puffers.

I have been amused in reading puffing advertisements in the newspapers. A little subscription school, in which half the pupils are abecedarians, is a college. The misfortune is that these vile pretensions finally induce the people to believe that there is a "royal road" to learning.

Town making introduces another species of puffing. Art and ingenuity have been exhausted in devising new ways of alluring purchasers to take lots and build in the new town. There are the fine rivers, the healthy hills, the mineral springs, the clear running water, the valuable forests, the fine steamboat navigation, the vast country adjacent, the central position, the admirable soil, and last of all the cheerful and undoubting predictions of what the town must one day be. I have read more than a hundred advertisements of this sort. Then the legislature must be tampered with in order to make the town either the metropolis, or at least the seat of justice.

A coarse caricature of this abomination of town making appeared in the St. Louis papers. The name was "Ne plus ultra." The streets were laid out a mile in width; the squares were to be sections, each containing six hundred and forty acres. The mall was a vast standing forest. In the center of this modern Babylon, roads were to cross each other in a meridional line at right angles.

In truth, while traveling on the prairies of the Illinois and Missouri, and observing such immense tracts of rich soil, remarking the beautiful simplicity of the limits of farms, introduced by our government, in causing the land to be all surveyed in exact squares, and thus destroying here the barbarous prescription, which has in the settled countries laid out the lands in ugly farms, and bounded them by zigzag lines—seeing the guardian genius, Liberty, hovering over the country—measuring the progress of the future, only by the analogy of the past—it will be difficult for the imagination to assign limits to the future growth and prosperity of the country.

I shall have occasion to remark upon the moving or migratory character of the western people generally. Though they have generally good houses, they might almost as well, like the Tartars, dwell in tents. Everything shifts under your eye. The present occupants sell, pack up, depart. Strangers replace them. Before they have gained the confidence of their neighbors, they hear of a better place, pack up, and follow their precursors.

I have spoken of the movable part of the community, and unfortunately for the Western country, it constitutes too great a proportion of the whole community. The general inclination here is too much like that of the Tartars. Next to hunting, Indian wars, and the wonderful exuberance of Kentucky, the favorite topic is new countries. They talk of them. They are attached to the associations connected with such conversations. They have a fatal effect upon their exertions. They only make such improvements as they can leave without reluctance

and without loss. I have everywhere noted the operation of this impediment in the way of those permanent and noble improvements which grow out of a love for that appropriated spot where we were born, and where we expect to die. There is a fund of virtuous habits, arising out of these permanent establishments, which give to our patriotism "a local habitation and a name." But neither do I at all believe the perverse representation of these same moving people, who have no affection for one spot more than another, and whose home is in the wild woods, or the boundless prairies, or wherever their dogs, their cattle, and their servants are about them. They lose, no doubt, some of the noble prejudices which are transmitted with durable mansions through successive generations. But they, in their turn, have virtues that are called into exercise by the peculiarities of their case and character, which are equally unknown. But whatever may be the effect of the stationary or the moving life upon the parties respectively, there can be no doubt about the result of this spirit upon the face of the country. Durable houses of brick or of stone, which are peculiarly called for, on account of the scarcity of timber, fences of hedge and ditch, barns and granaries of the more durable kind, the establishment of the coarser manufactories so necessary in a country like this, the planting of artificial forests, which on the wide prairies would be so beautiful and useful, all that accumulation of labor, industry, taste, and wealth that unite to beautify a family residence, to be transmitted as a proud and useful memento of the family—these improvements, which seem to be so naturally called for on these fertile plains, will not become general for many years. Scarcely has a family fixed itself, and enclosed a plantation with the universal fence, reared a suitable number of log buildings, in short, achieved the first rough improvements, that appertain to the most absolute necessity, than the assembled family about the winter fire begin to talk about the prevailing theme—some country that has become the rage, as a point of immigration. They offer their farm for sale, and move away.

The inducements to emigration arise, as most of our actions do, from mixed motives. There is more of the material of poetry than we imagine, diffused through all the classes of the community. And upon this part of the character it is that the disposition to emigration operates, and brings in aid the influence of its imperceptible but magic power. Very few, except the Germans, emigrate simply to find better and cheaper lands. The notion of new and more beautiful woods and streams, of a milder climate, deer, fish, fowl, game, and all those delightful images of enjoyment that so readily associate with the idea of the wild and boundless license of new regions; all that restless hope of finding in a new country, and in new views and combinations of things, something that we crave but have not.

I am ready to believe, from my own experience, and from what I have seen in the case of others, that this influence of imagination has no inconsiderable agency in producing emigration. Indeed, the saturnine and illiterate emigrant may not be conscious that such motives had any agency in fixing him in his purpose. They arrive, after long and diversified, but generally painful journeys, painful, especially if they have young and helpless members in their families, in the region for which they started. The first difficulty, and it is not a small one, is, among an infinite variety of choices, where to fix. The speculator, the surveyor, the different circles all propose different places, and each vaunts the exclusive excellence of his choice. If the emigrant is a reader, he betakes himself to the papers, and in the infinity of advertisements, his uncertainty is increased.

After the long uncertainty of choice is finally fixed—which is not till after the expenses and the lapse of a year—a few weeks' familiar acquaintance with the scene dispels the charms and the illusions of the imagination. The earth, the water, and the wood of these distant lands are found to be the same well-known realities of his own country. Hunting, though the game be plenty, is a laborious and unproductive business, and everything visionary and unreal gradually gives way to truth and reality.

In my view, after all the evils of the condition of an immigrant are considered, there is a great balance of real and actual advantages in his favor. There is much in that real and genuine American independence which is possessed by an industrious and frugal planter in a great degree. Any person, able and disposed to labor, is forever freed from the apprehension of poverty; and let philosophers in their bitter irony pronounce as many eulogies as they may on poverty, it is a bitter evil, and all its fruits are bitter. We need not travel these wilds in order to understand what a blessing it is to be freed forever from the apprehension of this evil. Even here there are sick, and there is little sympathy; no poor laws, no resource but in the charity of a people not remarkable for their feeling.

Thence it results that there are the more inducements to form families, and those ties, which are the cause, that while one is sick the rest are bound for his nursing and sustenance. A father can settle his children about him. A vigorous and active young man needs but two years of personal labor to have a farm ready for the support of a small family. There is less need of labor for actual support. The soil is free from stones, loose and mellow, and needs no manure, and it is very abundant in the productions natural to it, the principal of which are corn, fruits, and wheat. The calculation is commonly made that two days in a week contribute as much to support here, as the whole week at the North. The objection commonly made is that this ease of subsistence fosters idleness. But it is equally true that this depends entirely on the person, and a man of good principles and habits will find useful and happy employment for all that time which the wants of actual subsistence do not require.

One of the first things that a man, who is capable of learning anything in this country, learns is the folly of selecting his associates according to their country, or of having his friends and companions of the same country with himself. He sees good and bad, promiscuously, from all countries, and soon learns to try and weigh men by their character, and not by the place of birth. During the ten years of my acquaintance with the country, I have discovered these feelings lessening in every place. The time will come and is rapidly approaching when all local partialities will be merged in the pride of being a citizen of our great and free country, a country which is destined shortly to make a most distinguished figure among the nations.

II

Travel guides meticulously set down the best routes for westward migrants to follow, the equipment to bring, and the ways to organize the trip. These guides, not especially vital for migrants into the Midwest, were of crucial significance for those who took the long and difficult journey across the Great Plains. One typical set of instructions was issued by Randolph Marcy, an army captain who led such expeditions. The model company moving westward may have had more in common with Puritans crossing the Atlantic than with Daniel Boone types moving westward.

THE PRAIRIE TRAVELER, 1861

RANDOLPH MARCY

From Fort Leavenworth to Santa Fé, by the Way of the Upper Ferry of the Kansas River and the Cimarron

(Wood, water, and grass are found at all points where the absence of them is not stated.)

MILES FROM FORT LEAVENWORTH TO
  2.88   Salt Creek.
  9.59   Stranger's Creek.
13.54   "   "

In *The Prairie Traveller: A Handbook for Overland Expeditions*, by Randolph Marcy (New York, 1861), pp. 22–25, 276–79.

9.60	Grasshopper Creek.
4.54	Soldier's Creek.
2.45	Upper Ferry, Kansas River.
7.41	Pottawatomie Settlement.
3.89	White Wakarussi Creek.
7.78	" "
0.73	Road from Independence. No place to encamp.
7.97	Elm Creek. Water generally.
8.06	Diamond Spring.
15.46	Lost Spring. No wood.
9.25	Mud Creek. Water uncertain; no wood.
7.76	Cottonwood Creek.
6.16	Water Holes. Water generally; no wood.
12.44	Big Turkey Creek. No water.
7.83	Little Turkey Creek. Water uncertain; no wood.
18.19	Little Arkansas River.
10.60	Owl Creek. Water generally in holes above and below crossing.
6.39	Little Cow Creek. Water only occasionally.
2.93	Big Cow Creek. Water holes, ten miles (estimated). Water uncertain; no wood.
18.24	Bend of the Arkansas.
16.35	Pawnee Rock. Teams sometimes camp near here, and drive stock to the Arkansas to water. No wood.
5.28	Ash Creek. Water above and below crossing, uncertain.
6.65	Pawnee Fork. Best grass some distance above crossing.
	From Pawnee Fork to the lower crossing of the Arkansas, a distance of ninety-eight and one half miles, convenient camping places can be found along the Arkansas; the most prominent localities are therefore only mentioned. A supply of fuel should be laid in at Pawnee Fork to last till you pass Fort Mann, though it may be obtained, but inconveniently, from the *opposite* side of the Arkansas. Dry Route branches off at three and one half miles (estimated). It is said to be a good one, but deficient in water and without wood.
11.43	Coon Creek.
10.05	Fort Mann.
25.34	Lower Crossing of the Arkansas. A supply of wood should be got from this vicinity to last till you reach Cedar Creek.
15.68	Water hole. Water uncertain; no wood.
30.02	Two water holes. Water uncertain; no wood.
14.14	Lower Cimarron Springs. No wood.
20.00	Pools of Water. Water uncertain; no wood.
19.02	Middle Springs of the Cimarron. No wood.
12.93	Little Crossing of the Cimarron. No wood.
14.10	Upper Cimarron Springs. No wood. Pools of water, seven miles (estimated). No wood.
19.05	Cold Spring. A tree here and there in the vicinity. Pools of water, eleven miles (estimated). Water uncertain; no wood.
16.13	Cedar Creek. M'Nees' Creek, ten miles (estimated). Water indifferent and uncertain; scant pasture; no wood.
21.99	Cottonwood Creek. No water.

15.17   Rabbit Ear Creek. Ten miles (estimated), springs. Round Mound, eight miles (estimated). No water; no wood; no camping place. Rock Creek, ten miles (estimated). Grazing scant; no wood.

26.40   Whetstone Creek. Spring; no wood. Water, etc., to the left of the road.

14.13   Point of Rocks. Water and grass *up the canyon,* just after crossing the *point;* scattering shrub cedars on the neighboring heights.

16.62   Sandy Arroyo. Water uncertain; no wood. Grazing above the crossing; willows.

10.05   Rio Ocaté. Wood one third of a mile to right of road; grass in the canyon. Pond of water, thirteen and one half miles (estimated). No wood.

19.65   Wagon Mound.

21.62   Canyon del Lobo. Rio Moro, three and one half miles (estimated).

18.00   Las Vegas. Forage purchasable.

13.05   Tacolote. Forage purchasable. No grass to speak of.

14.00   San Miguel. Forage purchasable; no grass.

21.81   Ruins of Pecos. Grazing very scant. Water uncertain; no grass.

13.41   Stone Corral. No grass.

10.80   Santa Fé. Forage purchasable; no grazing.

Organization of Companies

After a particular route has been selected to make the journey across the plains, and the requisite number have arrived at the eastern terminus, their first business should be to organize themselves into a company and elect a commander. The company should be of sufficient magnitude to herd and guard animals, and for protection against Indians.

From fifty to seventy men, properly armed and equipped, will be enough for these purposes, and any greater number only makes the movements of the party more cumbersome and tardy.

In the selection of a captain, good judgment, integrity of purpose, and practical experience are the essential requisites, and these are indispensable to the harmony and consolidation of the association. His duty should be to direct the order of march, the time of starting and halting, to select the camps, detail and give orders to guards, and, indeed, to control and superintend all the movements of the company.

An obligation should then be drawn up and signed by all the members of the association, wherein each one should bind himself to abide in all cases by the orders and decisions of the captain, and to aid him by every means in his power in the execution of his duties; and they should also obligate themselves to aid each other, so as to make the individual interest of each member the common concern of the whole company. To insure this, a fund should be raised for the purchase of extra animals to supply the places of those which may give out or die on the road; and if the wagon or team of a particular member should fail and have to be abandoned, the company should obligate themselves to transport his luggage, and the captain should see that he has his share of transportation equal with any other member. Thus it will be made the interest of every member of the company to watch over and protect the property of others as well as his own.

In case of failure on the part of anyone to comply with the obligations imposed by the articles of agreement after they have been duly executed, the company should of course have the power to punish the delinquent member, and, if necessary, to exclude him from all the benefits of the association.

The advantages of an association such as I have mentioned are manifestly numerous. The animals can be herded together and guarded by the different members of the company in rotation, thereby securing to all the opportunities of sleep and rest. Besides, this is the only way to resist depredations of the Indians, and to prevent their stampeding and driving off animals; and much more efficiency is secured in every respect, especially in crossing streams, repairing roads, etc., etc.

When a captain has once been chosen, he should be sustained in all his decisions unless he commits some manifest outrage, when a majority of the company can always remove him, and put a more competent man in his place.

III

Migrants generally moved westward in successive steps, going in a typical sequence from western New York to Ohio, and then on to Michigan. In this way, they gradually accommodated themselves to frontier life. Occasionally, however, a family moved in one leap from settled Eastern communities to frontier communities, and the shock of displacement made them sensitive observers of the unique qualities of their new environment. One such person was Caroline Kirkland. Her memoir, A New Home, Who'll Follow? *reflects Eastern prejudices, and thereby points to much that was especially characteristic of frontier settlements.*

A NEW HOME, WHO'LL FOLLOW? 1839

CAROLINE S. KIRKLAND

When my husband purchased two hundred acres of wild land and drew with a piece of chalk on the barroom table the plan of a village, I little thought I was destined to make myself famous by handing down to posterity a faithful record of the advancing fortunes of that favored spot.

"The madness of the people" in those days of golden dreams took

In *A New Home, Who'll Follow?*, by Caroline S. Kirkland [pseud.] (n.p., 1839), pp. 8–9, 67–69, 82–83, 88–91, 111, 114–15.

more commonly the form of city building; but there were a few who contented themselves with planning villages on the banks of streams which never could be expected to bear navies, but which might yet be turned to account in the more homely way of grinding or sawing— operations which must necessarily be performed somewhere for the well-being of those very cities. It is of one of these humble attempts that it is my lot to speak, and I make my confession at the outset, warning any fashionable reader who may have taken up my book that I intend to be "decidedly low."

It did not require a very long residence in Michigan to convince me that it is unwise to attempt to stem directly the current of society, even in the wilderness, but I have since learned many ways of *wearing round* which give me the opportunity of living very much after my own fashion, without offending, very seriously, anybody's prejudices.

No settlers are so uncomfortable as those who, coming with abundant means as they suppose to be comfortable, set out with a determination to live as they have been accustomed to live. They soon find that there are places where the "almighty dollar" is almost power-less; or rather, that powerful as it is, it meets with its conqueror in the jealous pride of those whose services must be had in order to live at all.

It would be in vain to pretend that this state of society can ever be agreeable to those who have been accustomed to the more rational arrangements of the older world. The social character of the meals, in particular, is quite destroyed, by the constant presence of strangers, whose manners, habits of thinking, and social connections are quite different from your own, and often exceedingly repugnant to your taste. Granting the correctness of the opinion which may be read in their countenances that they are "as good as you are," I must insist that a greasy cookmaid, or a redolent stableboy can never be, to my thinking, an agreeable table companion—putting pride, that most terrific bug-bear of the woods, out of the question.

Some of my dear theorizing friends in the civilized world had dis-suaded me most earnestly from bringing a maid with me.

"She would always be discontented and anxious to return; and you'll find plenty of good farmer's daughters ready to live with you for the sake of earning a little money."

Good souls! how little did they know of Michigan! I have since that day seen the interior of many a wretched dwelling, with almost literally nothing in it but a bed, a chest, and a table; children ragged to the last degree, and potatoes the only fare; but never yet saw I one where the daughter was willing to own herself obliged to live out at service. She would "hire out" long enough to buy some article of dress perhaps, money to pay the doctor, or for some such special reason; but never as a regular calling, or with an acknowledgment of inferior station.

This state of things appalled me at first; but I have learned a better philosophy since. I find no difficulty now in getting such aid as I require, and but little in retaining it as long as I wish, though there is always a desire of making an occasional display of independence. Since living with one for wages is considered by common consent a favor, I take it as a favor; and, this point once conceded, all goes well. Perhaps I have been peculiarly fortunate; but certainly with one or two exceptions, I

have little or nothing to complain of on this essential point of domestic comfort.

To be sure, I had one damsel who crammed herself almost to suffocation with sweatmeats and other things which she esteemed very nice; and ate up her own pies and cake, to the exclusion of those for whom they were intended; who would put her head in at a door with, "Miss Clavers, did you hollar? I thought I *heered* a yell."

And another who was highly offended because room was not made for her at table with guests from the city, and that her company was not requested for tea visits. And this latter highborn damsel sent in from the kitchen a circumstantial account *in writing,* of the instances wherein she considered herself aggrieved; well written it was, too, and expressed with much naïveté, and abundant respect. I answered it in the way which "turneth away wrath." Yet it was not long before this fiery spirit was aroused again, and I was forced to part with my country belle.

I took especial care to be impartial in my own visiting habits, determined at all sacrifice to live down the impression that I felt *above* my neighbors. In fact, however we may justify certain exclusive habits in populous places, they are strikingly and confessedly ridiculous in the wilderness. What can be more absurd than a feeling of proud distinction, where a stray spark of fire, a sudden illness, or a day's contretemps may throw you entirely upon the kindness of your humblest neighbor? If I treat Mrs. Timson with neglect today can I with any face borrow her broom tomorrow? And what would become of me if, in revenge for my declining her invitation to tea this afternoon, she should decline coming to do my washing on Monday?

"Mother wants your sifter," said Miss Ianthe Howard, a young lady of six years' standing, attired in a tattered calico, thickened with dirt; her unkempt locks straggling from under that hideous substitute for a bonnet, so universal in the western country, a dirty cotton handkerchief, which is used, *ad nauseam*, for all sorts of purposes.

"Mother wants your sifter, and she says she guesses you can let her have some sugar and tea, 'cause you've got plenty."

This excellent reason, " 'cause you've got plenty," is conclusive as to sharing with your neighbors. Whoever comes into Michigan with nothing, will be sure to better his condition; but woe to him that brings with him anything like an appearance of abundance, whether of money or mere household conveniences. To have them, and not be willing to share them in some sort with the whole community, is an unpardonable crime. You must lend your best horse to *qui que ce soit*, to go ten miles over hill and marsh, in the darkest night, for a doctor; or your team to travel twenty after a "gal;" your wheelbarrows, your shovels, your utensils of all sorts, belong, not to yourself, but to the public, who do not think it necessary even to *ask* a loan, but take it for granted. The two saddles and bridles of Montacute spend most of their time travelling from house to house a-manback; and I have actually known a 'stray martingale to be traced to four dwellings two miles apart, having been lent from one to another, without a word to the original proprietor, who sat waiting, not very patiently, to commence a journey.

Then within doors, an inventory of your plenishing of all sorts would scarcely more than include the articles which you are solicited to lend. Not only are all kitchen utensils as much your neighbors as your own, but bedsteads, beds, blankets, sheets travel from house to house, a pleasant and effectual mode of securing the perpetuity of certain efflorescent peculiarities of the skin, for which Michigan is becoming almost as famous as the land " 'twixt Maidenkirk and John o' Groat's." Sieves, smoothing irons, and churns run about as if they had legs; one brass kettle is enough for a whole neighborhood; and I could point to a cradle which has rocked half the babies in Montacute. For my own part, I have lent my broom, my thread, my tape, my spoons, my cat, my thimble, my scissors, my shawl, my shoes; and have been asked far my combs and brushes: and my husband, for his shaving apparatus and his pantaloons.

Many English families reside in our vicinity, some of them well calculated to make their way anywhere; close, penurious, grasping, and indefatigable; denying themselves all but the necessaries of life, in order to add to their lands, and make the most of their crops; and somewhat apt in bargaining to overreach even the wary pumpkin-eaters, their neighbors: others to whom all these things seem so foreign and so unsuitable that one cannot but wonder that the vagaries of fortune should have sent them into so uncongenial an atmosphere. The class last mentioned generally live retired, and show little inclination to mingle with their rustic neighbors; and, of course, they become at once the objects of suspicion and dislike. The principle of "let-a-be for let-a-be" holds not with us. Whoever exhibits any desire for privacy is set down as "proud," or something worse; no matter how inoffensive, or even how benevolent he may be; and of all places in the world in which to live on the shady side of public opinion, an American backwoods settlement is the very worst, as many of these unfortunately mistaken emigrants have been made to feel.

The better classes of English settlers seem to have left their own country with high-wrought notions of the unbounded freedom to be enjoyed in this; and it is with feelings of angry surprise that they learn after a short residence here that this very universal freedom abridges their own liberty to do as they please in their individual capacity; that the absolute democracy which prevails in country places imposes as heavy restraints upon one's freewill in some particulars, as do the overbearing pride and haughty distinctions of the old world in others; and after one has changed one's whole plan of life, and crossed the wide ocean to find a Utopia, the waking to reality is attended with feelings of no slight bitterness. In some instances within my knowledge these feelings of disappointment have been so severe as to neutralize all that was good in American life, and to produce a degree of sour discontent which increased every real evil and went far toward alienating the few who were kindly inclined toward the stranger.

IV

The diary of Mrs. Miriam Colt, Went to Kansas, *starkly presents the inflated hopes and grandiose dreams that brought families to the West and kept them moving. The Colt family traveled from western New York to Kansas under the auspices of the Vegetarian Settlement Society, and while there was certainly something odd about this sponsorship, there is nothing unusual in the society's promises to prospective settlers. Railroad companies and real estate promoters did very much the same thing. The site, according to the prospectus, was to have an agricultural college and several common schools among its first institutions. Settlers would on arrival find mills in operation, houses built, and a city under way. What they found when they arrived, and how they dealt with it, emerges all too poignantly in Mrs. Colt's account.*

WENT TO KANSAS, 1862

MIRIAM COLT

May thirteenth

Can anyone imagine our disappointment [when arriving] this morning, on learning from this and that member that no mills have been built; that the directors, after receiving our money to build mills, have not fulfilled the trust reposed in them, and that in consequence, some families have already left the settlement.

Now *we all have come!* Have brought our fathers, our mothers, and our little ones, and find no shelter sufficient to shield them from the furious prairie winds, and the terrific storms of the climate!

In *Went to Kansas: Being a Thrilling and Ill-Fated Expedition to That Fairy Land—Its Sad Results,* by Miriam Colt (Boston, 1862), pp. 45–47, 52–55, 70–73, 98–99, 134–35, 140–41, 144–45, 278–85.

For a moment let me contrast the two pictures—the one we had made provision for and had reason to believe would be presented to us, with the one that meets our eyes:

Expected a sawmill would be in operation, a gristmill building, and a temporary boardinghouse erected to receive families as they should come into the settlement, until their own houses could be built.

Wherever there are mills in this southwestern world, there surely is to be a town. And how much of life, active life, would resound through a new settlement, from the noisy sawmill. How soon could comfortable houses be built. As it is, we find the families, some living in tents of cloth, some of cloth and green bark just peeled from the trees, and some wholly of green bark, stuck up on the damp ground, without floors or fires. These intelligent, but too confiding, families have come from the North, East, South, and West, to this *farther* West, to make pleasant homes; and now are determined to turn right about, start again on a journey—some know not where! Others have invested their all in the company. Now come lost means and blighted hopes.

We see that the city grounds, which have been surveyed (and a log cabin built in the center, where is to stand the large "central octagon building"), are one mile from here. It seems the company did not pitch their tents there on account of its being so wet, so chose this higher prairie until after the spring rains should be over. Two or three families of us, and a few single men, take to our wagons again, drive over the roadless prairie, and around the head of a creek, to become the first residents in the "Neosho, or Octagon City." Find the city, as we had seen, to contain only one log cabin, sixteen by sixteen, mudded between the logs on the inside, instead of on the outside; neither door nor window; the roof covered with "shakes" (western shingles), split out of

oak I should think, three and one-half feet in length, and about as wide as a sheet of foolscap paper.

The men have set themselves at work now to improve this dwelling. Some are laying a floor, or rather paving one, by drawing fresh dirt, spreading it all over the ground, then laying flat stones of irregular shape on to it, leaving them bound on all sides by the rich prairie soil. Others are laying a floor to the loft above of "shakes," which from their slivery sides and warping propensity, methinks, will present no very smooth surface to lie upon, when nothing, hardly, save one Indian blanket is to intervene between us and them.

May twenty-second

Members of the company who have concluded to remain in the Territory, think it time now to do what they can, under present disappointments, for the comfort of their families, and also for their future welfare. Some are building their cabins on their city lots, in their respective portions of the octagon; others, independent of the company, have become "squatter sovereigns," and will build their cabins on their claims.

Each claimant can claim and hold, by the preemption right, 240 acres of land—160 timber and 80 prairie. My husband, his father, and sister L. are each claimants; they have accordingly located their claims side by side, making 720 acres of land belonging to our family. It is two miles east from the "center octagon," and joining the Osage Indian lands. My husband says the timber on our claim is fine; there are different kinds of walnut and oak (some black walnuts four feet through), and that for several rods on the river is the prettiest bed of pebbles he ever saw, nice for walks. We intend, some time, to have walks made of them.

The Stewarts have located their claims two miles west from here; are building their cabin on a high prairie swell, where nature has planted the walnut and oak just sparsely enough for both beauty and shade.

Mr. Adams has made a cabin of "shakes" on his city lot, one-fourth of a mile north from the "center."

Mr. Herrimen, a little shed-like cabin of logs and bark, one-half mile a little west of north.

H. S. Clubb's dwelling is a cabin made of an old Indian wigwam and tenting, one mile southeast, on his city lot.

Father Cosgrove resides in a cabin one-half mile southeast, on his city lot, near the river.

The young men, and men without their families, board around in the cabins with the families. So we are all uncomfortably situated, for the want of proper building materials.

June fourth

Disappointment has darkened every brow, however hard they may have striven to rise above it. We are one hundred miles from a gristmill, and fifty from a post office. Mr. Clubb has petitioned to have the mail come here.

The Indians have gone away now on their hunt; it seems quiet and good to have our fear removed for a time. The people say we have had our hardest time here, but it does not seem so to me. I tell my husband, "We are a doomed ship; unless we go away, some great calamity will come upon us; and it is on me that the storm will burst with all its dark fury." Sometimes a voice speaks to me in thunder tones, saying, "Rise, rise! flee to the mountains—tarry not in all the plain. Haste away! Destruction's before thee, and sorrow behind." My husband says, "Miriam, don't feel so; I am afraid you will go crazy. I think it is your imaginings, caused by our disappointments and discomforts." I answer, "I hope it is, but I don't know why I should be so overpowered with such feelings; they come to me without being invited, and I cannot help giving them expression sometimes."

June seventh

My husband is up at his claim planting corn. Hopeful man! Whatever of calamity may be pent up in the black clouds for us, may Heaven grant that our lives may be spared! I can bear all pecuniary losses—go hungry, cold, barefoot, and sleep on the rough and uneven floor—but spare me my beloved husband and my darling children.

The *one plough* is broken. Father started off this morning to go twenty-five miles, down to the Catholic Mission, where is the nearest blacksmith, to get it mended.

June ninth

Father has returned with the mended plough—has had quite an interesting time going to and from the blacksmith's shop, a journey of fifty miles.

June tenth

Mr. Clubb has returned from Fort Scott, and the goods, groceries, seeds, and some provisions belonging to the company have arrived. They were bought with the company's money, still we are charged a very high price for them. Potatoes four dollars per bushel; can't afford to have even one meal of them—have cooked one for mother; they must, all that we have, be planted. Flour is dealt out to us in rations. Have just been to Mr. Clubb's with my small white bag; came home with a few pounds in one end strung over my shoulder. I must have resembled the Missourian woman, with her bag of cornmeal (for I felt as she looked), when I said, "shall I ever come to this?"

July thirteenth

Father's name is now added to the list of the sick. How can I stay this flood of tears, as I look about and see all but myself prostrated with sickness? So pale and weak, and amid so many discomforts. It is impossible for me to do for them as they require. I am weak myself; it seems when I go for water that I can never get back again. Have just been to the spring for my turn of water, one-half mile, which I bring in a six quart camp-pail and Indian coffee pot of the same dimensions.

It is all the way up hill from the spring. This is a long, long sabbath day. *"O, God, forsake us not utterly!"*

July sixteenth

Yesterday morning, father drove out to the settlement before his chill came on, and drove back last eve, after his fever was off. He went to see if he could get someone to stay with us for a few days. Our good neighbor, Mr. Stewart, sent his hired man, Mr. Buxton, this morning. He prepares wood, takes care of the oxen, cow and calf, and brings water. My husband is lying on our bed of prairie grass, on the floor; his fever is passing off. Mother lies on her bed in the other room; seems very sick.

August sixteenth

A letter has come over the long distance from our dear friend Mrs. V. She writes as follows:

Plainfield, Wis., July 22, 1856

My Dear Friends:

Arrived at home safely, and in much better health than when I left you. Arrived here at home just in two weeks from the time that we left the Neosho. Had a very pleasant journey. How happy I was, my dear friends, to find my father's family all well and happy, and O! how prosperous. They certainly have been signally blessed. The crops are most abundant; corn looks better than in Missouri. This is a beautiful country; it never looked so good to me before. I must tell you, Mr. Colt, that father says, and all the neighbors too, that there are thousands of acres of land to be taken in this vicinity, and any amount of wheat harvesting to be had on shares—no trouble. Father says there will be some place to stay in for the first few weeks. O, well, there is no *trouble*, no *difficulty* in the least; my parents and all the neighbors invite you to come; they will certainly insure you all profitable employment. Come, now! Schoolteachers are in great demand, both in the academies and district schools, around here. Oh! do come! The air is so pure and bracing—how can you be sick? It seems to infuse life and vigor immediately into me. Oh! if you would only come, you could live with us a while. Be sure to write immediately on the receipt of this. I must say again, oh! how I wish you would come! Our people here all want to see you; you certainly will not regret making a home here. How I hope you will come. That this may find you all well is the sincere wish and prayer of your friend,

E. V.

Dear, good friend. I could wish we were all transferred to your pleasant Wisconsin home; but my heart has so long vibrated between hope and fear that to get away from this place seems almost an impossibility. I ask my husband many times a day if he thinks we shall ever get away. He says, "I am determined to go now, let father do as he will."

August nineteenth

Have been saving a little water everyday now, for some days, to get enough to wash with, or make a pretension. Truly we are in a land where there is neither soap nor water; so how can we keep clean?

August thirtieth

Mr. Morris sent us word today that he will not be able to take us out of the Territory. He intends leaving with his family, in company with another, on account of the northern troubles.

Father has just returned from the cornfield, with a sledload of pumpkins that the Indians had not tugged away; he has piled them up in one corner of the cabin; says he is going to live on pumpkin pies after we go away. We know of no way now to get out of the Territory.

Sunday, August thirty-first

A bright, bright day! All nature is quiet; a silent adoration from prairie, wood, and dell.

My husband, though no dreamer, has just been relating to me the dream he dreamt last night. He said, "I dreamt that we left this place, and traveled a very long distance, until we came to a large river; then we stood on the bank considering how we were to get across it. Finally, we concluded to ford it; so you took one child and I the other, and soon came out on the other side. There we found a beautiful country—all kinds of fruit were growing spontaneously, and in abundance—every want was satisfied, and we were happy."

When we were expecting to leave, my husband gave the cow and calf to sister L.; told her that they were well worth forty dollars, and that the worth of them would take her out of the Territory anytime she wished to leave. His planes, augers, saws, and all such tools he has given to father; has divided the remainder of the money, keeping for ourselves just what, with the cheapest fare, would take us to some point on the other side of the Mississippi, either to Wisconsin or to New York.

September second

I was up this morning at early dawn, cooking for our journey, and bringing water to fill all empty vessels. Made myself and children ready again—got our good neighbor, Mr. Hobbs, to strap our trunks and take our bed of prairie grass from the loft, to be ready to place in the wagon, so that my husband and children can lie on it to ride through the days, and for us to sleep on nights. I then went for my last turn of water, and to pick my spike of flowers; bade farewell to all the windings of my path to the water, and to the trees, vines, grass, and flowers which had seemed to bow in silent sympathy at my sad lamentations. Soon the wagon was seen coming toward the creek, and the other two moving in a straight line on the prairie, with which we were soon to fall in rear. Our trunks were placed in the back end of the wagon, our bed in front, and our dinner pail so as to have it handy. Children were in a hurry to ride, and teamster to get up with the other wagons. I bade farewell to father, mother, and sister L. with a sad heart, and placed my children and self into the wagon; my husband still lingered; it was a time of heart-trial to him to leave his own father, mother, and sister in this wild land, when he had made such earnest appeals to them to leave. Father's tenacious will must bind his wife and daughter.

We start out upon the world again. Many a dark shade has passed over us since last spring. We move up along on to the high prairie.

Now I will take a look at the picture before me: here are my husband and children, very weak; we move along at a very slow pace; hundreds of miles are before us, and know not where we shall find a resting place. I must take the burden! How are we to reach the summit of the mountain that rises before us? May Heaven grant strength and courage!

V

One of the most famous outgrowths of frontier conditions was the vigilance committee, the posse that dispensed its own special brand of justice. These bands have been traditionally understood as more or less indistinguishable from the ruffians they pursued. But the story is actually far more complex. The vigilantes highlight the difficulty of establishing and maintaining order in a community where population growth has run far ahead of the transfer of institutions, where people settled in advance of courts, police, or other formal institutions of social control. In many ways, the bands stood outside the law because they had preceded the law.

A well-organized vigilance committee operated in the 1850s in San Francisco. In origin, the committee was a response to the sudden influx of thousands of migrants in search of gold in the hills. To a notable degree, it was composed of the most respectable classes of this new city, most typically the merchants, those who had most to lose in a reign of disorder. The documents below describe this venture, clarifying the motives and experiences of those who took the law into their own hands.

THE SAN FRANCISCO VIGILANCE COMMITTEE, 1851

Constitution of the San Francisco Vigilance Committee
Instituted the Eighth of June 1851

Whereas it has become apparent to the citizens of San Francisco that there is no security for life and property, either under the regulations of society as it at present exists or under the laws as now administered, therefore the citizens whose names are hereunto attached do unite themselves into an association for the maintenance of the peace and good order of society and the preservation of the lives and prop-

Originally entitled "Papers of the San Francisco Vigilance Committee of 1851." In *Publications of Pacific Coast History* (Berkeley, 1919), vol. 4, pp. 1–3, 634–37, 825–27.

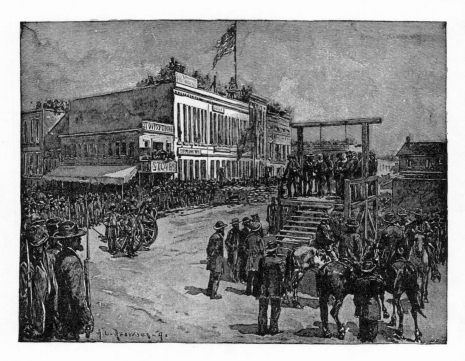

erty of the citizens of San Francisco and do bind themselves each unto the other to do and perform every lawful act for the maintenance of law and order and to sustain the laws when faithfully and properly administered but we are determined that no thief, burglar, incendiary assassin, professed gambler, and other disturbers of the peace shall escape punishment either by the quibbles of the law, the insecurity of prisons, the carelessness or corruption of the police, or a laxity of those who pretend to administer justice.

And to secure the objects of this association we do hereby agree:

First, that the name and style of the association shall be the "Committee of Vigilance for the protection of the lives and property of the citizens and residents of the City of San Francisco.

Secondly, that there shall be a room selected for the meeting and deliberations of the Committee at which there shall be some one or more members of the Committee appointed for that purpose in constant attendance at all hours of the day and night to receive the report of any member of the association or of any other person or persons whatsoever of any act of violence done to the person or property of any citizen of San Francisco and if in the judgement of the member or members of the Committee present it be such an act as justifies the interference of this Committee either in aiding in the execution of the laws or the prompt and summary punishment of the offender the Committee shall be at once assembled for the purpose of taking such action as a majority of the Committee when assembled shall determine upon.

Thirdly, that it shall be the duty of any member or members of the Committee on duty at the Committee room whenever a general assemblage of the Committee is deemed necessary to cause a call to be made by two strokes upon a bell.

Fourthly, that when the Committee have assembled for action the decision of a majority present shall be binding upon the whole Committee and that those members of the Committee pledge their honor and hereby bind themselves to defend and sustain each other in carrying out the determined action of this Committee at the hazard of their lives and their fortunes.

Fifthly, that there shall be chosen monthly a President, Secretary, and Treasurer and it shall be the duty of the Secretary to detail the members required to be in daily attendance at the Committee room. A Sergeant-at-Arms shall be appointed whose duty it shall be to notify such members of their detail for duty. The Sergeant-at-Arms shall reside at and be in constant attendance at the Committee room.

There shall be a standing Committee of Finance and qualification consisting of five each and no person shall be admitted a member of this association unless he be a respectable citizen and approved of by the Committee on qualification before admission.

[To this constitution were annexed the names of seven hundred and five citizens.]

Resignation of G. E. Schenck

Executive Chamber
San Francisco, September 14, 1851

To the Committee of Vigilance,
Gentlemen:
It is with great regret that we offer the annexed resignation of our Brother G. E. Schenck, who is about to leave the state. He has labored long and arduously with us throughout the trying scenes that have passed, has shown regard for their personal welfare, and for the lasting good and greatness, of this your adopted city and state.

With sentiments of great regard and esteem I beg to remain ever
Yours Truly etc.,
[Signed]   Geo. Everett Schenck

To,
   Stephen Payran,
   President Ex Committee

September 11, 1851
Executive Chamber

G. E. Schenck Esquire,
   of the Committee of Vigilance of San Francisco
Dear Sir:
In the name and on behalf of my colleagues constituting the executive body of our association to express our sincere regret at a separation with one whom we so fondly esteem.

We can never forget when with us at the inception of our duties you joined us with a willing heart and firm hand to relieve our adopted city from the many impending evils that hung over it.

We had suffered much and suffered long. The torch of the

incendiary had destroyed us many times, ruin so frequently fell to our lot that we became dismayed, the lives of many of our valuable citizens had been destroyed by the hands of assassins, it was under such a state of things that we banded ourselves together, having no alternative, our judiciary and subordinates, had become corrupt, desperate offenders were allowed to go forth in our midst to riot on our lives and property for their pecuniary advantage.

Although the day was dark, and danger stared us in the face, we essayed to meet the storm and test the consequence, the spirits of our revolutionary sires prompted us, virtue guided our acts, corrupt representatives yielded, felons and incendiaries fled, light has taken the place of darkness, and a calm has succeeded the storm, peace and security are restored.

You are about to revisit the scenes of your youth, to see eye to eye those whom you love; and with you will attend the sincere wishes of your colaborers that your fondest expectations may be realized.

We humbly trust that if you ever feel disposed to revisit us, that you may find the good seed sown by us in honesty bringing forth all that we so ardently have desired, that California may be the abode of virtue and innocence, and that such confidence may be felt in its institutions that yourself and all our brethren may be induced to bring out their wives and children, and thereby to strengthen what we have done, as to bid defiance to the vicious and evil minded.

Assure your friends, sir, that we are worthy of all commendation, that hereafter they may treat with us commercially with confidence.

You are granted leave of absence and a remittance of all dues until your return.

[signed]   Stephen Payran
President Ex[ecutive] Committee

Prisoners Arrested by the Committee of Vigilance

George Adams; larceny; handed over to authorities.
Thomas Ainsworth; larceny; handed over to authorities.
Ahone; keeper of a suspicious house; discharged.
William Alderson; convict; deported.
Alo; keeper of a suspicious house; discharged.
J. J. Arentrue; larceny and murder; handed over to authorities.
George Arthur; larceny; handed over to authorities.
William Barclay; convict; deported.
James Burns, *alias* Jimmy from Town; larceny; handed over to authorities.
Thomas Burns; convict, keeper of a suspicious house; deported.
Capt. Canning; murder; handed over to authorities.
Samuel Church; horse thief and deserter; handed over to army.
William Clay; convict; deported.
William Cummings; larceny; discharged.
Theodore Dahlgrén; larceny; honorably discharged.
Peter Davis; "desperate character"; discharged.
John Donnelly; convict; discharged.
David Earl; larceny; ordered to leave California.

Aaron Gainesborough; convict; ordered to leave California.
Samuel Gallagher; murder; handed over to authorities.
Richard Garland; convict; deported.
John Goff; convict; ordered to leave California.
W. F. Hance; murder in Panama; sent back to Panama.
W. H. Hays; larceny; ordered to leave California.
James Hetherington; keeper of a suspicious house; deported.
Lawrence Higgins; convict immigrant; deported.
Mary Ann Hogan; keeper of a suspicious house; discharged.
Howard; deserter; handed over to army.
John Jenkins; larceny; convict (?); hanged.
Daniel Jenks; larceny, ordered to leave California.
Emma Jones; convict; ordered to leave California.
Dr. Kennedy; assault; handed over to authorities.
Francois Le Bras; murder; handed over to authorities.
William Leonard; larceny; handed over to authorities.
William Lovegrove; larceny; discharged.
John McDonald; drunk; discharged.
Robert McKenzie; larceny; hanged.
John Matson; arson; discharged.
Robert Ogden; convict; ordered to leave California.
John Olligin; murder; discharged.
Daniel Peterson; larceny; discharged.
Justo Reyes; larceny; whipped; ordered to leave California.
James Roach; convict; deported.
Ben Robinson; arson; discharged.
Michael Ryan; suspected immigrant; deported.
Martin Sanphy; "bad citizen"; ordered to leave California.
Mrs. Jane Sanphy; larceny; discharged.
Thomas Scott; "bad man"; deported.
Henry Smith; horse stealing; honorably discharged.
James Smith; larceny; discharged.

VI

The frontier also bred its own peculiar brand of American religion—
revivalism. To many observers, evangelical preaching at camp
meetings represented the most primitive and crude form of religion.
They thought of revival meetings as excuses for drunkenness and
sexual license, and judged the revival ministers to be ignorant
rabble-rousers. But here, as in the case of vigilantes, Eastern
stereotypes miss the essential point. In fact, revivalism to an
extraordinary degree worked to uphold order on the frontier. It
also represented the triumph of a spirit of voluntarism. Here were
men and women organizing churches without state intervention,
and supporting them without state aid.

The most important analysis of revivalism during these years was made by Robert Baird, in his study Religion in the United States *(1844). His effort to defend the revivalist spirit led him to link this religious occurrence directly to the nature of frontier community life.*

RELIGION IN THE UNITED STATES OF AMERICA, 1844

ROBERT BAIRD

Neither the general government nor that of the states does anything directly for the maintenance of public worship. Religion is protected and indirectly aided by both; but nowhere does the civil power defray the expenses of the churches, or pay the salaries of ministers of the gospel, excepting in the case of a few chaplains connected with the public service.

Upon what then must religion rely? Only, under God, upon the efforts of its friends, acting from their own freewill, influenced by that variety of considerations which are ordinarily comprehended under the title of a desire to do good. This, in America, is the grand and only alternative. To this principle must the country look for all those efforts which must be made for its religious instruction.

Let us look for a moment at the work which, under God's blessing, has to be accomplished by this instrumentality.

The population of the United States at present (November 1842) is not far short of 18,000,000. Upon the voluntary principle alone depends the religious instruction of this entire population, embracing the thousands of churches and ministers of the gospel, colleges, theological seminaries, sunday schools, missionary societies, and all the other instrumentalities that are employed to promote the knowledge of the gospel from one end of the country to the other. Upon the mere unconstrained good will of the people, and especially of those among them who love the Savior and profess His name, does this vast superstructure rest.

At the first sight of this statistical view of the case, some of my readers will be ready to exclaim that the prospect is hopeless. Others will say, Woe to the cause of religion if the government does not put its shoulders to the wheel! But I answer, not only in my own name, but dare to do it in that of every well-informed American Christian: "No! we want no more aid from the government than what we receive, and what it so cheerfully gives. The prospect is not desperate so long as Christians do their duty in humble and heartfelt reliance upon God."

Americans [have] been trained to exercise the same energy, self-reliance, and enterprise in the cause of religion which they exhibit in other affairs. Thus, when a new church is called for, the people first inquire whether they cannot build it at their own cost, and ask help from others only after having done all they think practicable among

In *Religion in the United States of America*, by Robert Baird (London, 1844), pp. 288–89, 292, 298–99, 426–28, 433–44, 494–97.

themselves—a course which often leads them to find that they can accomplish by their own efforts what, at first, they hardly dared to hope for.

Besides, there has grown up among the truly American part of the population a feeling that religion is necessary even to the temporal well-being of society, so that many contribute to its promotion, though not themselves members of any of the churches.

These remarks point the reader to the true secret of the success of the voluntary plan in America. The people feel that they can help themselves, and that it is at once a duty and a privilege to do so. Should a church steeple come to the ground, or the roof be blown away, or any other such accident happen, instead of looking to some government official for the means of needful repair, a few of them put their hands into their pockets, and supply these themselves, without delay or the risk of vexatious refusals from public functionaries.

It is in the building of places of worship in the new settlements of the Western states, and in the villages that are springing up in the more recently peopled parts of those bordering on the Atlantic that we see the most remarkable development of the voluntary principle. Let me illustrate by a particular case what is daily occurring in both these divisions of the country.

Let us suppose a settlement commenced in the forest, in the northern part of Indiana, and that in the course of three or four years a considerable number of emigrants have established themselves within a mile or two of each other in the woods. Each clears away by degrees a part of the surrounding forest and fences in his new fields where the deadened trees still stand very thick. By little and little the country shows signs of occupation by civilized man.

In the center of the settlement a little village begins to form around a tavern and a blacksmith's shop. A carpenter places himself there as a convenient center. So do the tailor, the shoemaker, the wagon-maker, and the hatter. The merchant opens his magazine [store] there. And if there be any prospect of the rising city, though the deadened trees stand quite in the vicinity of the streets, becoming the seat of justice for a new county, there will soon be half a dozen young expounders of the law to increase the population and offer their services to those who have suffered or committed some injustice.

Things will hardly have reached this point before someone amid this heterogeneous population come from different points of the older states, intermixed with wanderers from Europe—Irish, Scotch, or German—proposes that they should think of having a church, or at least some place of worship. It is ten chances to one if there be not one or more pious women, or some pious man with his family, who sigh for the privileges of the sanctuary as once enjoyed by them in the distant east. What is to be done? Someone proposes that they should build a good large schoolhouse, which may serve also for holding religious meetings, and this is scarcely sooner proposed than accomplished. Though possibly made of mere logs and very plain, it will answer the purpose for a few years. Being intended for the meetings of all denominations of Christians, and open to all preachers who may be passing, word is sent to the nearest in the neighbourhood. Ere long some Baptist preacher in passing preaches in the evening, and is followed by a Presbyterian and a Methodist. Bye and bye the last of these arranges his circuit labors so as to preach there once in the fortnight, and then the minister of some Presbyterian congregation, ten or fifteen miles off, agrees to come and preach once a month.

Meanwhile, from the increase of the inhabitants, the congregations, on the sabbath particularly, become too large for the schoolhouse. A church is then built of framed beams and boards, forming no mean ornament to the village, and capable of accommodating some 200 or 300 people. Erected for the public good, it is used by all the sects in the place, and by others besides. But it will not be long before the Presbyterians, Methodists, or Baptists feel that they must have a minister on whose services they can count with more certainty, and hence a church also for themselves. And, at last, the house, which was a joint-stock affair at first, falls into the hands of some one of the denominations, and is abandoned by the others who have mostly provided each one for itself. Or, it may remain for the occasional service of some passing Roman Catholic priest, or Universalist preacher.

I have often been asked in Europe what measures are adopted by our churches in enforcing discipline—how unworthy persons, for instance, are prevented from coming to the Lord's table? The very question indicates familiarity with a state of things very different from what prevails in the United States—with a state of things in which the decisions of the ecclesiastical authority are enforced by the civil.

Church discipline with us, though wholly moral, is thought quite sufficient. The case must be rare, indeed, of anyone not the member of some recognized church coming forward to receive the sacrament in an evangelical church. But if he should, he does so on his own responsibility before God; the church is not to be blamed for his conduct. I know of one solitary occasion on which one of the office bearers whispered in the ear of a person who ought not to have been among the communicants that it would be better for his own soul, as well as due to the church, that he should retire, and he did so.

No difficulty whatever, I repeat, can arise on this subject. Our discipline is moral, and the people are too well instructed on the subject of their duties not to know what they should do, and what to abstain from doing. We have no *gens d'armes* or other police agents to enforce our discipline, and if such functionaries are ever seen about our churches in any character but that of worshippers, it is on extraordinary occasions, to keep order at the door; and their services are not often needed even for that purpose.

In regard to church members who subject themselves to censure for open sin, or gross neglect of duty, they are dealt with according to the established discipline of the body to which they belong; and that, in all our evangelical churches, is based upon the simple and clear directions given by our Lord and His apostles. Unworthy members after having been dealt with according to scriptural rule, are excluded until they give evidence of sincere contrition for their sin. Where the case is flagrant, and the sin persisted in, after all attempts to reclaim the offender have failed, he is openly excommunicated before the church and congregation. But whatever be the course pursued, unworthy men are excluded in all our evangelical churches as soon as their offense can be properly taken up by the church. I state this as a general fact. Once excluded, the world does not long remain ignorant of what has taken place, and the church thus avoids the charge of retaining persons of scandalous lives in her communion.

In order adequately to describe American preaching, one would require to be intimately acquainted with the churches of the country throughout its vast extent, but this knowledge it falls to the lot of few to possess. Some of the tourists from abroad that have visited the United States have affected to despise our "uneducated" and "ignorant" ministers, and have thought what they call the "ranting" of such men a fit subject of diversion for themselves. Such authors know little of the real worth of these humble, unlettered men. Their plain preaching, in fact, is often far more likely to benefit their usual hearers than would that of a learned doctor of divinity. Their language, though not refined, is intelligible to those to whom it is addressed. Their illustrations may not be classical, but they will probably be drawn either from the Bible or from the scenes amid which their hearers move, and the events with which they are familiar. To the labors of such men more than 10,000 neighborhoods in the United States are indebted for their general good order, tranquillity, and happiness, as well as for the humble but sincere piety that reigns in many a heart, and around many a fireside. To them the country owes much of its conservative character, for no men have inculcated more effectively those doctrines which promote obedience to law, respect for magistracy, and the maintenance of civil government, and never more than within the last year or two, during which they have had to resist the anarchical principles of self-styled reformers, both religious and political. No men are more hated and reviled by these demagogues, whose projects, I rejoice to say, find comparatively but a small and decreasing number of friends and advocates. To the influence of the pulpit, and that of the religious and sound part of the political press, we owe a return of better sentiments in several states. And in a late insurrectionary movement in Rhode Island, [Dorr's Rebellion] the leading journals of that state attest that the clergy of all denominations exerted a powerfully salutary influence.

A stranger upon visiting extensively our evangelical churches of all denominations would be struck, I am sure, with the order that prevails in them, and this applies equally to the smaller prayer meetings to be found in every parish and congregation that has any life in it, and to the greater assemblies that meet for public worship. Foreigners seem impressed with the idea that there is a great deal of disorder and lawlessness in the United States, and they infer that there must be no less insubordination in the religious commonwealth than they ascribe to the civil. But both opinions are totally unfounded. It does not follow because of a few disturbances arising from the disgraceful opposition made in some places to the slavery abolitionists, and the resentment of an exasperated populace against gangs of gamblers in others, that the whole country is a scene of continual commotion. In no part of the world have there been so few dreadful riots attended with loss of life as in the United States during those sixty years. There are bad men among us, and there are crimes, but after all, life is quite as safe among us as in any country I ever visited, and I have been in most of those that are considered civilized.

As for the church, a regard for law and order reigns to a degree not surpassed in any other country. There is no confusion of the respective rights of the ministry and people. The duties of both are well understood everywhere.

The little meetings of Christians held for prayer and the reading of the word—meetings so numerous, and almost always conducted by pious laymen! How seldom do private church members encroach by word or deed, at meetings of any kind, on the proper sphere of those who hold office in the churches! Indeed, on no one point are our churches more perfectly united in opinion than with respect to the necessity of maintaining due order and subordination. The ministry enjoys their full share of influence.

Experience has also taught us the necessity of maintaining order at meetings held during revivals—occasions on which, in consequence of the strong excitement of the most powerful feelings of the human heart, there is a special call for watchfulness in this respect. It is a sad mistake to multiply meetings unnecessarily during revivals, or to prolong them to unseasonable hours at night, to the exhaustion of strength, the loss of needed repose, and the unnatural and dangerous irritation of the nervous system. Yet these are the points in which the inexperienced are most liable to err. They begin a meeting, say, at seven o'clock in the evening. The preacher feels deeply, and the people are much interested. Instead of preaching for an hour, he is tempted, by the manifest attention of his hearers, to go on for an hour and a half or two hours, and instead of sending them home at half past eight o'clock, or at nine at the farthest, he dismisses them at ten or eleven o'clock, fatigued, yet excited, but here there is often a temptation of the adversary. Let the people be almost compelled to leave the house rather than unduly protract such meetings.

I consider hasty admissions to our churches to be the greatest of all the evils connected with revivals in some parts of the country, and among some denominations in particular. But this evil is not peculiar to revivals. It is quite as likely to occur when there is no revival as when there is. With all possible care it is difficult to keep a church pure, in a reasonable sense. The church must be kept as a living body of believers—a company of persons who have come out from the world and are determined to adorn the profession which they have made. In their organization and action, order, which is said to be "heaven's first law," must be maintained. In this opinion I am sure Christians of all denominations in the United States sincerely and entirely concur.

Chapter 8

The Common School

THE JACKSONIAN period witnessed the triumph of the common school, the establishment of free, tax-supported, public education. Before 1820, only a handful of communities took responsibility for primary education. By 1850, cities, towns, and villages all over the nation had founded schools. Education had become a primary responsibility of the state.

To later generations, schooling seemed so obviously a task for government to fulfill that it was difficult to imagine a time when citizens debated the propriety of using taxes to pay for such an enterprise. But in fact the establishment of the common schools was a controversial measure. It was the invention of one particular generation, not the inevitable culmination of colonial or Revolutionary developments. Why did the common school flourish in the Jacksonian period? What did proponents expect of it? Why was the controversy around the use of tax funds resolved so firmly and finally in favor of schooling?

The answers to these questions can be found first in the literature that supporters of public education produced during the antebellum decades. With great skill and sincerity, they tied the need for education to the fundamental welfare of the republic; so tight did they make this link that critics were hard pressed to challenge it. The founders of the common schools shared a very special view of childhood and human nature. This view assumed the power of the environment to effect change. It set forth a very particular definition of the needs of the republic (one which emphasized the prerequisites of virtue and intelligence for good citizenry) and had a very acute sensitivity to the problem of social order in the community (one which predicted the dissolution of the republic unless new means of social control were implemented). The foundation of the common schools rested on these premises.

Given the belief in the power of schooling to overcome the several dangers confronting the republic, education had to bear a heavy burden. It was not simply a matter of teaching students a basic knowledge of letters and numbers. Rather, the schools had to train students to political

participation, law-abiding behavior, and responsible community membership. In essence, the business of schools was not reading and writing
but citizenship, not education but social control.

This orientation probably had an important effect on the day-to-
day administration and conduct of the common schools. How did this
special focus on social order affect the nature of the curriculum? How
did it influence the routine of the classroom? What impact did it have
on the way students were to learn and on the way they were to behave
at school? The answers to these questions will enable us to measure the
impact of educational rhetoric on classroom reality.

Moreover, it is not accidental that the popularity of the common
school came at the same time that Americans began to rely upon institutions to care for the deviant and dependent. In the Jacksonian
period, the states erected penitentiaries for the criminal, insane asylums
for the mentally ill, and almshouses for the poor. In fact, many of the
leaders of the common-school movement were in the forefront of the
campaign to erect caretaker institutions, and the ways they defended
these programs were not at all dissimilar to the ways that they argued
for common schools. Yet why should schools have grown popular when
prisons did? Why should proponents of one of these programs support
the others? Did these similarities extend to the internal administration
of the institutions as well? To what extent were schools similar to
mental hospitals?

The materials that follow are addressed to these several considerations. The ideas of the common-school movement are captured effectively
in the writings of such spokesmen as Noah Webster and Horace Mann.
It is more difficult to re-create precisely the nature of the school day—
variety was probably as great as record keeping was primitive. Still, the
primers used in the classrooms do survive, as do some of the tests that
students had to take; and there are also seating plans and curriculum
outlines of the period. Finally, the prisons and hospitals published
annual reports, informing legislators of what went on behind the walls.
While clearly self-serving documents, they give us insights into the
goals and the conduct of these institutions. Taken together, these docu-

ments trace the origins and implications of reform movements in the Jacksonian era.

I

Noah Webster was one of the first spokesmen in the new nation to link the welfare of the republic with common schooling. Webster exemplified the patriotic enthusiasm of many of the first republicans— in every endeavor, the United States was to exhibit its uniqueness and superiority to Europe. As one part of this effort, Webster helped to organize a common American spelling, and he also worked to codify a distinctly American language. His dictionaries were, in effect, nationalist endeavors. So, too, Webster sought to give a distinctly American character to education. His essay On the Education of Youth, *which appeared in 1790, announced many of the themes that would be popular a generation later during the movement for common schools.*

ON THE EDUCATION OF YOUTH, 1790

NOAH WEBSTER

The education of youth is, in all governments, an object of the first consequence. The impressions received in early life usually form the characters of individuals, a union of which forms the general character of a nation.

The mode of education and the arts taught to youth have in every nation been adapted to its particular stage of society or local circumstances.

In despotic states education, like religion, is made subservient to government. In some of the vast empires of Asia children are always instructed in the occupation of their parents; thus the same arts are always continued in the same families. Such an institution cramps genius and limits the progress of national improvement; at the same time it is an almost immovable barrier against the introduction of vice, luxury, faction, and changes in government. This is one of the principal causes which have operated in preserving national tranquility for incredible periods of time.

In the complicated systems of government which are established among the civilized nations of Europe education has less influence in forming a national character; but there is no state in which it has not an inseparable connection with morals and a consequential influence upon the peace and happiness of society.

In *On the Education of Youth in America*, by Noah Webster (Boston, 1790). Reprinted in *Essays on Education in the Early Republic*, ed. Frederick Rudolph (Cambridge, Mass., 1965), pp. 43–47, 52–67.

Education is a subject which has been exhausted by the ablest writers. I am not vain enough to suppose I can suggest any new ideas but perhaps the manner of conducting the youth in America may be capable of some improvement. Our constitutions of civil government are not yet firmly established; our national character is not yet formed; and it is an object of vast magnitude that systems of education should be adopted and pursued which may not only diffuse a knowledge of the sciences but may implant in the minds of the American youth the principles of virtue and of liberty and inspire them with just and liberal ideas of government and with an inviolable attachment to their own country. It now becomes every American to examine the modes of education in Europe, to see how far they are applicable in this country and whether it is not possible to make some valuable alterations, adapted to our local and political circumstances. Let us examine the subject in two views. First, as it respects arts and sciences. Secondly, as it is connected with morals and government. In each of these articles let us see what errors may be found and what improvements suggested in our present practice.

The first error that I would mention is a too general attention to the dead languages, with a neglect of our own.

Indeed it appears to me that what is now called a *liberal education* disqualifies a man for business. Habits are formed in youth and by practice, and as business is in some measure mechanical, every person should be exercised in his employment in an early period of life, that his habits may be formed by the time his apprenticeship expires. An education in a university interferes with the forming of these habits and perhaps forms opposite habits; the mind may contract a fondness for ease, for pleasure or for books, which no efforts can overcome.

But the principal defect in our plan of education in America is the want of good teachers in the academies and common schools. By good teachers I mean men of unblemished reputation and possessed of abilities competent to their stations. To those who employ ignorant men to instruct their children, permit me to suggest one important idea: that it is better for youth to have *no* education than to have a bad one, for it is more difficult to eradicate habits than to impress new ideas.

Yet abilities are not the sole requisites. The instructors of youth ought, of all men, to be the most prudent, accomplished, agreeable, and respectable. In order to give full effect to instructions, it is requisite that they should proceed from a man who is loved and respected. But a low-bred clown or morose tyrant can command neither love nor respect, and that pupil who has no motive for application to books but the fear of a rod will not make a scholar.

The rod is often necessary in school, especially after the children have been accustomed to disobedience and a licentious behavior at home. All government originates in families, and if neglected there, it will hardly exist in society, but the want of it must be supplied by the rod in school, the penal laws of the state, and the terrors of divine wrath from the pulpit. The government both of families and schools should be absolute. There should in families be no appeal from one parent to another, with the prospect of pardon for offenses.

In schools the master should be absolute in command, for it is utterly impossible for any man to support order and discipline among children who are indulged with an appeal to their parents. A proper subordination in families would generally supersede the necessity of severity in schools, and a strict discipline in both is the best foundation of good order in political society.

If parents should say, "We cannot give the instructors of our children unlimited authority over them, for it may be abused and our children injured," I would answer, "They must not place them under the direction of any man in whose temper, judgment, and abilities they do not repose perfect confidence." The teacher should be, if such can be found, as judicious and reasonable a man as the parent.

There can be little improvement in schools without strict subordination; there can be no subordination without principles of esteem and respect in the pupils; and the pupils cannot esteem and respect a man who is not in himself respectable and who is not treated with respect by their parents.

From a strange inversion of the order of nature, the most important business in civil society is in many parts of America committed to the most worthless characters. The education of youth, an employment of more consequence than making laws and preaching the gospel, because it lays the foundation on which both law and gospel rest for success, this education is sunk to a level with the most menial services. In most instances we find the higher seminaries of learning entrusted to men of good characters and possessed of the moral virtues of social affections. But many of our [lower] schools, which, so far as the heart is concerned, are as important as colleges, are kept by men of no breeding, and many of them, by men infamous for the most detestable vices.

It is idle to suppress such truths; nay more, it is wicked. The practice of employing low and vicious characters to direct the studies of youth is in a high degree criminal; it is destructive of the order and peace of society.

Our legislators frame laws for the suppression of vice and immorality; our divines thunder from the pulpit the terrors of infinite wrath against the vices that stain the characters of men. And do laws and preaching effect a reformation of manners? Laws can only check the public effects of vicious principles but can never reach the principles themselves, and preaching is not very intelligible to people till they arrive at an age when their principles are rooted or their habits firmly established.

The only practicable method to reform mankind is to begin with children, to banish, if possible, from their company every low-bred, drunken, immoral character.

For this reason society requires that the education of youth should be watched with the most scrupulous attention. Education, in a great measure, forms the moral characters of men, and morals are the basis of government.

A good system of education should be the first article in the code of political regulations, for it is much easier to introduce and establish an effectual system for preserving morals than to correct by penal statutes the ill effects of a bad system.

Another defect in our schools, which, since the Revolution, is become inexcusable, is the want of proper books. The collections which are now used consist of essays that respect foreign and ancient nations. The minds of youth are perpetually led to the history of Greece and Rome or to Great Britain. Every child in America should be acquainted with his own country. As soon as he opens his lips, he should rehearse the history of his own country; he should lisp the praise of liberty and of those illustrious heroes and statesmen who have wrought a revolution in her favor.

A selection of essays respecting the settlement and geography of America, the history of the late Revolution and of the most remarkable characters and events that distinguished it, and a compendium of the principles of the federal and provincial governments should be the principal schoolbook in the United States.

Two regulations are essential to the continuance of republican governments: 1. Such a distribution of lands and such principles of descent and alienation as shall give every citizen a power of acquiring what his industry merits. 2. Such a system of education as gives every citizen an opportunity of acquiring knowledge and fitting himself for places of trust.

In several states we find laws passed establishing provision for colleges and academies where people of property may educate their sons, but no provision is made for instructing the poorer rank of people even in reading and writing. Yet in these same states every citizen who is worth a few shillings annually is entitled to vote for legislators. This appears to me a most glaring solecism in government. The constitutions are *republican* and the laws of education are *monarchical*. The *former* extend civil rights to every honest industrious man, the *latter* deprive a large proportion of the citizens of a most valuable privilege.

In our American republics, where government is in the hands of the people, knowledge should be universally diffused by means of public schools. Of such consequence is it to society that the people who make laws should be well informed that I conceive no legislature can be justified in neglecting proper establishments for this purpose.

Every small district should be furnished with a school, at least four months in a year, when boys are not otherwise employed. This school should be kept by the most reputable and well-informed man in the district. Here children should be taught the usual branches of learning, submission to superiors and to laws, the moral or social duties, the history and transactions of their own country, the principles of liberty and government. Here the rough manners of the wilderness should be softened and the principles of virtue and good behavior inculcated.

A tour through the United States ought now to be considered as a necessary part of a liberal education. Instead of sending young gentlemen to Europe to view curiosities and learn vices and follies, let them spend twelve or eighteen months in examining the local situation of the different states with an attention to the spirit and manners of the inhabitants, their laws, local customs, and institutions. Such a tour should at least precede a tour to Europe, for nothing can be more ridiculous than a man traveling in a foreign country for information when he can give no account of his own.

Americans, unshackle your minds and act like independent beings. You have been children long enough, subject to the control and subservient to the interest of a haughty parent. You have now an interest of your own to augment and defend: you have an empire to raise and support by your exertions and a national character to establish and extend by your wisdom and virtues. To effect these great objects, it is necessary to frame a liberal plan of policy and build it on a broad system of education. Before this system can be formed and embraced, the Americans must *believe* and *act* from the belief that it is dishonorable to waste life in mimicking the follies of other nations and basking in the sunshine of foreign glory.

II

More than any other individual, Horace Mann led the movement to establish common schools. Born in 1796 into a family of limited means in a small Massachusetts town, Mann worked his way through school, graduated from Brown University, and began to practice law. He found himself quickly drawn to government service; and since no other cause held greater appeal to him than education, in 1837 he became the first Secretary to the Massachusetts Board of Education. In that capacity he exercised practical leadership over the schools, and his system became a model for other states to emulate. He also used his position to persuade others of the merits of the program. His Twelfth Annual Report *for the State Board of Education summarizes the ideas most central to his concern for education.*

REPORT FOR THE MASSACHUSETTS BOARD OF EDUCATION, 1848

HORACE MANN

According to the European theory, men are divided into classes—some to toil and earn, others to seize and enjoy. According to the Massachusetts theory, all are to have an equal chance for earning, and equal security in the enjoyment of what they earn. The latter tends to equality of condition; the former to the grossest inequalities.

Now two or three things will doubtless be admitted to be true, beyond all controversy, in regard to Massachusetts. By its industrial condition, and its business operations, it is exposed, far beyond any other state in the Union, to the fatal extremes of overgrown wealth and

Originally entitled *Twelfth Annual Report,* Massachusetts State Board of Education (Boston, 1848). Reprinted in *The Republic and the School,* ed. Lawrence Cremin (New York, 1957), pp. 80–92, 98–101.

desperate poverty. Its population is far more dense than that of any other state. It is four or five times more dense than the average of all the other states, taken together; and density of population has always been one of the proximate causes of social inequality. According to population and territorial extent, there is far more capital in Massachusetts—capital which is movable, and instantaneously available—than in any other state in the Union; and probably both these qualifications respecting population and territory could be omitted without endangering the truth of the assertion. If this be so, are we not in danger of naturalizing and domesticating among ourselves those hideous evils which are always engendered between capital and labor, when all the capital is in the hands of one class, and all the labor is thrown upon another?

Now, surely, nothing but universal education can counterwork this tendency to the domination of capital and the servility of labor. If one class possesses all the wealth and the education, while the residue of society is ignorant and poor, it matters not by what name the relation between them may be called; the latter, in fact and in truth, will be the servile dependants and subjects of the former. But if education be equally diffused, it will draw property after it, by the strongest of all attractions.

For the creation of wealth, then—for the existence of a wealthy people and a wealthy nation—intelligence is the grand condition. The number of improvers will increase as the intellectual constituency, if I may so call it, increases. In former times, and in most parts of the world even at the present day, not one man in a million has ever had such a development of mind as made it possible for him to become a contributor to art or science. Let this development precede, and contributions, numberless, and of inestimable value, will be sure to follow.

In the possession of this attribute of intelligence, elective legislators will never far surpass their electors. By a natural law, like that which regulates the equilibrium of fluids, elector and elected, appointer and appointee, tend to the same level. It is not more certain that a wise and enlightened constituency will refuse to invest a reckless and profligate man with office, or discard him if accidentally chosen, than it is that a foolish or immoral constituency will discard or eject a wise man. This law of assimilation, between the choosers and the chosen, results not only from the fact that the voter originally selects his representative according to the affinities of good or of ill, of wisdom or of folly, which exist between them, but if the legislator enacts or favors a law which is too wise for the constituent to understand, or too just for him to approve, the next election will set him aside as certainly as if he had made open merchandise of the dearest interests of the people, by perjury and for a bribe.

Moral education is a primal necessity of social existence. The unrestrained passions of men are not only homicidal, but suicidal; and a community without a conscience would soon extinguish itself. Even with a natural conscience, how often has Evil triumphed over Good! From the beginning of time, Wrong has followed Right, as the shadow the substance. As the relations of men became more complex, and the business of the world more extended, new opportunities and new temptations for wrong-doing have been created. With the endearing relations of parent and child came also the possibility of infanticide and parricide; and the first domestic altar that brothers ever reared was stained with fratricidal blood. Following close upon the obligations to truth, came falsehood and perjury, and closer still upon the duty of obedience to the divine law, came disobedience. With the existence of private relations between men came fraud; and with the existence of public relations between nations came aggression, war, and slavery. And so, just in proportion as the relations of life became more numerous, and the interests of society more various and manifold, the range of possible and of actual offences has been continually enlarging.

The race has existed long enough to try many experiments for the solution of this greatest problem ever submitted to its hands; and the race has experimented, without stint of time or circumscription of space, to mar or modify legitimate results. Mankind have tried despotisms, monarchies, and republican forms of government. They have tried the extremes of anarchy and of autocracy. They have tried Draconian codes of law; and, for the lightest offences, have extinguished the life of the offender. They have established theological standards, claiming for them the sanction of divine authority, and the attributes of a perfect and infallible law; and then they have imprisoned, burnt, massacred, not individuals only but whole communities at a time, for not bowing down to idols which ecclesiastical authority had set up. These and other great systems of measures have been adopted as barriers against error and guilt; they have been extended over empires, prolonged through centuries, and administered with terrible energy; and yet the great ocean of vice and crime overleaps every embankment, pours down upon our heads, saps the foundations under our feet, and sweeps away the securities of social order, of property, liberty, and life.

But to all doubters, disbelievers, or despairers in human progress it may still be said, there is one experiment which has never yet been tried. It is an experiment which, even before its inception, offers the highest authority for its ultimate success. Its formula is intelligible to all; and it is as legible as though written in starry letters on an azure sky. It is expressed in these few and simple words: *"Train up a child in the way he should go, and when he is old he will not depart from it."* This declaration is positive. If the conditions are complied with, it makes no provision for a failure. Though pertaining to morals, yet, if the terms of the direction are observed, there is no more reason to doubt the result than there would be in an optical or a chemical experiment.

But this experiment has never yet been tried. Education has never yet been brought to bear with one hundredth part of its potential force upon the natures of children and, through them, upon the character of men, and of the race. In all the attempts to reform mankind which have hitherto been made, whether by changing the frame of government, by aggravating or softening the severity of the penal code, or by substituting a government-created for a God-created religion—in all these attempts, the infantile and youthful mind, its amenability to influences, and the enduring and self-operating character of the influences it receives, have been almost wholly unrecognized. Here, then, is a new agency, whose powers are but just beginning to be understood, and whose mighty energies, hitherto, have been but feebly invoked; and yet, from our experience, limited and imperfect as it is, we do know that, far beyond any other earthly instrumentality, it is comprehensive and decisive.

III

The steps by which the common school established itself in the various states may be followed in the sequence of events in Philadelphia. The first legislation establishing the legal obligations and powers of the community, the problems subsequent administrators faced, and their hopes for the system are clarified in the annual reports of the school district officials. First intended to serve only the children of the poor, the Philadelphia schools soon expanded to give education without cost to all the children of the city. The reasons for this shift are at the heart of the common school movement.

REPORTS OF THE PHILADELPHIA PUBLIC SCHOOLS, 1819–1850

An Act To Provide for the Education of Children at Public Expense, within the City and County of Philadelphia

Passed March 3, 1818

Be it enacted by the Commonwealth of Pennsylvania that the city and county of Philadelphia shall be and hereby are erected into a district, for the purposes of this act, to be denominated the First School District of the state of Pennsylvania. And be it further enacted by the authority aforesaid that the common and select councils shall appoint the requisite number of qualified taxable inhabitants to be directors of the public schools, that is to say, the select and common councils of the city of Philadelphia shall, in joint meeting, elect by ballot twenty-four directors. And be it further enacted by the authority aforesaid that the said controllers of the public schools shall determine upon the number of schoolhouses which shall be erected and shall limit the expense of erecting and establishing every such schoolhouse. They shall have the power to establish a model school, in order to qualify teachers for the sectional schools, or for schools in other parts of the state. They shall also have power to provide such suitable books as they shall deem necessary. And be it further enacted by the authority aforesaid that it shall be the duty of the assessors of every ward and township within the said district to require and receive once in every year from parents

In *Annual Report[s] of the Controllers of the Public Schools of the First School District of the State of Pennsylvania* (Philadelphia, 1819), pp. 4–6; (1821), pp. 4–5; (1826), pp. 6–7; (1836), pp. 8–12; (1850), pp. 116–19.

and guardians the names of all the indigent orphan children—children of indigent parents residing within the said school sections respectively, that is to say, the names of boys between the ages of six and fourteen years, and girls between the ages of five and thirteen years—and to inform the said parents and guardians of such children that they may send the said children to the proper school within the section in which they reside respectively, free of expense.

Annual Report for 1819

The controllers were organized on the sixth day of April 1818, and proceeded to establish schools for both sexes.

The whole number of children belonging to the public schools, under the care of the board, at the last quarterly report, was two thousand eight hundred and forty-five.

The boys are instructed in reading, writing, and arithmetic; and the girls are taught the same branches, as well as needlework in its useful and economical departments. The pupils attend with much regularity to their business, and exhibit gratifying proofs of improvement in their learning, as well as encouraging evidence of advancement in their morals.

The controllers feel authorized to express their opinion that the system of education under their care appears to them to be worthy of public confidence and support, whether it be regarded as valuable for its economy—practical in its communication of useful learning—or an efficient means whereby the minds of youth may be impressed with those great principles of morality and virtue so conducive to their own happiness and the welfare of our country.

Annual Report for 1821

Each successive year confirms the utility of the mode of instruction which has been adopted, and it is only to be regretted that many parents whose children might be brought under its auspices *criminally* withhold their offspring. How far legislative enactments can remedy this evil it may be difficult to determine, but it will be worthy of consideration whether the guardians of the poor ought not to be forbidden to confer relief upon pensioners whose children of suitable ages are not in regular attendance at the school of the district in which they reside. If the population of this description now suffered to spend their juvenile years in idleness, and who are thereby liable to the temptation and commission of crimes peculiarly incident to large cities, were subjected to the wholesome discipline of these schools, the moral culture and literary information which they afford would essentially contribute to render those neglected beings useful members of society. Within the last six months, another cause has operated to lessen the number of our pupils. The increase of manufactories in Philadelphia and its vicinity has produced a great demand for the labor of young persons, and has consequently withdrawn many children from the public schools. This evidence of returning business, and general prosperity, always inseparable from the occupation of the laboring classes, must be gratifying to every reflecting individual;

but if the employment of youth in those establishments be not accompanied by due attention to their mental and physical health and improvement, they will grow up unfit to discharge the duties of social life, and from bodily infirmity, and vicious habits, become burdens upon the community.

Annual Report for 1826

Of those children who have entered the schools, many have been withdrawn by their parents owing to the inducement of wages, which vary from fifty to one hundred and twenty-five cents per week, according to the demand for labor by the manufacturers. The rising generation may thus sustain irretrievable loss, in the abandonment of means for acquiring useful learning, as well as in the moral and physical evils to which, it is to be feared, they are often subjected in their tender years, by these employments. It is also a fact that a short training in the public schools renders the subject of it more profitable in the occupation mentioned; and in proportion to this valuable preparation, the scholars are sought for and engaged.

Without desiring improperly to interfere with the operations of any department of industry, the controllers cannot forbear again suggesting the necessity of legislative enactments to protect our youth from the ignorance and vice, and bodily deterioration, which combined private interests may thus produce. It would seem to be indispensable to require, by law, of those persons who employ large numbers of young persons in manufactories, not only to furnish them with useful school learning, but also to adopt regulations for the preservation of their health and morals. It will be unwise to delay a measure so vitally important to the welfare of the community until the influence of circumstances may render interposition unavailing.

An Act To Establish a General System of Education by Common Schools

Passed April 1, 1834

Whereas, it is enjoined by the Constitution, as a solemn duty, which cannot be neglected without a disregard of the moral and political safety of the people: Be it enacted by the commonwealth of Pennsylvania that the city and county of Philadelphia, and every other county in this commonwealth, shall each form a school division. And each of said districts shall contain a competent number of common schools for the education of every child within the limits thereof, who shall apply, either in person or by his or her parents, guardian, or next friend, for admission and instruction.

Annual Report for 1836

But eighteen years have rolled away since the original board opened its first school, with a few pupils, in a hired room; now they point their fellow-citizens to eleven magnificent edifices for the accommodation of our children, of whom they can proudly point to twelve thousand actually enrolled in more than fifty schools. Of our colleagues in this noble undertaking—the directors of all the sections—we demand, shall this work be stayed in its onward course? We know no barrier, we will recognize no limits to the extension of our schools, until the blessings of moral and intellectual culture is tendered to every solitary pupils, of every age, within our district. An ignorant people always has been and always will be a degraded and oppressed people— they are always at the mercy of the corrupt and designing. In vain shall we trust to physical strength to guard us from foreign hostility or domestic violence—to a seacoast girt with a thousand fortresses—or a frontier bristling with countless bayonets—to armies, fleets, or military skill—if we fail to cultivate the *moral* strength of our people—which is only founded upon *knowledge* and *self-respect—if we fail by Education to awake—guide—confirm the moral energies of our people, we are lost!*

Annual Report for 1837

Upon the general review of the year, the controllers are gratified with all the departments of the system—with the general fidelity and efficiency of the teachers, the augmentation of the means of early instruction, the certain prospect of unquestionable improvements, and the undeniable certainty of a perfect adaptation of the present organization to the wants of the compact population of the city and districts.

May they not be permitted again most earnestly to invoke the attention and lively interest of their fellow-citizens to this all-important enterprise—to implore their aid and countenance, their energetic efforts for the prosecution of a work upon which is to depend mainly the happiness and the security of our social fabric. Will they not judge of what is practicable from what has been already done? The stigma of poverty—once the only title of admission to our public schools—has, at the solicitation of the controllers, been erased from our statute book, and the schools of this city and county are now open to every child that draws the breath of life within our borders. What may not be accomplished by this mighty lever of universal education?

Scarcely nineteen years have elapsed since a few public spirited and philanthropic individuals, disgusted with the miserable provisions and fraudulent execution of the then existing laws for the gratuitous education of the poor, determined to attain a melioration of the system. Through the midst of violent and selfish opposition, their disinterested zeal bore them onward to a perfect triumph. The act of March 3, 1818, was the prize of their conflict.

Annual Report for 1850

OCCUPATIONS

It is a matter of very general interest and inquiry to know to what classes in society the students of the high school belong. The only available means of information on this point are the occupations of their parents. This is not always a certain criterion. The term "merchant," for instance, is one not very well defined, and means sometimes a man with an income of a few hundred dollars, and again one with an income of as many thousands. Still, there are other cases where the name of an occupation defines pretty clearly the class and condition of those who pursue it. Everyone understands the classification meant by clergymen, judges, carpenters, blacksmiths, seamstresses, and others that might be named. When a candidate is admitted to the school, the occupation of his parent or guardian is always registered and published, together with his residence. In the absence of any temptation to deceive, and with the certain means of detecting any deception, the register of occupations may be relied on as evidence, and as indicating with sufficient accuracy the classes in the community most immediately benefited by the school.

Occupations of the Parents or Guardians of Pupils Admitted from the First Opening of the School, October 22, 1838 to July 26, 1850: Agents 6, Aldermen 2, Apothecary 1, Artists 3, Bakers 18, Barbers 2, Blacksmiths 26, Boardinghouse keepers 9, Bookbinders 10, Booksellers 4, Brassfounders 6, Brewers 9, Bricklayers 21, Brickmakers 12, Brokers 18, Brushmakers 9, Cabinetmakers 28, Carpenters 108, Chairmakers 5, Clergymen 32, Clerks and Accountants 123, Coachmakers 5, Coal-dealers 8, Coopers 12, Cordwainers 98, Curriers 14, Customhouse officers 3, Dealers 5, Dentists 10, Distillers 7, Druggists 19, Dry goods merchants 5, Dyers 9, Engineers 7, Engravers 17, Farmers 30, Fishermen 5, Furriers 3, Gardeners 4, Gentlemen 4, Gilders 4, Glassblowers 4, Grocers 78, Hardware merchants 4, Hatters 26, Innkeepers 41, Ironfounders 6, Jewellers 11, Judges 5, Laborers 48, Lawyers 24, Locksmiths 3, Lumber merchants 4, Machinists 29, Mantua makers 28, Manufacturers 62, Mariners 30, Merchants 125, Millers 10, Milliners 5, Painters 9, Pawnbrokers 4, Peddlers 2, Physicians 45, Plasterers 14, Plumbers 4, Portrait painters 2, Potters 2, Printers 21, Prison keeper 1, Saddlers 27, Sailmakers 4, Seamstresses 18, Sea captain 1, Shipwrights 28, Silversmiths 4, Stonecutters 13, Stonemasons 3, Storekeepers 113, Tailors 69, Tanners 5, Teachers 36, Tinsmiths 15, Tobacconists 14, Traders 4, Umbrella makers 6, Victuallers 16, Watchmakers 11, Watchmen 14, Weavers 28, Widows 117, Miscellaneous 217, Total 2,130.

Another point on which inquiry is frequently made relates to the occupations of the pupils after leaving the school. Each pupil on leaving is requested to make a record of the business which he is about to follow. It no doubt often happens that a boy after following one kind of business for a few months changes it for another. In some cases also we are not able to ascertain the occupation of pupils after leaving school. Still, as a general rule, the record is a safe guide to one inquiring into the tendencies of the course of instruction pursued. It was very early a matter of anxiety with the controllers to avoid the error, not of *over*educating the pupils, but of so educating them as to give them a distaste for business. It was feared that the gift of intellectual culture would be accompanied with a disrelish for anything but intellectual employment, if not with a dislike of employment altogether. Such, without doubt, is often the result of education misdirected. The tendency in this respect of the course of instruction prescribed by the controllers would seem to be of the most encouraging kind. The alumni of the high school are already found scattered through the city in almost every walk of useful industry.

Occupations of the 1,467 pupils who Graduated or Left during the Eight Years, ending July 26, 1850: Architects 2, Bakers 2, Blacksmiths 32, Blind makers 2, Bookbinders 16, Bricklayers 30, Brickmakers 5, Cabinetmakers 8, Cadets 3, Carpenters 120, Chairmakers 3, Chemists 6, Clergymen 6, Clerks 137, Conveyancers 44, Coopers 8, Cordwainers 50, Curriers 12, Cutlers 2, Dentists 5, Druggists 44, Dyers 2, Engineers 24, Engravers 37, Farmers 70, Gas fitters 2, Gilders 4, Glasscutters 2, Grocers 11, Hatters 11, Ironfounders 2, Jewellers 12, Lawyers 17, Locksmiths 2, Machinists 65, Manufacturers 13, Mariners 31, Masons 4, Merchants 3, Millwrights 3, Moulders 2, Painters 13, Paperhanger 1, Physicians 19, Plasterers 2, Printers 54, Saddlers 14, Sailmakers 2, Ship carpenters 6, Ship joiners 2, Shipwrights 22, Stereotypists 2, Stonecutters 4, Storekeepers 332, Tailors 12, Teachers 55, Tinsmiths 4, Tobacconists 3, Turners 4, Type founders 4, Watchmakers 4, Weavers 4, Wheelwrights 7, Not ascertained 29, Deceased 6, Miscellaneous 8, Total 1,467.

IV

The several documents that follow begin to construct an image of school life in the Jacksonian period. They include a school seating chart, an outline for instruction, and the general rules of behavior for the common schools of Cheshire, Connecticut, 1826–1827. Together they reveal how vital order and discipline were to these institutions.

SCHOOL CURRICULUM AND RULES, CHESHIRE, CONNECTICUT 1826–1827

Curriculum: Outline of Instruction, As Conducted in Cheshire Primary School No. 1, Winter Term, 1826–1827

EDUCATION		
MORAL: GENERAL PRINCIPLES	PHYSICAL: GENERAL PRINCIPLES	INTELLECTUAL: GENERAL PRINCIPLES
Affections	Senses	Observation
Obedience	Play games	Memory
Truth	Exercises	Judgment
Temper		Method
Approbation		Abstraction
Amusements		Association
Rewards and		Invention
Punishments		Taste
		Imagination

In *American Journal of Education*, 3 (1828): 86–91, 94.

Moral Education

GENERAL PRINCIPLES

Elicit the affections, and direct them to their appropriate objects; to

The Instructor,
Associates,
Mankind,
Brutes,
The Creator.

Mild and conciliating measures only are to be used in the education of the affections and passions.

Reason and conscience carefully trained, and made the only objects of appeal.

Confidence in the instructor, induced by the affections, and by example, made the foundation of obedience.

Obedience made the basis of truth.

Approbation, founded on truth, and obedience.

Amusements—rewards and punishments—internal police, and process, made to exert a strictly *moral* influence.

AFFECTIONS

Employ the language of nature—attitude, gesture, countenance expressing joy, gladness, cheerfulness, satisfaction, contentment, complacency, approbation, love, with correspondent tones of voice—caressing.

Amusements adapted to the development of the affections.

Social inclinations furnished with proper objects.

Dress, manners, habits.

Instructor acknowledge his faults frankly to scholars, as an example for their imitation.

Desired emotions excited, by oratory, address, action, countenance.

Characteristic affections frequently exercised.

Address pupils familiarly on all occasions.

Mutual sympathy.

No competition—never blaming one, while another is praised—the selfish sympathies of two or more being never brought to desire the same object, at the same time.

Character of rewards, and the manner of their distribution, considered.

Pupils made as happy as possible, by the address and arrangements of the instructor.

Selfish passions eradicated as much as possible.

No individual comparisons—equal, and exact, and public justice given to all.

Attainment, not *place*, made the standard of merit.

The Cheshire School Rules

LAWS

Members of the school are required to comply with the following rules:

1. That they appear at the schoolroom at the appointed hours for exercises to commence, or be denied entrance, unless a reasonable excuse from parents is preferred.
2. That they arrange their books, slates, etc., in good order on entrance.
3. That they keep their own, and so far as concerned, the books, and school apparatus of others, from defacement.
   That they do not soil, deface, or scatter any object in or near the schoolroom.
4. That they do not, without permission, address anyone during school exercises, save the instructor, and then, in all practicable cases, to prefer an address in writing, through the superintendent.
5. That they treat the superintendent with respect.
6. That they articulate their lessons in such voice as to be distinctly heard at any part of the schoolroom.
7. That they practice no deception in their lessons.
8. That they pursue their studies in silence.
9. That they follow the order of instruction faithfully.
10. That an excuse be given for imperfect lessons.
11. That they do not leave their seats without permission.
12. That they do not unnecessarily interrupt or retard the studies of their companions.
13. That they do not express inability to perform any given exercise previous to attempt.
14. That they suffer the consequences of forgetting and talebearing.
15. That they exercise mutual kindness and forbearance.
16. That they endeavor to promote the happiness of their companions.
17. That they *"Behave to their companions as they desire their companions to behave to them."*

OBEDIENCE

Induce the confidence of scholars, by affection and conduct, as the foundation for obedience.

Example—precept—practice, founded on reason.

Preventives, rather than punishments.

Few laws—those clearly defined, and rendered familiar by habitual practice.

Integrity, and honesty, without dissimulation, on the part of instructor.

Diminish temptations, by arrangement.

Self-government induced by appealing to reason and conscience.

Punishment, uniform, certain, immediate.

Ridicule, and raillery, used for the cure of little misdemeanors and habits.

Natural consequences of obedience and disobedience employed to encourage, or punish.

Punishments, private and solitary, to induce obedience.

TRUTH

Never require children to accuse themselves; ask them no questions where it is for their interest to deceive.

Clear ideas of right and wrong fixed in the minds of children.

Honesty and integrity respected, commended, rewarded.

Confidence deserved before it is given.

Avoid presenting temptations and dissimulation.

Fear banished; truth valued more than any pecuniary consideration.

TEMPER

Induce the affections which form and sweeten the temper.

Never irritate intentionally.

Appeal to hope and reason—not to fear.

Sympathy of surrounding persons.

APPROBATION

Train conscience, by frequent appeal to it.

Induce habitual obedience, as far as possible.

No personal emulation; general praise bestowed.

Beware of the counterfeits of approbation, pride, and vanity—cultivate the judgment carefully.

AMUSEMENTS

Controlled by the instructor.

Amusements *moralized* as much as possible, exercising a good influence on the affections and passions, improving and elevating the mind.

Adapted to the understandings, feelings, and habits of children.

REWARDS AND PUNISHMENTS

Moralized, of an intellectual nature, addressed to the understanding and the feelings.

REWARDS	PUNISHMENTS
Self-approbation	Self-condemnation
Affection of instructor	Loss of instructor's affection
Success	Defeat
Consequences of obedience	Consequences of disobedience
Caressing	Neglect
Encouragement	Ridicule; raillery
Self-government	Governed by the instructor
Proposed for imitation	Contempt
Hope; with attendants	Fear; and its attendants
Esteem; confidence; love	Aversion; jealousy
Perusal of library books	Wooden books
Knowledge; usefulness	Ignorance; beggary
Happiness	Misery; despair

Seating Chart

SCHOOL APPARATUS

Every scholar is furnished with a:

Slate, pencil, and sponge.
Desk.
Class books.

Writing books; pen, ink, but no
rule.
Cubes, beans, etc.

And for general use are furnished:

Books.
Cubes.
Tangible letters.

Prints.
Material substances, etc.

SCHOOLROOM

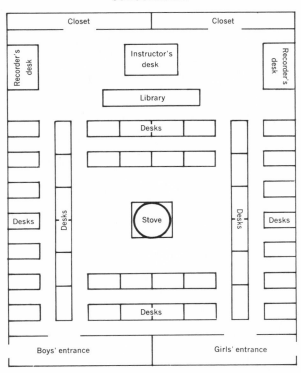

V

*Another indication of the character of the school experience in the
antebellum period comes from the textbooks most often read in the
classrooms. Lyman Cobb had the good fortune to compose one of
the most popular volumes; his* New North American Reader, *pub-*

lished in 1844, was used in many different regions of the country. The passages below make quite clear that the teaching of reading was part of a general exercise at teaching morality and good order. And imagine what it was like for students to review these passages day after day.

NEW NORTH AMERICAN READER, 1844

LYMAN COBB

READING LESSON

Danger of Bad Habits

A man's case may be pronounced to be desperate when his mind is brought into such a state as that the necessary means of reformation shall have lost their effect upon him; and, this is the natural consequence of confirmed habits of vice, and a long-continued neglect of the means of religion and virtue.

In order to be the more sensible of this, you are to consider that vice is a habit, and therefore of a subtle and insinuating nature. By easy, pleasing, and seemingly harmless actions men are often betrayed into a progress which grows everyday more alarming. Our virtuous resolutions may break with difficulty. It may be with pain and reluctance that we commit the first acts of sin, but the next are easier to us; and use, custom, and habit will at last reconcile us to anything, even things the very idea of which might at first be shocking to us.

Vice is a thing not to be trifled with. You may, by the force of vigorous resolution, break off in the early stages of it; but habits, when they have been confirmed, and long continued, are obstinate things to contend with, and are hardly ever entirely subdued. When bad habits seem to be overcome, and we think we have got rid of our chains, they may perhaps only have become, as it were, invisible; so that when we thought we had recovered our freedom and strength, so as to be able to repel any temptation, we may lose all power of resistance on the first approach of it.

A man who has contracted a habit of vice and been abandoned to sinful courses for some time *is never out of danger*. He is exactly in the case of a man who has long labored under a chronic disease and is perpetually subject to a relapse.

The reason is that a relapse does not find a person in the condition in which he was when the first fit of illness seized him. That gave his constitution a shock, and left him enfeebled, so as to be less able to sustain another shock.

In the very same dangerous situation is the man who has ever been addicted to vicious courses. He can never be said to be perfectly recovered, whatever appearances may promise, but is always in danger

In *New North American Reader, or Fifth Reading Book*, by Lyman Cobb (New York, 1844), pp. 25–28, 123–25.

of a fatal relapse. He ought, therefore, to take the greatest care of himself.

He ought, therefore, to have the greatest distrust of himself, and set a double watch over his thoughts, words, and actions, for fear of a surprise. For if once, through the force of any particular temptation, he should fall back into his former vicious courses, and his former disposition should return, his case will probably be desperate.

Questions—When may a man's condition or case be pronounced desperate? Of what is this the natural consequence? What is of a subtle and insinuating nature? How are men often betrayed into a progress which becomes alarming? To what will use, custom, and habit at last reconcile us? With what should we not trifle? Who is *never out of danger*? Why is a relapse very dangerous? Who is always in danger of *a fatal relapse*? Will all young persons remember that *habits*, whether *good* or *bad,* formed in youth, will generally remain with them through life, and never practice *any vice*, or contract *any bad habit*?

READING LESSON

The Schoolmaster

There are prouder themes for the eulogist than this. The praise of the statesman, the warrior, or the orator furnishes more splendid topics for ambitious eloquence; but no theme can be more rich in dessert or more fruitful in public advantage.

The enlightened liberality of many of our state governments, by extending the common school system over their whole population, has brought elementary education to the door of every family.

In this state, it appears, from the Annual Reports of the [New York] Secretary of the State, 1829, there are, besides the fifty incorporated academies and numerous private schools, about nine thousand school districts, in each of which instruction is regularly given. These contain at present half a million of children taught in the single state of New York.

Of what incalculable influence, then, for good or for evil, upon the dearest interests of society, must be the estimate entertained for the character of this great body of teachers, and the consequent respectability of the individuals who compose it!

What else is there in the whole of our social system of such extensive and powerful operation on the national character? There is one other influence more powerful, and but one. It is that of the *Mother.* The forms of a free government, the provisions of wise legislation, the schemes of the statesman, the sacrifices of the patriot are as nothing compared with these.

If the future citizens of our republic are to be worthy of their rich inheritance, they must be made so principally through the virtue and intelligence of their *mothers.*

But next in rank and in efficacy to that pure and holy source of moral influence is that of the *schoolmaster.* It is powerful already. What would it be if in every one of those school districts which we now count

by annually increasing thousands, there were to be found one teacher well informed without pedantry, religious without bigotry or fanaticism, proud and fond of his profession, and honored in the discharge of its duties? How wide would be the intellectual, the moral influence of such a body of men!

The schoolmaster's occupation is laborious and ungrateful; its rewards are scanty and precarious. He may indeed be, and he ought to be, animated by the conscientiousness of doing good, that best of all consolations, that noblest of all motives. But that too must be often clouded by doubt and uncertainty.

Obscure and inglorious as his daily occupation may appear to learned pride or worldly ambition, yet to be truly successful and happy, he must be animated by the spirit of the same great principles which inspired the most illustrious benefactors of mankind.

If he bring to his task high talent and rich acquirement, he must be content to look into distant years for the proof that his labors have not been wasted; that the good seed which he daily scatters abroad does not fall on stony ground and wither away, or among thorns, to be choked by the cares, the delusions, or the vices of the world. He must regard himself as sowing the seeds of truth for posterity and the care of heaven.

VI

The good order of the school was not very different from the good order of the new asylums for the mentally ill. Indeed, the psychiatrists of the nineteenth century diagnosed mental illness as a disease which resulted from disorder—the chaos that followed excessive ambition, or excessive concern with moneymaking, or excessive learning. Americans, they feared, were particularly liable to insanity—it was the price we paid for our free and open institutions. This diagnosis of the social causes of insanity led the psychiatrists to think that they had discovered a cure for the malady: in well-ordered and disciplined settings, the insane would learn the rigid rules for living that they had heretofore neglected. The description of the asylum routine comes from the Pennsylvania Hospital for the Insane, located in Philadelphia. It was a private hospital whose routine exemplified the best that was available for the treatment of the mentally ill in this period.

REPORT OF THE PENNSYLVANIA HOSPITAL FOR THE INSANE, 1843

The following is a sketch of the *regular duties of each day.*

The watchman rings the bell at a quarter before 5 A.M. when all persons engaged about the premises are expected to arise, and immediately commence the performance of their various duties. The attendants unlock the chamber doors, and give the patients a kind greeting, see that they are properly prepared for breakfast, and commence ventilating and arranging the halls and chambers, in which labor they receive voluntary assistance from many of the patients.

Half an hour before breakfast, which is at half past 6 A.M., they call at the physician's office for whatever medicine is to be given to the patients, and which they always find ready and in cups, labeled with each individual's name. No medicine is kept in the wards.

After breakfast, the beds are made, and every part of the wings placed in order, so as to be ready for inspection at the visit of the physician. At this visit, every patient is seen and spoken to, and all their rooms examined.

After the morning visit, the patients who are employed at outdoor labor commence their work—others engage in indoor employment—or walk, ride, or occupy themselves in reading, or various kinds of amusements. At half-past twelve, dinner is taken in different dining rooms. At all the meals, the attendants either wait upon the patients, or a portion of them preside at the different tables. In the afternoon, those who labor return to their work; and everyday in fine weather, some of the patients ride, and most of them take long walks in the open air, generally within but frequently outside of the enclosure. At 6 P.M., tea is ready, and no patients go out after sunset without special permission.

In the evening, the different parlors and halls are handsomely lighted, and the patients engage in reading, writing, or some of the various amusements, always at hand, among themselves or with some of the officers or attendants.

At half-past seven, medicine is given for the evening, and afterward such patients as wish it are allowed to retire. All are expected to do so by half-past nine. At 10 P.M., the house is closed, and all light in the wards extinguished.

In *Second Annual Report*, Pennsylvania Hospital for the Insane (Philadelphia, 1843), pp. 23–29, 34–35.

Remedial Means Employed in the Hospital

Of the strictly *medical* treatment, we can, of course, in a report of this kind speak only in a very general manner. In a large proportion of the recent cases that have been admitted, we have found derangement of the health of some kind, and the remedies have been varied according to circumstances.

In nearly all cases, our patients have a full and nutritious, but plain diet—they go to the dining rooms, where the tables are supplied with meats, and a great variety of vegetables, of which they are allowed to partake till satisfied.

In the *moral* treatment of the insane, so much may be effected by *attendants*, who are constantly in intercourse with the patients, who see them at all hours and under all circumstances, that although much has been done, we cannot help hoping the time is not far distant when greater inducements will be offered to persons of superior qualifications to engage in these stations, where active benevolence can be most profitably employed.

Printed rules are furnished to the attendants when entering upon the performance of their duties, and to which they are expected to conform in every particular. In these rules and on frequent occasions, we endeavor to impress the attendants with a true view of the importance and responsibility of their stations.

We insist on a mild and conciliatory manner under all circumstances, and roughness or violence we never tolerate. We are not satisfied with the simple performance of special duties, but wish to see an active interest felt in all the patients—a desire to add to their comfort, and to advance their cure—judicious efforts to interest or amuse them— a watchful care over their conduct and conversation, and a constant, sympathizing intercourse, calculated to win their attachment, and command their respect and confidence.

Employment and Amusements

The importance of furnishing the insane with suitable means of employment and amusement is now so well understood that we shall merely indicate those to which our patients have resorted during the past year.

At the head of the list, we place *outdoor labor*, on account of its importance in many of the curable cases, and its value in even those that are the most chronic and incurable. It is one of the means of treatment for which ample provision should be made in every well-conducted institution; and the importance of the farm can only be properly estimated by calculating the value of one of the best means for the restoration of the insane.

Although many of our patients previous to their admission had unfortunately never been accustomed to labor, nor to habits of industry, still a considerable number of the males have assisted in most of the operations connected with haymaking, and securing the harvest.

Farming and gardening are probably two of the very best means of giving exercise to insane patients; and the latter has this year produced the most pleasant effects in several instances. One of the regular gardeners before he commenced outdoor work was rarely more than a month without a period of excitement, requiring seclusion for several days, and during which he was guilty of nearly every description of mischief. During this summer he has had no recurrence of these attacks.

The incurable patients who labor show its good effects by their quietness in the halls—their orderly deportment and their sound rest at night.

The *workshop* is a valuable acquisition to our means of employment. It is a handsome frame building twenty by forty feet, two stories high, and situated near the gateway. The lower story is intended for carpenter work, turning, basket making, etc. The upper room is plastered, and may be used for mattress making, and other pursuits requiring space, or for some of the amusements of the patients.

Many of our cases, generally among the convalescent, have already been pleasantly and profitably employed in this building, and the interest they have felt in their work—the entire change in their thoughts, and the active use of their muscles—have rarely failed to contribute to the rapidity and certainty of their cure.

We have not as yet attempted any kind of work by which to ascertain the amount of income that might be derived from the workshop. Our great object thus far has been to induce our patients *to labor*; for the kind of work we have cared but little, and whatever object appeared most likely to excite a new train of thought has received our approbation.

Several of the patients, male and female, assist in keeping the house in order—preparing food for cooking and arranging the dining rooms; others take charge of particular departments of business—one attends the furnaces at the wash house, another superintends all the *mangling* in the ironing room; one who in the afternoon devotes himself to the classics, spends a part of each morning in cleaning the area around the whole building; and several are found always ready to assist where their services can be useful.

Simple seclusion in chambers properly secured has been resorted to during the past year, in by far the greater number of cases that have appeared to require restraint of any kind. In others, leather wristbands, secured by a belt around the body, or mittens of the same material, or of canvas, have been employed in rare cases, and two patients have occasionally been kept on their beds with much advantage, by an apparatus also of leather, but admitting of much freedom of motion.

The so-called tranquilizing chair has not been seen in our wards, nor is the muff or straitjacket among our regular means of restraint. The latter contrivance was used in two cases—only with the exceptions just indicated, no species of personal restraint has been resorted to, but those previously mentioned—and of these the use has been comparatively rare. For nearly three months after opening the house, not an article for restraint was used in the hospital. We have frequently, during the whole fortnight, had a family of more than one hundred patients without any kind of restraint upon the person of a single individual—not more than two or three confined to their rooms, and not more than half a dozen who were not able to take their meals in the dining rooms, at tables regularly furnished with crockery, knives, forks, and glasses.

From this freedom of action, and from these indulgences, we have found nothing but advantage and encouragement to promote still less dependence upon restraining apparatus as a means of controlling the insane. To save the attendants trouble or labor is never admitted as a reason for its application—the positive benefit of the patient is the only one that is sound or justifiable, except under very peculiar circumstances.

We allow restraint to be applied only by order of one of the physicians—and even the seclusion of a patient is to be promptly reported.

We have not dispensed with all restraining apparatus, because, under some circumstances, mild means of the kind are much less annoying to the patient, and effect the object in view with less irritation and more certainty, than the constant presence of even the best instructed attendants.

The great objection to the employment of restraint, and the positive injury produced by it, does not come so much from its application, as from its abuse, by being too long continued. Restraint or simple seclusion may be required for a week or a day, or it is possible that a single hour will be more beneficial than either; and it ought never to be forgotten that when either ceases to be useful, from that moment it becomes positively injurious.

VII

Nowhere was the emphasis on obedience more pronounced than in the child-rearing literature of the Jacksonian period. Practically every tract instructed parents first and foremost to train their children to respect authority, to obey commands immediately and without argument. And in each instance, they held out the most dire consequences should parents fail in this task, from children drowning to children growing up to become criminals. Affection between child and parent was important, not as an end in itself, but as a way of securing more prompt and willing obedience. One of the most widely read of the advice-to-parents books was John Abbott's The Mother at Home. *Abbott, like his fellow authors, insisted that not only the good order of the family but also the good order of society demanded this training to obedience. In no other way would children learn to resist temptations at loose in the community, and grow up to become law-abiding and hard-working citizens.*

THE MOTHER AT HOME, 1834

J O H N   A B B O T T

It is a great trial to have children undutiful when young. But it is a tenfold greater affliction to have a child grow up to maturity in disobedience and become a dissolute and abandoned man. How many parents have passed days of sorrow, and nights of sleeplessness, in consequence of the misconduct of their offspring! How many have had their hearts broken, and their gray hairs brought down with sorrow to the grave, solely in consequence of their own neglect to train up their children in the nurture and admonition of the Lord! Your future happiness is in the hands of your children. They may throw gloom over all your prospects, embitter every enjoyment, and make you so miserable that your only prospect of relief will be in death.

That little girl whom you now fondle upon your knee, and who plays, so full of enjoyment, upon your floor, has entered a world where temptations are thick around. What is to enable her to resist these temptations but established principles of piety? And where is she to obtain these principles but from a mother's instructions and example? If, through your neglect now, she should hereafter yield herself to temptation and sin, what must become of your peace of mind? O mother! little are you aware of the wretchedness with which your beloved daughter may hereafter overwhelm you.

This is a dreadful subject. But it is one which the mother must feel and understand. There are facts which might here be introduced, sufficient to make every parent tremble. We might lead you to the dwelling of the clergyman, and tell you that a daughter's sin has murdered the mother; and sent paleness to the cheek, and trembling to the frame, and agony to the heart of the aged father.

No matter what your situation in life may be, that little child, now so innocent, whose playful endearments and happy laugh awaken such thrilling emotions in your heart, may cause you years of unalleviated misery.

And, mother! look at that drunken vagrant, staggering by your door. Listen to his horrid imprecations, as, bloated and ragged, he passes along. That wretch has a mother. Perhaps, widowed and in poverty, she needs the comfort and support of an affectionate son. You have a son. You may soon be a widow. If your son is dissolute, you are doubly widowed; you are worse, infinitely worse, than childless. You cannot now endure even the thought that your son will ever be thus abandoned. How dreadful then must be the experience of the reality!

I once knew a mother who had an only son. She loved him most ardently, and could not bear to deny him any indulgence. He, of course, soon learned to rule his mother. At the death of his father, the poor woman was left at the mercy of this vile boy. She had neglected her

In *The Mother at Home*, by John Abbott (New York, 1834), pp. 2–3, 10–15, 18–23.

duty when he was young, and now his ungovernable passions had become too strong for her control. Self-willed, turbulent, and revengeful, he was his mother's bitterest curse. His paroxysms of rage at times amounted almost to madness. One day, enraged with this mother, he set fire to her house, and it was burned to the ground with all its contents, and she was left in the extremest state of poverty.

You have watched over your child through all the months of its helpless infancy. You have denied yourself that you might give it comfort. When it has been sick, you have been unmindful of your own weariness and your own weakness, and the livelong night you have watched at his cradle, administering to all its wants. When it has smiled, you have felt a joy which none but a parent can feel, and have pressed your much-loved treasure to your bosom, praying that its future years of obedience and affection might be your ample reward. And now, how dreadful a requital for that child to grow up to hate and abuse you; to leave you friendless, in sickness and in poverty; to squander all his earnings in haunts of iniquity and degradation!

How entirely is your earthly happiness at the disposal of your child! His character is now in your hands, and you are to form it for good or for evil. If you are consistent in your government, and faithful in the discharge of your duties, your child will probably, through life, revere you. If, on the other hand, you cannot summon resolution to punish your child when disobedient; if you do not curb his passions; if you do not bring him to entire and willing subjection to your authority you must expect that he will be your curse. In all probability, he will despise you for your weakness. Unaccustomed to authority at home, he will break away from all restraints, make you wretched by his life, and disgraceful in his death.

"A good boy generally makes a good man," said the mother of Washington. "George was always a good boy." Here we see one secret of his greatness. George Washington had a mother who taught him to be a good boy and instilled into his heart those principles which raised him to be the benefactor of his country, and one of the brightest ornaments of the world. The mother of Washington is entitled to a nation's gratitude. She taught her boy the principles of obedience, and moral courage, and virtue. She, in a great measure, formed the character of the hero and the statesman. It was by her own fireside that she taught her playful boy to govern himself; and thus was he prepared for the brilliant career of usefulness which he afterward pursued. We are indebted to God for the gift of Washington; but we are no less indebted to Him for the gift of his inestimable mother. Had she been a weak, and indulgent, and unfaithful parent, the unchecked energies of Washington might have elevated him to the throne of a tyrant, or youthful disobedience might have prepared the way for a life of crime and a dishonoured grave.

The question has probably often presented itself to your mind "How shall I govern my children, so as to secure their virtue and happiness?" This question I shall now endeavor to answer.

Obedience is absolutely essential to proper family government. Without this, all other efforts will be in vain. You may pray with and for your children; you may strive to instruct them in religious truth; you may be unwearied in your efforts to make them happy, and to gain their affection. But if they are suffered to indulge in habits of disobedience, your instructions will be lost, and your toil in vain. And by obedience I do not mean languid and dilatory yielding to repeated threats, but prompt and cheerful acquiescence in parental commands. Neither is it enough that a child should yield to arguments and persuasions. It is essential that he should submit to your authority.

I will suppose a case in illustration of this last remark. Your little daughter is sick; you go to her with the medicine which has been prescribed for her, and the following dialogue ensues:

"Here, my daughter, is some medicine for you."
"I don't want to take it, mamma."
"Yes, my dear, do take it; for it will make you feel better."
"No it won't, mother. I don't want it."
"Yes it will, my child. The doctor says it will."
"Well, it don't taste good, and I don't want it."

The mother continues her persuasions, and the child persists in its refusal. After a long and wearisome conflict, the mother is compelled either to throw the medicine away, or to resort to compulsion, and force down the unpalatable drug. Thus, instead of appealing to her own supreme authority, she is appealing to the reason of the child; and, under these circumstances, the child of course refuses to submit.

A mother, not long since, under similar circumstances, not being able to persuade her child to take the medicine, and not having sufficient resolution to compel it, threw the medicine away. When the physician next called, she was ashamed to acknowledge her want of government, and therefore did not tell him that the medicine had not been given. The physician, finding the child worse, left another prescription, supposing the previous one had been properly administered. But the child had no idea of taking the nauseous dose, and the renewed efforts of the mother were unavailing. Again the fond and foolish, but cruel parent, threw the medicine away; and the fever was left to rage unchecked in its veins. Again the physician called, and was surprised to find the inefficacy of his prescriptions, and that the poor little sufferer was at the verge of death. The mother, when informed that her child must die, was in an agony, and confessed what she had done. But it was too late. The child died. And think you that mother gazed upon its pale corpse with any common emotions of anguish? Physicians will tell you that many children have thus been lost. Unaccustomed to obedience when well, they are still more adverse to it when sick. The efforts which are made to induce a stubborn child to take medicine often produce such an excitement as entirely to counteract the effect of the prescription; and thus is a mother often called to weep over the grave of her child, simply because she has not taught that child to obey.

The first thing therefore to be aimed at is to bring your child under perfect subjection. Teach him that he must obey you. Sometimes give him your reasons; again, withhold them. But let him perfectly understand that he is to do as he is bidden. Accustom him to immediate and cheerful acquiescence in your will. This is obedience. And this is absolutely essential to good family government. Without this, your family will present one continued scene of noise and confusion; the toil of rearing up your children will be almost insupportable; and, in all probability, your heart will be broken by their future licentiousness or ingratitude.

Chapter 9

The American Art Union

AN INTENSE ambivalence marked American attitudes toward culture and artistic production in the antebellum period. Americans were, on the one hand, acutely hostile to art and artists. They associated paintings with the overopulent walls of aristocratic and decadent Europeans; and they thought of artists as parasitic, as morally obnoxious as their upper-class patrons. Art, they believed, traditionally flourished amid gross disparities of wealth and power, disparities which they did not wish to re-create here. And yet other considerations blunted this hostility and suspicion. Americans, after all, wished to demonstrate the superiority of republican society in all its aspects. The best answer to European critics who labeled the new country rude and boorish would be to create splendid works of art, to make an esthetic contribution as notable and original as their constitutional one. Somehow, then, Americans had to turn out great art without corrupting themselves in the process.

Another stimulus to artistic production in the young republic was the eagerness of citizens to commemorate great moments in their history, to build appropriate monuments to the founding fathers and their victories. By 1820, most of those who had signed the Declaration of Independence or fought in the Revolutionary War had died, and those who had heard about these events firsthand, from parents or older siblings, were themselves advancing in age. The time had arrived, therefore, to celebrate the past; the nation's debt to these heroic figures had to be properly acknowledged. Furthermore, the monuments themselves would help to keep alive the spirit of the founding fathers. Veneration for George Washington was at once veneration for the republic. Appreciating the valor shown at Bunker Hill would perpetuate ideals of citizenship. In essence, monument building was one way to encourage and promote patriotic fervor.

This perspective on monument building carried over to other forms of artistic production as well. The solution to the paradox of producing great art without endangering republican values was to insist that art

193

self-consciously serve the nation. It was to be popularly supported and popularly oriented. The heroes on American canvases were to be Americans; the message of the painting was to promote the good order and solidarity of the society. Art, ultimately, was to serve social needs, not esthetic ones. The responsibility of the artist was not to some inner standard of taste, but to the moral character of the republic. Rather than endanger the society, the artist was to uplift it.

The character of American culture during the first half of the nineteenth century reflected this judgment. The artist was assured of support; his work was held in repute. But his position depended upon his willingness and ability to serve the public welfare. This solution clearly did not always enhance the quality of the artistic productions themselves.

These many themes were reflected in the formation of the American Art Union. The Union was an ingenious plan for supporting American artists and popularizing their works. A peculiarly American invention, the Union was the democratic answer to the problem of patronage and distribution. Under its influence, cultural needs were joined to social ones.

I

The organization and activities of the American Art Union reveal the connections between artistic productions and social goals. Under the Art Union plan, members were to purchase tickets for a lottery; the winner of the lottery would receive one large oil painting, and every subscriber would receive at least one print. The sums gathered through this scheme would be used to support worthy artists, and, at the same time, guarantee their works wide circulation. The selection below reveals how the Art Union viewed its own contribution to the state of American culture.

AMERICAN ART UNION BULLETIN, 1849

PLAN OF THE AMERICAN ART UNION

The American Art Union, in the City of New York, was incorporated by the Legislature of the State of New York for the promotion of the fine arts in the United States. It is managed by gentlemen who are chosen annually by the members, and receive no compensation. To accomplish a truly national object, uniting great public good with private gratification at small individual expense, in a manner best suited to the situation and institutions of our country, and the wants, habits, and tastes of our people, the Committee have adopted the following plan.

In *Bulletin for 1849*, American Art Union (New York, 1849), pp. 3–4, 8–11, 14–17.

Every subscriber of five dollars is a member of the Art Union for the year, and is entitled to all its privileges.

The money thus obtained (after paying necessary expenses) is applied:

First, to the production of a large and costly original engraving from an American painting, together with a set of outlines, or some other similar work of art.

Of this engraving every member receives a copy for every five dollars paid by him.

Members entitled to duplicates are at liberty to select from the engravings of previous years.

Second, to the purchase of paintings and sculpture, statuettes in bronze, and medals by native or resident artists.

These works of art are publicly exhibited at the Gallery of the Art Union till the annual meeting in December, when they are publicly distributed by lot among the members, each member having one share for every five dollars paid by him.

Each member is thus certain of receiving in return at least the value of the five dollars paid, and may also receive a painting or other work of art of great value.

Third, the institution keeps an office and free picture gallery always open, well attended, and hung with fine paintings where the members in New York receive their engravings, paintings, etc., and where the business of the institution is transacted.

What Has the American Art Union Accomplished?

The new gallery of the American Art Union has been opened to the public. The occasion is a proper one for "taking an observation," ascertaining where we are at present, whether we are sailing on our true course, and how much progress we have made in the voyage.

In material prosperity we have certainly abundant cause for self-congratulation. As a society, we have advanced with unexampled rapidity. So far as the number of members and the amount of subscriptions are concerned, the annual increase has been sufficiently large to gratify the expectations of the most sanguine. The change which a period of only eight years has brought about is believed to be unparalleled in the history of similar institutions. The six hundred and eighty-six members of the year 1840 have multiplied to sixteen thousand and upward in 1848, and the income of the former year, scarcely four thousand dollars, has grown in the same period to more than eighty-five thousand. Then the operations of the society beyond the city of New York were exceedingly limited; now many thousand letters are annually received and answered by the Corresponding Secretary, besides a great number of printed circulars and other communications which are constantly dispatched to our agents.

The contrast in the local habitations of the Art Union, at different periods, is not less striking. Only six years ago the Board held its meetings in a small dark apartment in the rear of a bookstore, which was thus used free of rent, through the courtesy of a friend of Art. We have at present in actual use for our own business, two galleries, also a

committee chamber and office, besides large apartments in the base-
ment for packing, storage, and other purposes; and all these properly
lighted, warmed, ventilated, and furnished.

It is now apparent to all who examine the subject that a mode has
been discovered by which Art may be encouraged to a proper extent as
liberally in an economical republic as in a prodigal monarchy. That
great moving principle of civilization which has effected such wonders
in its application to traveling, to commerce, and to the useful arts; the
principle of the combination of the limited means of many individuals
to accomplish some great end has been found to serve equally well in
the promotion of painting, sculpture, and engraving, and to be capable
when carried out of supplying to these as generous a support as they
have ever derived from crowned heads or wealthy aristocracies. The
Art Union is now their steady and reliable patron. It expends a larger
sum upon them than all other patrons upon the continent united; and
under its auspices the most ambitious and laborious enterprises in their
several departments may be undertaken and accomplished.

Has the Art Union Developed Talent among Artists?

Increasing subscription lists and growing revenues and large halls
are not the only or the best tests of the benefits of any institution. A far
more important matter to be settled is whether it advances the ends for
which it was established. Does the American Art Union promote the
development of artistic power? Does it elevate the taste and increase the
knowledge of the people in matters of Art? We maintain the affirmative
of both these questions. To the first of them we say that the association
has already raised the compensation of artists for works of undoubted
excellence to the rates paid in Europe for similar productions, and is
always a ready and willing customer for such works at the advanced
prices. It has stimulated many to attempt a higher range of subjects,
and to bestow upon their paintings longer preparatory study, and more
careful and laborious execution than heretofore. It has brought into
notice a considerable number of men of decided ability who would have
remained entirely unknown or, at any rate, advanced with much less
rapidity excepting for this assistance. Great injustice is constantly
done both to the Art Union and the artists by comparing the works of
the latter, not with their own previous efforts, but either with the
elaborate masterpieces of European schools or with some fanciful
standard in the mind of the critic. This comparison is well enough
when the abstract merit of our own men is to be estimated, but when the
question relates to the progress they have made from year to year, and
to the worth of any peculiar influence under which they have labored, a
fairer mode is to compare each man with himself. It will be found that
those who speak most contemptuously of Art Union pictures are persons
who know nothing of the history of Art in America. They forget that
genius has manifested itself here in many other departments, more
conspicuously than in the fine arts—that at the time when our society
commenced its efforts, the American School (if it may be so called)
showed but little vitality, excepting in landscape and portraiture, that
the most, after all, the Art Union could do was to offer generous prices

and impartial judgments—it could not create genius, but only provide that genius, if it existed, should certainly be discovered and as certainly rewarded.

We must not forget to mention the immense benefit conferred by the Art Union in providing a sure and convenient avenue by which talent, no matter how obscure and humble its possessor, may make itself known to the public at large. This advantage is entirely independent of that conferred by the purchases of pictures by the committee, and must be conceded even by those who find the greatest fault with the character of these purchases. We allude to the great public galleries of this institution, which are well warmed, lighted, and ventilated, opened constantly to the public, and thronged daily by thousands of citizens. In these galleries any artist or amateur, whatever may be his station or his birthplace, the poor apprentice as well as the accomplished master, the unknown and friendless emigrant as well as the President of the Academy, may deposit his work (provided it be not utterly worthless) for public inspection. The only distinction recognized in these rooms is that of merit. As conspicuous a place is given to the nameless aspirant to fame, if his productions deserve it, as to the reigning favorite of the hour. No jealousies or secret enmities, no influential connections or low intrigues are allowed to control the arrangement of these apartments. We do not believe that in any part of the world, even among the most cultivated and refined nations of Europe, has there ever been afforded such an easy and accessible mode by which artists may bring their works before the people as this.

Has the Art Union Increased the Taste and Knowledge of the People in Matters of Art?

So much for the question as to what the Art Union has done to develop artistic power; let us now attend to the equally important inquiry whether it has not also done much to elevate popular taste and increase the knowledge of the people in matters of Art. To answer this statistically, we may say that in the course of its ten year's existence, the society has distributed through the whole country nearly thirteen hundred paintings, seven hundred medals, more than fifty thousand engravings. It has constituted five hundred agencies in different parts of the country. It has kept open nearly ever since its institution a free gallery, in which not only have works been exhibited which were sent to the rooms to be purchased, but many others also, of the highest merit, belonging to individuals and deposited there for the gratification and improvement of the public. Finally, it has established a journal of the fine arts, which contains original and selected essays and much information respecting the progress of Art at home and abroad. This is given gratuitously to the members, and more than sixty-seven thousand copies of the different numbers have been printed and distributed.

It is well known to all who have studied the subject that a very general and strongly marked increase of interest in the fine arts has manifested itself within five or six years past in the United States. The growing subscription lists of the Art Union by themselves show this. Drawing is beginning to be taught in common schools. Exhibitions of paintings and statuary are more frequent and better attended. A greater number of houses are decorated with objects of taste. A decided improvement in the sale of prints is observed. Illustrated literature is eagerly welcomed and largely purchased. Societies upon the plan of the Art Union have sprung up in Philadelphia, Boston, Cincinnati, and elsewhere. Better taste is exhibited in architecture, both public and private, and in the furniture and adornment of houses. Books relating to Art have been sold in larger quantities than ever before in the same periods, and in parts of the country also where previously no interest had been felt in such matters.

Every unprejudiced mind must connect these novel manifestations with the progress of the American Art Union, and ascribe to its agency, in a very great degree, this newly awakened interest in the fine arts. After making due allowance for the great diffusion of illustrated books and newspapers, which have undoubtedly exercised an important influence, the greatest part of the credit for this movement must be awarded to our institution. Its secretaryships, its free gallery, its annual distribution of paintings, its various publications of prints and pamphlets have continually attracted public attention to the cause to which it is devoted. A periodic stimulus has been created which year after year has brought the subject freshly and pleasantly before the people.

II

The burdens of serving their society did not seem onerous to many American artists of the period. Indeed, to an astonishing degree, they found themselves comfortable with the charge. One such notable artist was the sculptor Horatio Greenough. Born in Boston in 1805, he was actually the first American to devote all his energies to sculpture. After graduating from Harvard in 1824, he studied in Rome, and then went to Florence, where he spent most of his later years. But his residence abroad did not in the least diminish his enthusiasm for an American art form. He executed an enormous statue of George Washington for the Capitol rotunda, and another piece for one of its entranceways. In 1851, a year before his death, he wrote a memoir of his life in art, giving clear expression to his national sentiments.

EXPERIENCES OF A YANKEE STONECUTTER, 1852

HORATIO GREENOUGH

The susceptibility, the tastes, and the genius which enable a people to enjoy the fine arts, and to excel in them, have been denied to the Anglo-Americans, not only by European talkers, but by European thinkers. The assertion of our obtuseness and inefficiency in this respect has been ignorantly and presumptuously set forth by some persons, merely to fill

In *Travels, Observations, and Experiences of a Yankee Stonecutter*, by Horatio Greenough (Boston, 1852), pp. 116–20, 122–26.

up the measure of our condemnation. Others have arrived at the same conclusions after examining our political and social character, after investigating our exploits and testing our capacities. They admit that we trade with enterprise and skill, that we build ships cunningly and sail them well, that we have a quick and far-sighted apprehension of the value of a territory, that we make wholesome homespun laws for its government, and that we fight hard when molested in any of these homely exercises of our ability; but they assert that there is a stubborn, antipoetical tendency in all that we do, or say, or think; they attribute our very excellence in the ordinary business of life to causes which must prevent our development as artists.

Enjoying the accumulated result of the thought and labor of centuries, Europe has witnessed our struggles with the hardships of an untamed continent, and the disadvantages of colonial relations, with but a partial appreciation of what we aim at, with but an imperfect knowledge of what we have done. Seeing us intently occupied during several generations in felling forests, in building towns, and constructing roads, she thence formed a theory that we are good for nothing except these pioneer efforts. She taunted us, because there were no statues or frescoes in our log cabins; she pronounced us unmusical, because we did not sit down in the swamp with an Indian on one side, and a rattlesnake on the other, to play the violin. That she should triumph over the deficiencies of a people who had set the example of revolt and republicanism was natural; but the reason which she assigned for those deficiencies was not the true reason. She argued with the depth and the sagacity of a philosopher who should conclude, from seeing an infant imbibe with eagerness its first aliment, that its whole life would be occupied in similar absorption.

It is true that before the Declaration of Independence Copley had in Boston formed a style of portrait which filled Sir Joshua Reynolds with astonishment; and that West, breaking through the bar of Quaker prohibition, and conquering the prejudice against a provincial aspirant, had taken a high rank in the highest walk of art in London. Stuart, Trumbull, Allston, Morse, Leslie, Newton followed in quick succession, while Vanderlyn won golden opinions at Rome, and bore away high honors at Paris. That England, with these facts before her, should have accused us of obtuseness in regard to art, and that we should have pleaded guilty to the charge, furnishes the strongest proof of her disposition to underrate our intellectual powers, and of our own ultra docility and want of self-reliance.

Artists have arisen in numbers; the public gives its attention to their productions; their labors are liberally rewarded. It seems now admitted that wealth and cultivation are destined to yield in America the same fruits that they have given in Italy, in Spain, in France, Germany, and England. It seems now admitted that there is no anomalous defect in our mental endowments; that the same powers displayed in clearing the forest and tilling the farm will trim the garden. It seems clear that we are destined to have a school of art. It becomes a matter of importance to decide how the youth who devote themselves to these studies are to acquire the rudiments of imitation, and what influences are to be made to act upon them. This question seemed at one time to have been decided. The friends of Art in America looked to Europe for an example, and with the natural assumption that experience had made the old world wise in what relates to the fine arts, determined upon forming academies as the more refined nations of the continent have ended by doing. We might as well have proposed a national church establishment. That the youth must be taught is clear—but in framing an institution for that object, if we look to countries grown old in European systems, it must be for warning rather than example.

The above reflections have been drawn from us by the oft-repeated expressions of regret which we have listened to, "that from the constitution of our society, and the nature of our institutions, no influences can be brought to bear upon art with the vivifying power of court patronage." We fully and firmly believe that these institutions are more favorable to a natural, healthful growth of art than any hotbed culture whatever. We cannot—as did Napoleon—make, by a few imperial edicts, an army of battle painters, a hierarchy of drum-and-fife glorifiers. Nor can we, in the lifetime of an individual, so stimulate this branch of culture, so unduly and disproportionately endow it, as to make a Walhalla start from a republican soil. The monuments, the pictures, the statues of the republic will represent what the people love and wish for—not what they can be made to accept, not how much taxation they will bear.

III

The social function of art was no less attractive a theme for the most talented painter in antebellum America, Thomas Cole. Cole (1801–1848) was the founder and leading spirit of the Hudson River School, that group of artists who made the dramatic scenery of northern and western New York the focus of their painting. As Cole insisted, the choice of these rough and dramatic scenes was important for two reasons: first, it would focus Americans' attention on the sublime and beautiful, somehow making them more refined and less aggressive in their mutual dealings. Second, and no less important, this scenery was so appealing and attractive that it served to answer those European critics who argued that nothing of real value existed in this New World worthy of an artist's attention. Cole's statement clearly reflects both the social and patriotic concerns of the artists of the period.

ESSAY ON AMERICAN SCENERY, 1836

THOMAS COLE

The essay which is here offered is a mere sketch of an almost illimitable subject—American scenery. It is a subject that to every American ought to be of surpassing interest; for, whether he beholds the Hudson ming-

In *The American Monthly Magazine*, 1 (1836): 1–12.

ling waters with the Atlantic, explores the central wilds of this vast continent, or stands on the margin of the distant Oregon, he is still in the midst of American scenery—it is his own land; its beauty, its magnificence, its sublimity—all are his; and how undeserving of such a birthright, if he can turn toward it an unobserving eye, an unaffected heart!

The spirit of our society is to contrive but not to enjoy—toiling to produce more toil—accumulating in order to aggrandize. The pleasures of the imagination, among which the love of scenery holds a conspicuous place, will alone temper the harshness of such a state; and, like the atmosphere that softens the most rugged forms of the landscape, cast a veil of tender beauty over the asperities of life.

There are those who through ignorance or prejudice strive to maintain that American scenery possesses little that is interesting or truly beautiful—that it is rude without picturesqueness, and monotonous without sublimity—that being destitute of those vestiges of antiquity whose associations so strongly affect the mind, it may not be compared with European scenery. But from whom do these opinions come? From those who have read of European scenery, of Grecian mountains, and Italian skies, and never troubled themselves to look at their own; and from those traveled ones whose eyes were never opened to the beauties of nature until they beheld foreign lands, and when those lands faded from the sight were again closed and forever; disdaining to destroy their transatlantic impressions by the observation of the less fashionable and unfamed American scenery. Let such persons shut themselves up in their narrow shell of prejudice—I hope they are few—and the community increasing in intelligence will know better how to appreciate the treasures of their own country.

A very few generations have passed away since this vast tract of the American continent, now the United States, rested in the shadow of primeval forests, whose gloom was peopled by savage beasts and scarcely less savage men; or lay in those wide grassy plains called prairies. And, although an enlightened and increasing people have broken in upon the solitude, and with activity and power wrought changes that seem magical, yet the most distinctive, and perhaps the most impressive, characteristic of American scenery is its wildness.

It is the most distinctive because in civilized Europe the primitive features of scenery have long since been destroyed or modified—the extensive forests that once overshadowed a great part of it have been felled, rugged mountains have been smoothed, and the once tangled wood is now a grassy lawn; the turbulent brook a navigable stream, crags that could not be removed have been crowned with towers, and the rudest valleys tamed by the plough.

And to this cultivated state our western world is fast approaching; but nature is still predominant, and there are those who regret that with the improvements of cultivation the sublimity of the wilderness should pass away; for those scenes of solitude from which the hand of nature has never been lifted affect the mind with a more deep-toned emotion than aught which the hand of man has touched. Amid them the consequent associations are of God the Creator—they are His undefiled works, and the mind is cast into the contemplation of eternal things.

I will now venture a few remarks on what has been considered a grand defect in American scenery—the want of associations such as arise amid the scenes of the old world. He who stands on Mont Albano and looks down on ancient Rome has his mind peopled with the gigantic associations of the storied past; but he who stands on the mounds of the West, the most venerable remains of American antiquity, *may* experience the emotion of the sublime, but it is the sublimity of a shoreless ocean un-islanded by the recorded deeds of man.

Yet American scenes are not destitute of historical and legendary associations—the great struggle for freedom has sanctified many a spot, and many a mountain, stream, and rock has its legend, worthy of poet's pen or the painter's pencil. But American associations are not so much of the past as of the present and the future. Seated on a pleasant knoll, look down into the bosom of that secluded valley, begirt with wooded hills. You see no ruined tower to tell of outrage, no gorgeous temple to speak of ostentation; but freedom's offspring—peace, security, and happiness—dwell there, the spirits of the scene. On the margin of that gentle river the village girls may ramble unmolested, and the glad schoolboy, with hook and line, pass his bright holiday; those neat dwellings, unpretending to magnificence, are the abodes of plenty, virtue, and refinement. And in looking over the yet uncultivated scene, the mind's eye may see far into futurity. Where the wolf roams, the plough shall glisten; on the gray crag shall rise temple and tower— mighty deeds shall be done in the now pathless wilderness; and poets yet unborn shall sanctify the soil.

Yet I cannot but express my sorrow that the beauty of such land-scapes are quickly passing away—the ravages of the ax are daily increasing—the most noble scenes are made desolate, and oftentimes with a wantonness and barbarism scarcely credible in a civilized nation. The wayside is becoming shadeless, and another generation will behold spots, now rife with beauty, desecrated by what is called improvement; which, as yet, generally destroys Nature's beauty without substituting that of Art. This is a regret rather than a complaint; such is the road society has to travel; it may lead to refinement in the end, but the traveler who sees the place of rest close at hand dislikes the road that has so many unnecessary windings.

I will now conclude, in the hope that the importance of cultivating a taste for scenery will not be forgotten. Nature has spread for us a rich and delightful banquet. Shall we turn from it? We are still in Eden; the wall that shuts us out of the garden is our own ignorance and folly.

IV

Probably the most perceptive and widely read art critic in mid-nine-teenth-century America was James Jackson Jarvis. A noted collector of art, Jarvis skillfully and persuasively helped to define the role of art and the artist in American society. For Jarvis, too, the link between esthetics and social order was at the heart of what he called the "art idea." As he put it, "We cannot make the world more beautiful without making it better, morally and socially."

THE ART IDEA, 1864

JAMES JACKSON JARVIS

The chief expressions in America of the art idea, under the forms of painting, sculpture, and architecture, traced to their present condition, we perceive a steady, and of late a rapid advance of each in quality and variety, showing that the unfolding of the art idea bears fruit in objects of taste and beauty, suited to all degrees of knowledge and feeling. Art, like nature, adds so much to enjoyment, and in such manifold ways, that we do not recognize the full extent of our obligations to her. But what she has done is as nothing compared with her power in reserve. Every good picture, statue, or bit of architecture is one more joy for the human race. We perceive that as a people or as individuals, it is a duty incumbent on all, in the interests of civilization, to make life as lovely as possible in manners, dress, and buildings; to adorn our homes, streets, and public places; in short, to infuse beauty by the aid of art into all objects, and to make unceasing war upon whatever deforms and debases, or tends to ugliness and coarseness.

We cannot make the world more beautiful without making it better, morally and socially. The art idea is the beautifier, an angel messenger of glad tidings to every receptive mind. Upward of four million visitors enjoyed Central Park, New York, the last year. We cite the park as an example of the carrying out of the art idea because, beside a barren site, it owes nothing to nature. Art here has done everything, even to

In *The Art Idea: Sculpture, Paintings, and Architecture in America,* by James Jackson Jarvis (New York, 1864). Reprint edition (Cambridge, Mass., 1960), pp. 247–53, 262–63, 266–67, 270–71.

nursing and training nature herself. An institution like this, combining art, science, and nature in harmonious unity, is a great free school for the people, of broader value than mere grammar schools; for, besides affording pleasing ideas and useful facts, it elevates and refines the popular mind by bringing it in intimate contact with the true and beautiful under circumstances conducive to happiness and physical well-being. What matter if it should cost a score of millions of money? Is it not so much saved from prisons, priests, police, and physicians? By it bodies are temporarily rescued from dirt and misery, and opportunities given the eye to look up to the clear vault of heaven, and take into the mind the healing significance of nature and art. In many it awakens the first consciousness of their spiritual birthright. To all it operates as a magnetic charm of decent behavior, giving salutary lessons in order, discipline, and comeliness, culminating in mutual goodwill and a better understanding of humanity at large, from its democratic intermingling of all classes, under quickening, many-sided, various refinements and delights. It is, too, a far cheaper amusement for the million than theaters, not to speak of the exchange of foul air for pure, noxious gaslight for health-giving sunlight, dubious morality and nerve-exhausting incitements for glorious music, invigorating games, boating, and exercise, the humanizing sight of merry childhood, the zoological and horticultural gardens.

In one direction we have already gone far enough. Anglo-Saxons, in their one-sided idea of home, are becoming selfish and unpatriotic. A home is a nursery and safeguard of domestic virtue, a protection of individuality, lest it be merged entirely into the mass. But man's selfhood being asserted and trained, he owes allegiance to the community. Home

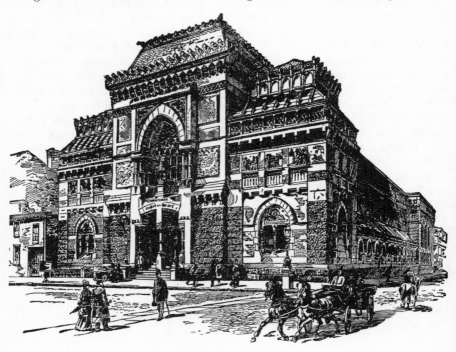

is indeed the primary school of life and the sanctuary of its affections. As such it should be jealously guarded. We would make it as sacred in spirit as the holy of holies of the Temple itself. But any virtue pushed to excess becomes a vice. An American home has become something more than its original intent. It distracts the individual too much from mankind at large; tempts him to center therein wealth, luxury, and every conceivable stimulus of personal ease, pride, and display. The tendency is to narrow his humanity by putting it under bonds to vanity and selfishness. The family is made an excuse for neglecting the responsibilities of citizenship. As with trade, short-sighted, he forgets that the welfare of the neighbor in the code of Christian ethics is put upon the par with one's own, and that as he neglects it, the state drifts toward anarchy and turmoil. New Yorkers make too much money to care whether their city is given over or not to scoundrelism. They pay a blackmail to villainy, in order to shirk their duties as citizens and patriots, to make money as traders, or luxuriate as heads of fashionable families. Easy enough to see where this will end. Riots are the legitimate results. Home or business, viewed from the point of view of selfishness, becomes a curse instead of a blessing.

If we could expand the low-toned rivalry of individuals for wealth and power into a generous competition of cities and states in the growth of public institutions and the founding of parks, galleries of science and art, libraries, fine taste in architecture, schools of ideas, and whatever dignifies and advances human nature morally, intellectually, and esthetically, individuals competing with one another to be associated in noble enterprises with the same zeal and lavish expenditure they now devote to excel in costly houses, equipages, dress, and the gratification of appetites, we should shortly see the true golden age dawn. We are no illusionist. We do not look for this tomorrow, or the day after. But there are young minds to be formed on nobler ideas than have yet largely obtained. We are earnest in our advocacy of a larger measure of public spirit; of a collective local pride, and rivalry in good works; of the diminution of the selfishness of the home feeling by the substitution of a more generous sentiment, expanding love of the individual into a love of the people.

The inquiry now arises by what means, in America, may the knowledge and appreciation of art be best promoted?

The first duty of art, as we have already intimated, is to make our public buildings and places as instructive and enjoyable as possible. They should be pleasurable, full of attractive beauty and eloquent teachings. Picturesque groupings of natural objects, architectural surprises, sermons from the sculptor's chisel and painter's palette, the ravishment of the soul by its superior senses, the refinement of mind and body by the sympathetic power of beauty—these are a portion of the means which a due estimation of art as an element of civilization inspires the ruling will to provide freely for all. If art be kept a rare and tabooed thing, a specialty for the rich and powerful, it excites in the vulgar mind envy and hate. But proffer it freely to the public, and the public soon learns to delight in and protect it as its rightful inheritance. It also tends to develop a brotherhood of thought and feeling. During the civil strifes of Italy art flourished and was respected. Indeed, to some extent it operated as a sort of peace society, and was held sacred when nothing else was. Even rude soldiers, amid the perils and necessities of sieges, turned aside destruction from the walls that sheltered it. The history of art is full of records of its power to soften and elevate the human heart.

The desire for art being awakened, museums to illustrate its technical and historical progress, and galleries to exhibit its master-works, become indispensable. The most common means of popularizing art and cultivating a general taste is by galleries or museums. But even in Europe these have been only quite recently established.

To stimulate the art feeling, it is requisite that our public should have free access to museums, or galleries, in which shall be exhibited, in chronological series, specimens of the art of all nations and schools, including our own, arranged according to their motives and the special influences that attended their development. After this manner a mental and artistic history of the world may be spread out like a chart before the student, while the artist, with equal facility, can trace up to their origin the varied methods, styles, and excellences of each prominent epoch. A museum of art is a perpetual feast of the most intense and refined enjoyment to everyone capable of entering into its phases of thought and execution, and of analyzing its external and internal being and tracing the mysterious transformations of spirit into form.

Connected with it there might be schools of design for studying the nude figure, antique casts, and modern works. Also, for improvement in ornamental manufacture, the development of architecture, and whatever aids to refine and give beauty to social life.

Were we to wait long enough, fashion and interest here, as in England, would provide galleries and means of instruction in art for the people. But the spirit which animates such efforts is in the main ego-tistical. Better is it by far that the people act for themselves, supplying their own demands for esthetic enjoyment. Surely, the means already exist among us for beginning institutions which could in time grow to be the people's pride.

For immediate wants it would be sufficient to provide a suitable locality where such wealth of art as we possess could be got together in orderly shape. As the people grow into an appreciation of the value of art institutions, they will as freely provide for their permanent support and growth, either by private liberality or state aid, as they now do for more common education. That America possesses the population calculated to sustain and enjoy such institutions we have evidence in the progressively increasing interest awakened by every fresh appeal to its intellect and taste.

V

The federal buildings in Washington, D.C. provided some of the first opportunities for public sponsorship of artistic endeavors. Not surprisingly, Congress, in the role of patron, had very fixed ideas

*on the proper subject matter for decorating a government struc-
ture, and they did not invariably coincide with the particular
ambitions of the artist. One such conflict is described in the
correspondence of Washington Allston, one of the leading painters
of this period, and G. C. Verplanck, a New York congressman. Not
all artists, it is clear, flourished under a system in which art was
to serve the nation.*

THE LETTERS OF WASHINGTON ALLSTON,
1830–1832

From Allston to Verplanck

Cambridge, Mass., March 1, 1830

My Dear Sir:

I did not get your letter of the seventeenth until the night before
last and I shall endeavor to answer it in a businesslike manner.

I thank you for this additional instance of the friendship with
which you honor me. And yet I fear there are certain formidable,
and to my present apprehension, insurmountable obstacles to my
profiting by your kindness. The subjects from which I am to choose,
you say, are limited to American history. The most prominent of these,
indeed the only ones that occur to me, are in our military and naval
achievements. Herein lies my difficulty. I know that I have not any
talent for battlepieces; and, perhaps, because they have always appeared
to me, from their very nature, incapable of being justly represented,
for, to say nothing of the ominous prelude of silent emotion, when you
take away the excessive movement, the dash of arms, the deadly roll
of the drum, the blast of the trumpet, and the still more fearful din of
human thunder, giving a terrific life to the whole—and all this must
be taken from the painter—what is there left for his canvas?

Such being my opinion, you will easily believe that I could have
no hope of succeeding in subjects of this nature. Indeed I know from
past experience that I must fail when the subject is not of myself, that
is, in relation to the powers of my art, essentially exciting. In a pecuniary
view it has been, perhaps, my misfortune to have inherited a patrimony,
since it has lasted only just long enough to allow my mind to take its
own course till its habits of thought had become rigid and too fixed to
be changed when change was desirable. As an artist I cannot, in spite
of many troubles, regret this freedom of action, since I feel of such that
I owe to it whatever professional skill I may possess. But of late years,
since the source of this liberty has been dried up, and the cold current
of necessity has sprung up in its stead, I have sometimes, as a man,
almost felt the possession to have been a misfortune, for necessity,
I find, has no inspiration; she has not with me even the forcing power.

I trust you know me too well to doubt my patriotism because I
cannot be inspired to paint an American battle. I yield in love of country

In *The Life and Letters of Washington Allston*, ed. Jared B. Flagg (New York,
1922), pp. 230–39, 254–58.

to no man; no one has gloried more in the success of her arms, or more sincerely honored the gallant spirits whose victories have given her a name among nations. But they need not my pencil to make their deeds known to posterity.

But may there not be some eligible subject in our civil history? For myself I can think of none that would make a picture; of none, at least, that belongs to high art. But such a subject might possibly have occurred to you. If so, and I find it one from which I can make such a picture as you would have me paint, both for my own credit and that of the nation, be assured I will most gladly undertake it.

There is another class of subject, however, in which, were I permitted to choose from it, I should find exciting matter enough, and more than enough, for my imperfect skill, that is, from Scripture. But I fear this is a forlorn hope. Yet why should it be? This is a Christian land, and the Scriptures belong to no country, but to man. Should the government allow me to select a subject from them, I need not say with what delight I should accept the commission. With such a source of inspiration and the glory of painting for my country, if there be anything in me, it must come out. Would it might be so! But let us suppose it. Well, supposing such a commission given, there's a subject already composed *in petto*, which I have long intended to paint as soon as I am at liberty—the three Marys at the tomb of the Savior, the angel sitting on a stone before the mouth of the sepulcher. I consider this one of my happiest conceptions. I see now before me; I wish I could see them on the walls at Washington.

Now as to the price, should such a dream, I will not call it hope, be realized, it would be eight thousand dollars, which I believe was the price given to Colonel Trumbull for each of his pictures. I should not indeed refuse ten thousand, should Uncle Sam take the generous fit upon him to offer it; but eight is my price for that particular composition, which would consist of four figures, seven feet high; the picture itself (an upright) twelve or thirteen feet high and ten or twelve wide.

Pray do not let any part of this letter get into print. I beg you will not think from anything I have said that I intent any disrespect to the painters of battles. There are many of deserved reputation which show great skill in their authors; it would be unjust not to mention, as holding the very first rank, Mr. West's "Wolf," and the "Death of Warren and Montgomery," and the "Sortie," by Colonel Trumbull.

Ever most truly yours,

W. Allston

From Verplanck to Allston

Washington, March 9, 1830

My Dear Sir:

Your letter only convinces me the more that we must, if we can, have one specimen of "high art" on the wall of the Capitol. By American history mere revolutionary history is not meant. To Scripture I fear we cannot go in the present state of public opinion and taste. But does our anterevolutionary history present no subject? The "Landing of the

Pilgrims," a threadbare subject in some respects, has never been viewed with a poet's and painter's eye. What think you of that, or of any similar subject in our early history? Your townsman, Dr. Holmes, has recently published a very useful, though not important, book of "Annals." A hasty glance over the first volume of this would perhaps suggest some idea. If not, I still fall back upon the "Pilgrims."

Yours truly,

G. C. Verplanck

From Allston to Verplanck

Cambridgeport, March 29, 1830

My Dear Sir:

Your letter duly come to hand; as you full well know that I cannot be insensible to such persevering kindness I will not trouble you with a repetition of thanks, but proceed to answer them in as businesslike a way as I can.

To the first subject you propose, "The Landing of the Pilgrims" (not unpicturesque), I have a personal objection. It has already been painted by an old friend of mine, Colonel Sargent, a high-minded, honorable man, to whom I would on no account give pain; which I could not avoid doing were I to encroach on what, at the expense of several years' labor, he has a fair right to consider his ground.

I will not trouble you with my objections to the other subject, the "Leave-taking of Washington," lest I have no room for one of my own choosing, which I should be glad to have you approve, namely: "The First Interview of Columbus with Ferdinand and Isabella" at court after the discovery of America, accompanied by natives, and so forth, exhibited in evidence of his success. As you have read Irving's book it is unnecessary for me to describe the scene. Here is magnificence, emotion, and everything, the very truimph of "matter" to task a painter's powers. The announcement and the proof of the birth of a New World. This is not thought of now for the first time. I have long cherished it as one of the dreams which the future, if the future were spared to me, was one day to embody. But to business; the size of a picture from this would be not less than eighteen feet by twelve, perhaps twenty by fourteen; and the price fifteen thousand dollars. As to its class, I know not what subject could be said more emphatically to belong to America and her history than the triumph of her discoverer. We, who now enjoy the blessings of his discovery, cannot place him too high in that history which without him would never have been.

Faithfully yours,

W. Allston

From Verplanck to Allston

House of Representatives, May 29, 1830

My Dear Sir:

We (that is our Committee) had determined to try the taste and liberality of Congress by recommending an appropriation for a picture from you on your terms and choice, restricting you only to American history, in which Columbus would, of course, be included; but, unfortunately, for the present our bill for the improvement of the public buildings has been crowded out by the press of other business, and must lie over till next winter.

Though our proposed alterations in the buildings are important both to comfort and taste, there was nothing pressing in the bill now passing, and I only regret the delay on your account. Next winter we shall have the opportunity of taking up the bill early, and I hope with better success. But the extent to which Congress will go in these matters depends much on accidental circumstances.

Allston to Cogdell [Allston's Later Thoughts on the Incident]

Cambridgeport, February 27, 1832

Dear Cogdell:

It gives me great pleasure that I can bestow sincere praise on your group of Hagar and Ishmael. It is decidedly your best work, and much exceeds what I had expected; it really does you great honor. And though it has many faults, they are by no means of a kind to outweigh its merits. The attitudes of both mother and child are well conceived, and they group well together. But its chief merit lies in the general conception and the expression, which are certainly the principal points in a work of art. It has indeed great power of expression.

Now, after this praise, will you allow me, my friend, to say a few words of a prudential nature. Do not let it tempt you to give up a certainty for an uncertainty. I say this because my nephew informs me that when he left Carolina, you talked, as he had heard, of going to Italy, to make art your profession; if so, you must of course give up your office at the Customhouse, which, if I understand you aright, is now your principal means of support. What I am about to say, however, I do not give in the shape of advice; for I as much dislike giving advice as asking it. I shall merely express my opinion on the subject, leaving you to weigh it as you think fit, and to decide for yourself.

If by making the art your profession you are to depend on it as the means of support for yourself and family, I cannot but think that you look to a very precarious source. What may be the prospects of employment from private individuals you can judge as well as I, and I no better than you, for I can have no definite knowledge as to it unless I were myself a sculptor. It has often, however, been doubted by Greenough's friends here, notwithstanding the high and general estimation in which he stands as well for his private character as for his talents, whether he will be able to support himself in Boston from private employment alone. And if Boston cannot afford him sufficient, I know not in what other city of the Union he can expect it. His resource, they think, must be at Washington, in works for the government, or in Europe. Indeed, it seems to be the opinion of most persons that employment for the general government is the only hope for a sculptor who is to live by his profession in our country. And whether it is that people have been but little accustomed to it, or from some other cause, so far as I have observed, the interest taken in sculpture is by no means so general as that taken in pictures. Then the prices which a sculptor must charge, even to defray his expenses, are such as very few in our country are either able or willing to give for works of art. So I do not see much prospect even of a bare support, unless he is content to confine himself to busts that are portraits. But even supposing there were sufficient demand for sculpture, are you prepared to coin your brain for bread—at all times and under all circumstances, of depression, of illness, and the numberless harassments of unavoidable debt? To produce an original work of the imagination, requiring of all human efforts a pleasurable state of the mind, with a dunning letter staring you in the face? With an honest heart yearning to give everyone his due, and an empty purse, I know from bitter experience that the fairest visions of the imagination vanish like dreams never to be recalled, before the daylight reality of such a visitor. Poverty is no doubt a stimulus to general industry, and to many kinds of mental effort, but not to the imagination; for the imagination must be abortive—is a nonentity—if it have not peace as its immediate condition. Pictures that would have otherwise brought me hundreds, not to say thousands, have crumbled into nothing under its pressure, and been thrown aside as nothing worth. I say these things not querulously but that you might know what it is to be an artist by profession, with no other income than the product of the brain—which, to be at all available, must at least be at peace. And I give them in their naked reality solely from a conscientious regard for your peace and happiness as a man. The love I bear my art you well know; no one could love it more. And yet, with all this love, which I still bear it, I thus speak of it as a profession. Because I must speak the truth. But, understand me, when I speak of it thus as a profession, it is when that profession is associated with poverty.

Your office allows you, I suppose, the half of each day to yourself, and secures to you the means of devoting one half of the year to the pursuit of the art, in the way you like best, and independent of the world. Ah, that word independent has a charm which I well know how to value, from having known its reverse. But I still have hope, and I look for repossession of it yet.

VI

Few military events were as famous in the United States as the Revolutionary War battle at Bunker Hill, and it is not surprising that one of the first proposed memorials was to commemorate this incident. In 1824 a group of New Englanders, including Daniel Webster and Edward Everett, tried to raise funds from the public for this enterprise, and the following solicitation vividly captures the early ideology of monument building.

THE BUNKER HILL MONUMENT ASSOCIATION, 1824

Fifty years have now nearly elapsed since the curtain rose on this momentous scene of our national drama, the battle of the seventeenth of June 1775. This long period has laid down in the soil which they combined to liberate most of the high-minded men who raised their hands or their voices in those trying times. A few only remain, the venerable witnesses of what we may do to show our gratitude toward those to whom we owe all "that makes it life to live," our liberty. The presence of these few Revolutionary patriots and heroes among us seems to give a peculiar character to this generation. It binds us by an affecting association to the momentous days, the searching trials, the sacrifices, and dangers, to which they were called. The feeble hands and gray hairs of those who, before we were living, faced death, that we, their children, might be born free, are a sight which this generation ought not to behold without emotion; a sight which calls upon us not to delay those public expressions of gratitude which soon will be too late for those we would most wish to honor.

Now, in the days of our independence, of our prosperity, of our growing internal wealth, of our participation in all the world's commerce, of our enjoyment of everything which can make a people happy, we ought to remember the sacrifices and losses of our fathers. No grateful mind can, from the fruits of this unexampled welfare, refuse to bestow a trifle upon a work proposed as a decent and becoming tribute to the memory of the great and good men to whose disinterestedness in putting to hazard their property and lives we owe our being, our rights, our property, our all.

The spot itself on which this memorable action took place is extremely favorable for becoming the site of a monumental structure. Competent judges have pronounced the heights of Charlestown to excel any spot on our coast, in their adaptation to the object in view. Their position, with the expanse of the harbor of Boston, and its beautiful islands in front, has long attracted the notice of the stranger. An elevated monument on this spot would be the first landmark of the mariner in his approach to our harbor; while the whole neighboring country, with their rich fields, villages, and spires, the buildings of the university, the bridges, the numerous ornamental country seats and improved plantations would be spread out as in a picture, to the eye of the spectator on the summit of the proposed structure.

Nor are these the only natural advantages of the spot. Though essentially rural in many of its features, it rises above one of our most flourishing towns, the seat of several important national establishments, where the noble ships of war of the American republic seem to guard the approach to the spot where her first martyrs fought and bled. Its immediate vicinity to Boston, and its convenient distance from Salem,

In *The History of the Bunker Hill Monument Association,* by George Washington Warren (Boston, 1877), pp. 112–13, 116–17.

makes the access to it direct from the centers of our most numerous, wealthy, and active populations, and will be the means of keeping continually in sight, or bringing frequently to view, to the great masses of the community, the imposing memorial of an event which ought never to be absent from their memory, as its effects are daily and hourly brought home to the business and bosoms of every American citizen.

In forming an estimate of the cost of the structure proposed, a single eye has been had to the principle which dictates its erection. Everything separated from the idea of substantial strength and severe taste has been discarded, as foreign from the grace and serious character both of the men and events to be commemorated. With this principle in view, it has been ascertained that a monumental column, of a classic model, with an elevation to make it the most lofty in the world, may be erected of our fine Chelmsford granite for about thirty-seven thousand dollars.

The general propriety and expediency of erecting public monuments of the kind proposed are acknowledged by all. They form not only the most conspicuous ornaments with which we can adorn our towns and high places, but they are the best proof we can exhibit to strangers that our sensibility is strong and animated toward those great achievements and greater characters to which we owe all our national blessings. There surely is not one among us who would not experience

a strong satisfaction in conducting a stranger to the foot of a monumental structure rising in decent majesty on this memorable spot.

Works of this kind also have the happiest influence in exciting and
nourishing the national and patriotic sentiment. Our government has
been called, and truly is a government of opinion; but it is one of
sentiment still more. It is not the judgment only of this people, which
dictates a preference for our institutions, but it is a strong, deep-seated,
inborn sentiment; a feeling, a passion for liberty. It is a becoming
expression of this sentiment to honor, in every way, the memories and
characters of our fathers; to adorn a spot where their noble blood was
spilt, and not surrender it uncared for to the plough. Years, it is to be
remembered, are rapidly passing away; and the glorious traditions of
our national emancipation which we received from them will descend
more faintly to our successors. The patriotic sentiment which binds us
together more strongly than compacts or constitutions will, if permitted,
grow cold from mere lapse of time. We owe these monuments, therefore,
not less to the character of our posterity than to the memory of our
fathers. These events must not lose their interest. Our children and our
children's children have a right to these feelings, cherished and kept
by a worthy transmission. It is the order of nature that the generation
to achieve nobly should be succeeded by a generation worthily to record
and gratefully to commemorate. We are not called to the fire and the
sword; to meet the appalling array of armies, to taste the bitter cup of
imperial wrath and vengeance proffered to an ill-provided land. We are
chosen for the easier, more grateful, but not less bound duty of com-
memorating and honoring the labors, sacrifices, and sufferings of the
great men of those dark times.

There is one point of view in which we seem to be strongly called
upon to engage in the erection of works like that proposed. The beautiful
and noble arts of design and architecture have hitherto been engaged in
arbitrary and despotic service. The pyramids and obelisks of Egypt, the
monumental columns of Trajan and Aurelius have paid no tribute to
the rights and feelings of man. Majestic and graceful as they are, they
have no record but that of sovereignty, sometimes cruel and tyrannical,
and sometimes mild; but never that of a great, enlightened, and
generous people. Providence, which has given us the senses to observe,
the taste to admire, and the skill to execute these beautiful works of art,
cannot have intended that, in a flourishing nation of freemen, there
should be no scope for their erection. Our fellow-citizens of Baltimore
have set us a noble example of redeeming the arts to the cause of free
institutions, in the imposing monument they have erected to the memory
of those who fell in defending their city. If we cannot be the first to
set up a structure of this character, let us not be other than the first
to improve upon the example; to arrest and fix the feelings of our
generation on the important events of an earlier and more momentous
struggle; and to redeem the pledge of gratitude to the high-souled heroes
of that trying day.

For a work calculated to appeal, without distinction, to every
member of the community, we trust we need no apology for respectfully
soliciting your cooperation and interest. The monument must be erected
by the union of all the classes and members of society, and the smallest

assistance, by contribution or encouragement, will aid in the great
design.

Daniel Webster,	Jesse Putnam,
H. A. S. Dearborn,	Isaac P. Davis,
Benjamin Gorham,	Seth Knowles,
George Blake,	Edward Everett,
John C. Warren,	George Ticknor,
Samuel D. Harris,	Theodore Lyman, Jr.,
William Sullivan,	*Directors*

Edward Everett, $\begin{cases} \textit{Secretary of the Standing} \\ \textit{Committee of the Directors} \end{cases}$

Chapter 10

Abolitionist Societies

BEGINNING IN THE 1830s and continuing up to the outbreak of the Civil War, ardent opponents of slavery organized themselves into societies to further their cause. Under the organizational network of these societies, they urged the abolition of slavery in the United States in public meetings, newspapers, pamphlets, and petitions. Their impact far outweighed their numbers. Indeed, the content of their message and the ways in which they spread it were so novel that the movement created a furor among contemporaries, and to this day has remained the subject of heated debate among historians.

The rhetoric of the abolitionists is in and of itself worth close scrutiny. Abolitionism was part of a large reform effort; those eager to improve the condition of slaves also devoted their efforts to uplifting other disadvantaged groups, namely women, the criminal, the poor, and the insane. Hence, to understand the causes behind the concern for the slave is to explore the motives of other reform efforts as well. What view of society did the abolitionists share? How did they understand the possibility of social change within the United States? What constituted for them an optimal social organization, and how did they set out to achieve it?

Moreover, the activities of the abolitionists have sparked a heated debate on the issue of whether or not these leaders were "fanatics." Many contemporaries, and later historians, too, insisted that the abolitionists did far more harm than good. By exciting the passions of the people, by whipping up public emotions, they made reasoned compromise impossible. The tragedy of the Civil War is laid at their feet. If not for their frenzied activities, sensible statesmanship could have amicably settled the issues dividing North and South. The abolitionists themselves and their defenders offer a far different interpretation. For them, the very notion of a fanatic for freedom is absurd. Rather, abolitionists were the keepers of the American conscience. Their activities made it impossible for the country to tolerate the moral disgrace that was slavery. Hence, any effort to understand the coming of the Civil War must focus on the merits of the abolitionist movement.

The activities of the abolitionist societies command attention for they were, in many ways, notably modern. Abolitionists were among the first groups in American society to employ all available means to mold public opinion. In this way, their efforts clarify for us the mechanisms that could be used in the early republic for purposes of persuasion, and to break the barriers of regional insularity.

Finally, the public's response to the abolitionists was so violent as to prompt a whole series of questions about the forces of order and disorder operating in antebellum society. Abolitionists' meetings were often broken up by force, their presses smashed, their lives threatened, and several of them were actually murdered—all this in Northern not Southern, communities. Why did a movement so essentially verbal in its approach provoke such incredibly hostile physical reactions? Why did antislavery words lead men to take to the streets? By exploring this phenomenon, the underlying tensions in American society during the period before the Civil War are revealed.

I

An especially articulate statement of the abolitionists' ideology appeared in the writings and speeches of Wendell Phillips. Born in Boston in 1811, Phillips first became interested in the movement when a mob attacked abolitionist William Lloyd Garrison in Boston in 1835. Soon Phillips was writing for Garrison's paper, The Liberator, *and addressing innumerable public meetings as well. He was also concerned with other causes. Before the Civil War it was women's rights, and after the war, worker's welfare. His speech, reprinted below, delivered in Boston in 1853 before a meeting of the Massachusetts Anti-Slavery Society, presents the abolitionist's response to critics who labeled them uncompromising fanatics on the slavery issue.*

THE PHILOSOPHY OF THE
ABOLITION MOVEMENT, 1853

WENDELL PHILLIPS

I wish, Mr. Chairman, to notice some objections that have been made to our course ever since Mr. Garrison began his career, and which have been lately urged again. I know these objections have been made a thousand times, that they have been often answered. But there are times when justice to the slave will not allow us to be silent. There are many

In *Speeches, Lectures, and Letters,* by Wendell Phillips (Boston, 1863), pp. 98–100, 105–111, 126–27, 151–53.

in this country who have had their attention turned, recently, to the antislavery cause. They are asking, "Which is the best and most efficient method of helping it?" Engaged ourselves in an effort for the slave, which time has tested and success hitherto approved, we are very properly desirous that they should join us in our labors, and pour into this channel the full tide of their new zeal and great resources. Long experience gives us a right to advise. They are our spiritual children.

The charges to which I refer are these: that, in dealing with slaveholders and their apologists, we indulge in fierce denunciations, instead of appealing to their reason and common sense by plain statements and fair argument; that we might have won the sympathies and support of the nation if we would have submitted to argue this question with a manly patience; but, instead of this, we have outraged the feelings of the community by attacks, unjust and unnecessarily severe, on its most valued institutions, and gratified our spleen by indiscriminate abuse of leading men who were often honest in their intentions, however mistaken in their views; that we have utterly neglected the ample means that lay around us to convert the nation, submitted to no discipline, formed no plan, been guided by no foresight, but hurried on in childish, reckless, blind, and hot-headed zeal, bigots in the narrowness of our views, and fanatics in our blind fury of invective and malignant judgment of other men's motives. I reject with scorn all these implications that *our* judgments are uncharitable, that *we* are lacking in patience, that *we* have any other dependence than on the simple truth, spoken with Christian frankness, yet with Christian love.

I claim, before you who know the true state of the case, I claim for the antislavery movement with which this society is identified, that, looking back over its whole course, and considering the men connected with it in the mass, it has been marked by sound judgment, unerring foresight, the most sagacious adaptation of means to ends, the strictest self-discipline, the most thorough research, and an amount of patient and manly argument addressed to the conscience and intellect of the nation, such as no other cause of the kind, in England or this country, has ever offered.

We must plead guilty, if there be guilt in not knowing how to separate the sin from the sinner. With all the fondness for abstractions attributed to us, we are not yet capable of that. We are fighting a momentous battle at desperate odds—one against a thousand. Every weapon that ability or ignorance, wit, wealth, prejudice, or fashion can commond, is pointed against us. The guns are shotted to their lips. The arrows are poisoned. Fighting against such an array, we cannot afford to confine ourselves to any one weapon. The cause is not ours, so that we might, rightfully, postpone or put in peril the victory by moderating our demands, stifling our convictions, or filing down our rebukes, to gratify any sickly taste of our own, or to spare the delicate nerves of our neighbor. Our clients are three millions of Christian slaves, standing dumb suppliants at the threshold of the Christian world. They have no voice but ours to utter their complaints, or to demand justice. The press, the pulpit, the wealth, the literature, the prejudices, the political arrangements, the present self-interest of the country are all against us. God has given us no weapon but the truth, faithfully uttered, and addressed, with the old prophets' directness, to the conscience of the individual sinner. The elements which control public opinion and mold the masses are against us. We can but pick off here and there a man from the triumphant majority. We have facts for those who think, arguments for those who reason; but he who cannot be reasoned out of his prejudices must be laughed out of them; he who cannot be argued out of his selfishness must be shamed out of it by the mirror of his hateful self held up relentlessly before his eyes. We live in a land where every man makes broad his phylactery, inscribing thereon, "All men are created equal," "God hath made of one blood all nations of men." It seems to us that in such a land there must be, on this question of slavery, sluggards to be awakened, as well as doubters to be convinced.

What is the denunciation with which we are charged? It is endeavoring, in our faltering human speech, to declare the enormity of the sin of making merchandise of men, of separating husband and wife, taking the infant from its mother, and selling the daughter to prostitution, of a professedly Christian nation denying, by statute, the Bible to every sixth man and woman of its population, and making it illegal for "two or three" to meet together, except a white man be present! What is this harsh criticism of motives with which we are charged? It is simply holding the intelligent and deliberate actor responsible for the character and consequences of his acts. Is there anything inherently wrong in such denunciation or such criticism? All that we ask the world and thoughtful men to note are the principles and deeds on which the American pulpit and American public men plume themselves.

The South is one great brothel, where half a million of women are flogged to prostitution or, worse still, are degraded to believe it honorable. The public squares of half our great cities echo to the wail of families torn asunder at the auction block; no one of our fair rivers that has not closed over the Negro seeking in death a refuge from a life too wretched to bear; thousands of fugitives skulk along our highways, afraid to tell their names, and trembling at the sight of a human being; free men are kidnapped in our streets, to be plunged into that hell of slavery; and now and then one, as if by miracle, after long years, returns to make men aghast with his tale. The press says, "It is all right"; and the pulpit cries, "Amen." They print the Bible in every tongue in which man utters his prayers; and get the money to do so by agreeing never to give the book, in the language our mothers taught us, to any Negro, free or bond, south of Mason and Dixon's line. The press says, "It is all right"; and the pulpit cries, "Amen."

Prove to me now that harsh rebuke, indignant denunciation, scathing sarcasm, and pitiless ridicule are wholly and always unjustifiable.

Our aim is to alter public opinion. Did we live in a market, our talk should be of dollars and cents, and we would seek to prove only that slavery was an unprofitable investment. Were the nation one great, pure church, we would sit down and reason of "righteousness, temperance, and judgment to come." Had slavery fortified itself in a college, we would load our cannons with cold facts, and wing our arrows with arguments. But we happen to live in the world—the world made up of thought and impulse, of self-conceit and self-interest, of weak men and wicked. To conquer, we must reach all. Our object is not to make every man a Christian or a philosopher, but to induce everyone to aid in the abolition of slavery. To change public opinion, we use the very tools by which it was formed. That is, all such an honest man may touch.

But there are some persons about us who pretend that the anti-slavery movement has been hitherto mere fanaticism, its only weapon angry abuse. My claim is this: that neither the charity of the most timid of sects, the sagacity of our wisest converts, nor the culture of the ripest scholars, though all have been aided by our twenty years' experience, has yet struck out any new method of reaching the public mind, or originated any new argument or train of thought or discovered any new fact bearing on the question.

We are charged with lacking foresight, and said to exaggerate. This charge of exaggeration brings to my mind a fact I mentioned, last month. The theaters in many of our large cities bring out, night after night, all the radical doctrines and all the startling scenes of "Uncle Tom." They preach immediate emancipation, and slaves shoot their hunters to loud applause. Two years ago, sitting in this hall, I was myself somewhat startled by the assertion of my friend Mr. Pillsbury, that the theaters would receive the gospel of antislavery truth earlier than the churches. A hiss went up from the galleries, and many in the audience were shocked by the remark. I asked myself whether I could endorse such a statement, and felt that I could not. I could not believe it to be true. Only two years have passed, and what was then deemed rant and fanaticism, by seven out of ten who heard it, has proved true. The theater, bowing to its audience, has preached immediate emancipation, and given us the whole of "Uncle Tom"; while the pulpit is either silent or hostile, and in the columns of the theological papers the work is subjected to criticism, to reproach, and its author to severe rebuke.

Every thoughtful and unprejudiced mind must see that such an evil as slavery will yield only to the most radical treatment. If you consider the work we have to do, you will not think us needlessly aggressive, or that we dig down unnecessarily deep in laying the foundations of our enterprise. A money power of two thousand millions of dollars, as the prices of slaves now range, held by a small body of able and desperate men; that body raised into a political aristocracy by special constitutional provisions; cotton, the product of slave labor, forming the basis of our whole foreign commerce, and the commercial class thus subsidized; the press bought up; the pulpit reduced to vassalage; the heart of the common people chilled by a bitter prejudice against the black race; our leading men bribed, by ambition, either to silence or open hostility—in such a land, on what shall an abolitionist rely? On a few cold prayers, mere lip service, and never from the heart? On a church resolution, hidden often in its records, and meant only as a decent cover for servility in daily practice? On political parties, with their superficial influence at best, and seeking ordinarily only to use existing prejudices to the best advantage? Slavery has deeper root here than any aristocratic institution has in Europe. How shall the stream rise above its fountain? Where shall our church organizations or parties get strength to attack their great parent and molder, the Slave Power? Mechanics say nothing but an earthquake, strong enough to move all Egypt, can bring down the pyramids.

Experience has confirmed these views. The abolitionists who have acted on them have a "short method" with all unbelievers. They have but to point to their own success, in contrast with every other man's failure. To waken the nation to its real state, and chain it to the consideration of this one duty, is half the work. So much we have done. Slavery has been made the question of this generation. To startle the South to madness, so that every step she takes, in her blindness, is one step more toward ruin, is much. This we have done. Witness Texas and the Fugitive Slave Law. To have elaborated for the nation the only plan of redemption, pointed out the only exodus from this "sea of troubles," is much. This we claim to have done in our motto of *Immediate, Unconditional Emancipation on the Soil.* The closer any statesmanlike mind looks into the question, the more favor our plan finds with it. The Christian asks fairly of the infidel, "If this religion be not from God, how do you explain its triumph, and the history of the first three centuries?" Our question is similar. If our agitation has not been wisely planned and conducted, explain for us the history of the last twenty years! Experience is a safe light to walk by, and he is not a rash man who expects success in future from the same means which have secured it in times past.

II

The work of the Grimké sisters Angelina and Sarah, on behalf of abolitionism demonstrates many of the favorite tactics of these organizations. Trained by Theodore Weld (who later became Angelina's husband), the sisters went out in the 1830s to address and organize women's auxiliaries. They soon grew famous, stimulating controversy not only about slavery but also about women's rights. The pamphlet below, composed by Angelina Grimké upon her conversion to abolitionism, was addressed specifically to the women of the South. It presents the ideas and the techniques that the sisters used in their efforts to influence public opinion.

APPEAL TO THE CHRISTIAN WOMEN OF THE SOUTH, 1836

ANGELINA GRIMKÉ

Respected Friends,

It is because I feel a deep and tender interest in your present and eternal welfare that I am willing thus publicly to address you. Some

In *The Anti-Slavery Examiner*, I (1836): 1–3, 16–20, 23–24, 26, 28–30, 32–33, 35–36.

of you have loved me as a relative, and some have felt bound to me in Christian sympathy, and gospel fellowship; and even when compelled by a strong sense of duty, to break those outward bonds of union which bound us together as members of the same community, you were generous enough to give me credit, for sincerity as a Christian, though you believed I had been most strangely deceived. I thanked you then for your kindness, and I ask you *now*, for the sake of former confidence, and former friendship, to read the following pages in the spirit of calm investigation and fervent prayer. I have felt for you at this time, when unwelcome light is pouring in upon the world on the subject of slavery, light which even Christians would exclude, if they could, from our country, or at any rate from the southern portion of it, I know that even professors of His name would, if they could, build a wall of adamant around the Southern states whose top might reach unto heaven, in order to shut out the light. But believe me, when I tell you, their attempts will be as utterly fruitless as were the efforts of the builders of Babel; and why? Because moral, like natural light, is so extremely subtle in its nature as to overleap all human barriers. All the excuses and palliations of this system must inevitably be swept away, just as other "refuges of lies" have been, by the irresistible torrent of a rectified public opinion. All that sophistry of argument which has been employed to prove that although it is sinful to send to Africa to procure men and women as slaves, who have never been in slavery, that still is not sinful to keep those in bondage who have come down by inheritance, will be utterly overthrown. We must come back to the good old doctrine of our forefathers who declared to the world, "this self evident truth that *all* men are created equal, and that they have certain *inalienable* rights among which are life, *liberty,* and the pursuit of happiness."

But after all, it may be said, our fathers were certainly mistaken, for the Bible sanctions slavery, and that is the highest authority. Now the Bible is my ultimate appeal in all matters of faith and practice, and it is to *this test* I am anxious to bring the subject at issue between us. Let us then begin with Adam and examine the charter of privileges which was given to him. "Have dominion over the fish of the sea, and over the fowl of the air, and over every living thing that moveth upon the earth." In this charter, although the different kinds of *irrational* beings are so particularly enumerated, and supreme dominion over *all of them* is granted, yet *man* is *never* vested with this dominion *over his fellow-man;* he was never told that any of the human species were put *under his feet. Man* then, I assert *never* was put *under the feet of man,* by that first charter of human rights which was given by God.

But perhaps you will be ready to query, why appeal to *women* on this subject? *We* do not make the laws which perpetuate slavery. *No* legislative power is vested in *us; we* can do nothing to overthrow the system, even if we wished to do so. To this I reply, I know you do not make the laws, but I also know that *you are the wives and mothers, the sisters and daughters of those who do;* and if you really suppose *you* can do nothing to overthrow slavery, you are greatly mistaken. You can do much in every way: four things I will name. 1. You can read on this subject. 2. You can pray over this subject. 3. You can speak on this subject. 4. You can *act* on this subject. I have not placed reading before praying because I regard it more important, but because, in order to pray aright, we must understand what we are praying for; it is only then we can "pray with the understanding and the spirit also."

1. Read then on the subject of slavery. Search the Scriptures daily, whether the things I have told you are true. Other books and papers might be a great help to you in this investigation, but they are not necessary, and it is hardly probable that your committees of vigilance will allow you to have any other.

In the great mob in Boston, last autumn, when the books and papers of the Anti-Slavery Society were thrown out of the windows of their office, one individual laid hold of the Bible and was about tossing it out to the ground, when another reminded him that it was the Bible he had in his hand. "O! 'tis all one," he replied, and out went the sacred volume, along with the rest. We thank him for the acknowledgment.

Read the *Bible* then, it contains the words of Jesus, and they are spirit and life. Judge for yourselves whether *he sanctioned* such a system of oppression and crime.

2. Pray over this subject. Pray to your Father, who seeth in secret, that He would open your eyes to see whether slavery is *sinful*, and if it is, that He would enable you to bear a faithful, open, and unshrinking testimony against it, and to do whatsoever your hands find to do, leaving the consequences entirely to Him. Pray also for the poor slave, that he may be kept patient and submissive under his hard lot, until God is pleased to open the door of freedom to him without violence or bloodshed. Pray too for the master that his heart may be softened.

3. Speak on this subject. It is through the tongue, the pen, and the press that truth is principally propagated. Speak then to your relatives, your friends, your acquaintances on the subject of slavery; be not afraid if you are conscientiously convinced it is *sinful*, to say so openly, but calmly, and to let your sentiments be known. If you are served by the slaves of others, try to ameliorate their condition as much as possible; never aggravate their faults, and thus add fuel to the fire of anger already kindled, in a master and mistress's bosom; remember their extreme ignorance, and consider them as your heavenly Father does the *less* culpable on this account, even when they do wrong things. Discountenance *all* cruelty to them, all starvation, all corporal chastisement; these may brutalize and *break* their spirits, but will never bend them to willing, cheerful obedience. If possible, see that they are comfortably and *seasonably* fed, whether in the house or the field; it is unreasonable and cruel to expect slaves to wait for their breakfast until eleven o'clock, when they rise at five or six. Do all you can to induce their owners to clothe them well, and to allow them many little indulgences which would contribute to their comfort. Above all, try to persuade your husband, father, brothers, and sons that *slavery is a crime against God and man*, and that it is a great sin to keep *human beings* in such abject ignorance; to deny them the privilege of learning to read and write.

4. Act on this subject. Some of you *own* slaves yourselves. If you believe slavery is *sinful*, set them at liberty. If they wish to remain with

you, pay them wages, if not let them leave you. Should they remain
teach them, and have them taught the common branches of an English
education.

But some of you will say, we can neither free our slaves nor teach
them to read, for the laws of our state forbid it. Be not surprised when
I say such wicked laws *ought to be no barrier* in the way of your duty,
and I appeal to the Bible to prove this position. What was the conduct
of Shiphrah and Pauh, when the king of Egypt issued his cruel mandate,
with regard to the Hebrew children? *"They* feared *God,* and did *not* as
the King of Egypt commanded them, but saved the men children alive."
Did these *women* do right in disobeying that monarch?

What was the conduct of Daniel, when Darius made a firm decree
that no one should ask a petition of any man or God for thirty days?
Did the prophet cease to pray? No!

Did Daniel do right thus to *break* the law of his king? Let his
wonderful deliverance out of the mouths of the lions answer.

But some of you may say, if we do free our slaves, they will be
taken up and sold, therefore there will be no use in doing it. Peter and
John might just as well have said, we will not preach the gospel, for
if we do, we shall be taken up and put in prison, therefore there will be
no use in our preaching. *Consequences,* my friends, belong no more to
you, than they did to these apostles. Duty is ours and events are God's.
If you think slavery is sinful, all *you* have to do is to set your slaves at
liberty, do all you can to protect them, and in humble faith and fervent
prayer, commend them to your common Father.

I know that this doctrine of obeying *God,* rather than man, will be
considered as dangerous, and heretical by many, but I am not afraid
openly to avow it, because it is the doctrine of the Bible; but I would
not be understood to advocate resistance to any law however oppressive,
if, in obeying it, I was not obliged to commit *sin.* If for instance, there
was a law which imposed imprisonment or a fine upon me if I manu-
mitted a slave, I would on no account resist that law, I would set the
slave free, and then go to prison or pay the fine. If a law commands
me to *sin I will break it;* if it calls me to *suffer,* I will let it take its course
unresistingly. The doctrine of blind obedience and unqualified submission to *any human* power, whether civil or ecclesiastical, is the
doctrine of despotism, and ought to have no place among republicans
and Christians.

But you will perhaps say, such a course of conduct would inevitably expose us to great suffering. Yes! my Christian friends, I believe
it would, but this will *not* excuse you or anyone else for the neglect of
duty. If prophets and apostles, martyrs and reformers had not been
willing to suffer for the truth's sake, where would the world have been
now? If they had said, we cannot speak the truth, we cannot do what
we believe is right, because the *laws of our country or public opinion are
against us,* where would our holy religion have been now?

The Ladies' Anti-Slavery Society of Boston was called last fall to a
severe trial of their faith and constancy. They were mobbed by "the
gentlemen of property and standing," in that city at their anniversary
meeting, and their lives were jeopardized by an infuriated crowd; but
their conduct on that occasion did credit to our sex, and affords a full

assurance that they will *never* abandon the cause of the slave. The pamphlet, "Right and Wrong in Boston," issued by them in which a particular account is given of that "mob of broadcloth in broad day," does equal credit to the head and the heart of her who wrote it. I wish my Southern sisters could read it; they would then understand that the women of the North have engaged in this work from a sense of *religious duty,* and that nothing will ever induce them to take their hands from it until it is fully accomplished. Northern women may labor to produce a correct public opinion at the North, but if Southern women sit down in listless indifference and criminal idleness, public opinion cannot be rectified and purified at the South. It is manifest to every reflecting mind that slavery must be abolished; the era in which we live, and the light which is overspreading the whole world on this subject, clearly show that the time cannot be distant when it will be done. Now there are only two ways in which it can be effective, by moral power or physical force, and it is for *you* to choose which of these you prefer. Slavery always has and always will produce insurrections whenever it exists, because it is a violation of the natural order of things, and no human power can much longer perpetuate it. The opposers of abolitionists fully believe this; one of them remarked to me not long since, there is no doubt there will be a most terrible overturning at the South in a few years, such cruelty and wrong must be visited with divine vengeance soon. Abolitionists believe, too, that this must inevitably be the case if you do not repent, and they are not willing to leave you to perish without entreating you to save yourselves from destruction; well may they say with the apostle, "am I then your enemy because I tell you the truth," and warn you to flee from impending judgments.

The *women of the South can overthrow* this horrible system of oppression and cruelty, licentiousness and wrong. Such appeals to your legislatures would be irresistible, for there is something in the heart of man which *will bend under moral suasion.* There is a swift witness for truth in his bosom, which *will respond to truth* when it is uttered with calmness and dignity. If you could obtain but six signatures to such a petition in only one state, I would say, send up that petition, and be not in the least discouraged by the scoffs and jeers of the heartless, or the resolution of the house to lay it on the table. It will be a great thing if the subject can be introduced into your legislatures in any way, even by *women,* and *they* will be the most likely to introduce it there in the best possible manner, as a matter of *morals* and *religion,* not of expediency or politics.

Great fault has been found with the prints which have been employed to expose slavery at the North, but my friends, how could this be done so effectually in any other way? Until the pictures of the slave's sufferings were drawn and held up to public gaze, no Northerner had any idea of the cruelty of the system, it never entered their minds thas such abominations could exist in Christian, republican America; they never suspected that many of the *gentlemen* and *ladies* who came from the South to spend the summer months in traveling among them, were petty tyrants at home. To such hidden mourners the formation of Anti-Slavery Societies was as life from the dead, the first beams of hope which gleamed through the dark clouds of despondency

and grief. Prints were made use of to effect the abolition of the In-
quisition in Spain, and Clarkson employed them when he was laboring
to break up the slave trade, and English abolitionists used them just as
we are now doing. They are powerful appeals and have invariably done
the work they were designed to do, and we cannot consent to abandon
the use of these until the *realities* no longer exist.

Sisters in Christ, I have done. As a Southerner, I have felt it was
my duty to address you. I have endeavored to set before you the ex-
ceeding sinfulness of slavery, and to point you to the example of those
noble women who have been raised up in the church to effect great
revolutions, and to suffer for the truth's sake. I have appealed to your
sympathies as women, to your sense of duty as *Christian women.* I have
attempted to vindicate the abolitionists, to prove the entire safety of
immediate emancipation, and to plead the cause of the poor and oppressed. I have done—I have sowed the seeds of truth, but I well know
"*God only* can give the increase."

Farewell—Count me not your "enemy because I have told you the
truth," but believe me in unfeigned affection,

Your sympathizing Friend,
Angelina E. Grimké

Published by the American Anti-Slavery Society, corner of Spruce and Nassau
Streets. Price 6¼ cents single. 62½ cents per dozen. $4 per hundred.—Please
Read and Circulate—

III

*The abolitionist societies produced capsule guides for would-be anti-
slavery proponents. Anyone reading this fact sheet, they hoped,
should be able to spread the message effectively, persuade his own
audiences, and effectively rebut opponents. The manual reprinted
here has a double significance for the reader today. It offers both
insights into the content of the antislavery message and clarifies
the ways by which proponents tried to extend its appeal.*

ANTISLAVERY MANUAL, 1837

LAROY SUNDERLAND

Immediate Emancipation

We mean by this,

1. That the slave owner, so far as he is personally concerned,
should *cease immediately* to hold or to use human beings as his *property.*

In *Anti-Slavery Manual Containing a Collection of Facts and Arguments on
American Slavery,* by LaRoy Sunderland (New York, 1837), pp. 79, 100–101,
118–20, 129–33.

And is there one slave owner in the nation who cannot do this? If there be one, then he must be set down as *non compos mentis,* or an idiot.

2. That the master, so far as he is personally concerned, should immediately offer to employ those whom he has held as his property, as free hired laborers; he should not turn them loose upon society, uncared for and unprotected, but he should treat them as *men,* and give them the liberty of choice, whether to remain in his employ at fair wages, or not.

3. So far as the state is concerned, it should annihilate the right of man to hold man as property; and all who are now slaves should be *immediately brought under the protection and restraint of suitable and impartial laws.* But the want of action on the part of any state government should not, and need not, hinder anyone from doing his duty as above described.

Reasons for Discussing the Subject of Slavery at the North

1. Because it is *American* slavery.
2. Because the North contributes its share toward its support.

Its money in building prisons in the District of Columbia, where slaves are kept.

Its representatives and senators in Congress who virtually vote for its continuance.

Its portion of men, Christians and ministers of the gospel, who go to the South and become slaveholders.

3. We are obligated by the United States' laws to deliver up slaves who escape to us for refuge.

4. Because Northern blood is liable to be spilt in case of insurrection at the South.

5. Because the slaveholding principle exists at the North, as really as at the South. The continuance of the system is justified here by Christians and ministers, on the same ground on which it is justified there, by the slaveholders themselves.

6. We discuss this subject at the North, because as long as slavery exists in this nation our own liberties are insecure. See the case of Dr. Crandall, a citizen of New York, who was incarcerated in Washington jail, for eight months, merely on suspicion of his being an abolitionist. Other citizens from the North have, by simply venturing to the South, lost both their liberty and their lives.

7. Because it is our right and privilege to discuss this question. The United States and the state in which we live have guaranteed to us the freedom of speech, and of the press.

8. Because God has commanded his servants to open their mouths for such as cannot plead for themselves.

9. Because to neglect this subject would endanger the salvation of souls, for whom Christ died.

10. Because slavery is a reproach to the nation which every lover of his country should be anxious to do away.

11. Because we should do, as we would be done by.

12. Because, without discussion, slavery will never be abolished, and it must be discussed here or nowhere, in the nation.

Abolitionists

Their Principles

1. We hold that Congress has no right to abolish slavery in the Southern states.

2. We hold that slavery can only be lawfully abolished by the legislatures of the several states in which it prevails, and that the exercise of any other than moral influence to induce such abolition is unconstitutional.

3. We believe that Congress has the same right to abolish slavery in the District of Columbia, that the state governments have within their respective jurisdictions, and that it is their duty to efface so foul a blot from the national escutcheon.

4. We believe that American citizens have the right to express and publish their opinions of the constitutions, laws, and institutions of any and every state and nation under heaven; and we mean never to surrender the liberty of speech, of the press, or of conscience.

5. We have uniformly deprecated all forcible attempts on the part of the slaves to recover their liberty. And were it in our power to address them, we would exhort them to observe a quiet and peaceful demeanor, and would assure them that no insurrectionary movement on their part would receive from us the slightest aid or countenance.

6. We would deplore any servile insurrection, both on account of the calamities which would attend it, and on account of the occasion which it might furnish of increased severity and oppression.

7. We are charged with sending incendiary publications to the South. If by the term *incendiary* is meant publications containing arguments and facts to prove slavery to be a moral and political evil, and that duty and policy require its immediate abolition, the charge is true. But if this term is used to imply publications encouraging insurrection, and designed to excite the slaves to break their fetters, the charge is utterly and unequivocally false.

8. We are accused of sending our publications to the slaves, and it is asserted that their tendency is to excite insurrections. Both the charges are false. These publications are not intended for the slaves, and were they able to read them, they would find in them no encouragement to insurrection.

9. We are accused of employing agents in the slave states to distribute our publications. We have never had one such agent. We have sent no *packages* of our papers to any person in those states for distribution, except to five respectable resident citizens, at their own request. But we have sent, by mail, single papers addressed to public officers, editors of newspapers, clergymen and others.

10. We believe slavery to be sinful, injurious to this and every other country in which it prevails; we believe immediate emancipation to be the duty of every slaveholder, and that the immediate abolition of slavery, by those who have the right to abolish it, would be safe and wise.

11. We believe that the education of the poor is required by duty, and by a regard for the permanency of our republican institutions. There are thousands and tens of thousands of our fellow-citizens, even in the free states, sunk in abject poverty, and who on account of their complexion, are virtually *kept* in ignorance, and whose instruction in certain cases is actually prohibited by law! We are anxious to protect the rights and to promote the virtue and happiness of the colored portion of our population, and on this account we have been charged with a design to encourage intermarriage between the whites and blacks. This charge has been repeatedly, and is again, denied, while we repeat that the tendency of our sentiments is to put an end to the criminal amalgamation that prevails wherever slavery exists.

12. We are accused of acts that tend to a dissolution of the Union, and even of wishing to dissolve it. We have never "calculated the value of the Union," because we believe it to be inestimable; and that the abolition of slavery will remove the chief danger of its dissolution; and one of the many reasons why we cherish and will endeavor to preserve the Constitution is that it restrains Congress from making any law abridging the freedom of speech or of the press.

Such, fellow-citizens, are our principles. Are they unworthy of republicans and of Christians?

Objections Answered

1. "The Bible recognizes, and of course in some circumstances, justifies slavery."

One sentence is sufficient to dispose of this argument. *Slaveholders refuse the Bible to their slaves.* Strange that they should fear to add *moral chains* to the *physical!*

2. "Abolitionists are too sweeping in their denunciations. Slavery is not always, as they affirm, a *sin*, because slaves are often treated with kindness."

So are horses. Is it right to put a man to the place of a horse, provided that horse is a beloved and favorite one? And would you judge it kind treatment, if you were, under any circumstances, robbed of your liberty, and bought and sold like a beast?

3. "The slaves are unfit for freedom."

Are they all unfit? If not, then you must be an immediate abolitionist in regard to those who are fit. If they are, then how can any of them ever be made fit, for some, nay, many of them, have already enjoyed long enough all the possible influences which can be supposed to fit men for freedom while in a state of slavery.

4. "Slaves are paid wages, inasmuch as they receive from their masters food and clothing."

"It takes two to make a bargain." You might as well call the grease a man puts on his cart wheels the wages of the ox of the cart, as to call the food and clothing of the slave his wages.

5. "Many slaves have religious privileges. Their masters labor for the salvation of their souls."

So long as the slaves are kept in ignorance of the Bible, and of their own rights as *men*, and consequently of their duties to God and man; and so long as their persons and purity are not protected either by public opinion or by the laws, their piety must be of a doubtful character.

6. "Slaveholders know that slavery is a curse, and are opposed to it, but cannot get rid of it."

If they know it to be a curse, they seem not to believe that their slaves are curses, or, if they do, they are very loth to part with curses.

IV

In 1840, two brothers, Arthur and Lewis Tappan, having made fortunes as New York merchants, turned their energies to the antislavery campaign. Determined to bring as much organizational efficiency to the spreading of the antislavery message as to selling goods, they founded the American and Foreign Antislavery Society. Each year they issued an annual report to their members, describing the many activities that the society had carried out. It was, as the report of 1849 reprinted below demonstrates, an impressive list of activities, one indicator of the modernity of their techniques.

REPORT OF THE AMERICAN AND FOREIGN ANTISLAVERY SOCIETY, 1849

The past year has been distinguished for the increasing prevalence of antislavery sentiments, and especially for attention to the political aspects of the cause. Venal politicians have been rebuked, arrested in their career of iniquity, and taught a lesson that will never, it is believed, be forgotten. The people have been aroused, and have evinced a determination if not to put an end to slavery, to prevent its extension on this continent. At the same time, the moral and religious aspects of the cause have not been overlooked. Many friends of the Redeemer, heretofore repelled by the erroneous doctrines of persons advocating the antislavery cause, have been led to see that it is the cause of God and humanity, and that all who profess to be the friends of the slave are not disunionists, and do not speak the truth in unrighteousness.

It is now acknowledged, even by the opponents of abolitionists, that the abolition of American slavery is the great question of the age; and men who have hitherto remained passive upon the subject now feel that the encroachments of the slavocracy are becoming intolerable; that the point where inactive forbearance ceases to be a virtue is at hand; that the grasping spirit of slavery must be arrested, and the foul system overthrown and swept away forever.

The part taken by the Executive Committee of this Society the past year has been cautious, watchful, and prudent. With limited means, in the midst of political excitement, aware of the imprudence of those who call themselves, par excellence, the friends of the slave, they have not been eager to startle the community by new projects, or arouse them by spasmodic efforts; they have contented themselves by using the resources committed to them with economy, in diffusing truth with firmness and perseverance, and in aggressive movements both in the free and slave states, as opportunities and openings occurred. "Make haste slowly" has been their maxim, in the peculiar condition of the country and of the antislavery cause, in convincing of error and sin—in effecting reformation—leaving to others the odious task of vituperation, projects of disunion, efforts to rend the churches, destroy the constitution, and break down the government of their country. The Committee have been desirous of pursuing a course that would commend the cause to the approbation, and enlist the cooperation, of good men of all religious denominations and political parties. To accomplish this great object they have not deemed it necessary or wise to adulterate truth, to possess or exhibit a compromising spirit. Associates thus gained are not worth the pains taken to obtain their adhesion. The course pursued the past year will be continued, but the Committee hope with more abundant means at command, with more ability in their use, and with greater accessions to their members.

Some progress has been made in the plan, announced in the last

In *Annual Report for 1849*, American and Foreign Antislavery Society (New York, 1849), pp. 20–29.

Annual Report, of publishing the slave laws of the several states and territories. The laws of the District of Columbia relating to slaves and free people of color, under the title of the *Black Code of the District of Columbia,* have been published, prepared by William G. Snethen, Esq., counselor at law, Washington City, who has also in readiness for publication laws of similar character of the State of Maryland, to be followed by the slave laws of other states, and published whenever sufficient funds shall have been contributed for the object. A copy of the *Black Code* was sent to each member of Congress, and to each of the judges of the Supreme Court of the United States. Aid has been furnished Rev. John G. Fee, of Kentucky, in the publication of his work entitled "An Antislavery Manual," and in giving it an extensive circulation in that state and elsewhere.

The Committee published the past year, as usual, a large edition of the *Liberty Almanac.* In it they gave a succinct history of the formation of this Society, vindicated its founders in reference to the aspersions frequently heaped upon them by disappointed and selfish individuals and cabals from whom they had felt compelled to separate, and proved that the original object of the Society—the entire extinction of slavery and the slave trade, and the equal security, protection, and improvement of the people of color—had been pursued to the extent of the means furnished. This publication contained also valuable reminiscences respecting the restriction of slavery; discussions on the Wilmot Proviso and the Oregon Bill; the compromises of the Constitution; the slave power politically and morally considered—together with a mass of intelligence, antislavery, and miscellaneous. No better way can be devised, it is thought, for the dissemination of valuable matter relating to the great object of our association than by the cheap and popular method referred to.

A new and large edition of the Society's *Address to Non-Slaveholders of the United States* has been published, and a portion of it, with considerable additions, is in the press for distribution in New Mexico and California. Applications have been received and responded to, from different slave states, for books and pamphlets of an antislavery character; and the Committee are advised that native citizens of such states are circulating essays showing the safety and advantages of emancipation, with much effect; and they know of no way in which the friends of the cause can better aid the progress of antislavery principles than by liberal appropriations for such objects.

Applications have been received from several individuals for aid in sustaining newspapers in slave states and territories that will advocate, though not exclusively, the emancipation of slaves, or the prohibition of slavery; and the Committee are in possession of facts with regard to the prevalence of antislavery feeling and action in slave states, produced by Northern agitation, that are highly encouraging.

Under the advice of the Committee, and with funds furnished by its members and others, suits or other legal processes have been commenced for the liberation of persons claiming their liberty under the laws of the states in which they have been held in bondage. In one of these cases, where slaves, emancipated by the will of a slaveholder in Maryland, were kept in slavery nearly fourteen years by the unprincipled executor, a decree has been obtained, after an expensive and protracted litigation in the various courts, restoring fifteen persons to liberty. This result was achieved by the joint cooperation and at the mutual expense of members of this Committee and friends of justice in Maryland.

Correspondence has been maintained with other societies, and with individual friends of emancipation in this and other countries, and intelligence has been reciprocated. Publications have been received from various quarters.

Letters were recently addressed by the Corresponding Secretary to a considerable number of influential and intelligent abolitionists in different states, asking their opinion and advice with reference to the best course to be taken by the Society in the present position of the antislavery cause in this country. Great unanimity on the following sentiments was expressed in the replies: that the present is a favorable time to awaken the public conscience with regard to the moral and religious aspects of the cause; that an organization, based upon an earnest abhorrence of the sinfulness of slavery, and bringing its influence to bear upon the social, civil, and ecclesiastical defenses of the system, is greatly needed; a hope that judicious, prayerful, and persevering action may soon bring about an application of antislavery principles to Bible, tract, missionary, and Sunday-school operations, and induce all the organizations in these departments of benevolence to give the slave population an importance proportioned to their hard and bitter necessities.

V

For all their fervor, the abolitionists relied exclusively upon verbal persuasion to end slavery. Their critics, on the other hand, had frequent recourse to violence. In the 1830s, over one hundred incidents of violence were directed at the abolitionists, and all of these were in the North, not the South. Why did citizens, often led by business leaders in the community, react so violently to the abolitionist message? Why were the forces of law and order so ineffective in containing them? These questions emerge vividly in the incidents that surround the first murder of an abolitionist, the death of Elijah Lovejoy in Alton, Illinois, on November 3, 1837. Lovejoy was a Presbyterian minister, who at the age of thirty-one joined the abolitionist struggle. He published an antislavery newspaper in St. Louis, but in 1836, after public opposition to his writings there grew too great, he moved to Alton. Again he edited an abolitionist paper, but this time he was determined to ride out criticism. When in 1836 a mob destroyed his press, he ordered a second; when the second was smashed, he ordered a third; and when the third went the way of its predecessors, a fourth. The document below describes what happened when a fourth press arrived.

NARRATIVES OF RIOTS AT ALTON, 1838

EDWARD   BEECHER

It often happens that events, in themselves of no great importance, are invested with unusual interest in consequence of their connection with principles of universal application or with momentous results. Of this kind are the events which preceded and led to the death of the Rev. Elijah P. Lovejoy: the first martyr in America to the great principles of the freedom of speech and of the press.

Of these events I propose in the following pages to give an account. The facts are of a nature sufficiently astounding in any age or at any time: the destruction of four printing presses in succession; the personal abuse of the editor, from time to time by repeated mobs; and his final and premeditated murder!

Still more astounding are they when we consider the country in which they occurred. Had it been in revolutionary France; or in England, agitated by the consequent convulsion of the nations; there had been less cause for surprise. But it was not. It was in America—the land of free discussion and equal rights.

Still more are we amazed when we consider the subjects, the discussion of which was thus forcibly arrested. Had it been an effort to debauch and pollute the public mind by obscenity and atheism; or by injurious and disorganizing schemes; the rise of public indignation had at least found a cause; though the friends of truth and righteousness are not the men who employ mobs as their chosen instruments of persuasion. But it was none of these. It was solely the advocacy of the principles of freedom and equal rights.

Were these principles of recent origin, and the opinions of a sect, it might have caused less surprise. But they are the sacred legacy of ages—the doctrines of our nation's birth; of natural justice; and of God.

All these things are astonishing: but there is one fact that may justly excite amazement still more deep and overwhelming; the opinions and feelings elicited by events like these. Had an earthquake of indignation convulsed the land; had the united voices of every individual of every party rebuked and remedied the wrong; all had been well. But during the progress of the scenes there have been found those in reputation as wise and good who have been unsparing in their censure on the sufferers, and stimulated the evildoers by sympathy or feeble rebuke. And after the final and dreadful catastrophe, only a faint tribute has been given by them to certain abstract principles of free inquiry as generally good; and a decent regret for their violation has been expressed. But the full tide of indignation has been reserved for the audacious man who dared to speak and act as a freeman; and though lawlessly inflicted, his penalty has been declared to be deserved.

What are we to say of facts like these? They at least open a deep chapter in human nature, and in the condition of our country. They are

In *Narratives of Riots at Alton* (New York, 1838). Reprint edition, (New York, 1965), pp. 3–4, 60–66.

the result of principles neither superficial nor accidental. They penetrate to the very vitals of society and indicate a crisis in our national life.

That as a nation we are radically unsound and lost, they do not to my mind indicate. But that there are in the body politic causes of tremendous power tending to that result, they do evince. And the question on which all turns is now before us as a nation; and on its decision our life or death depends. Have we coolness of thought left sufficient to discern them, and energy of moral feeling enough to react?

As these events are of a nature to rouse and demand public attention, I hope that an impartial narration of them will be candidly and thoughtfully read; and as I have been an actor in the leading events from the beginning—an eyewitness of most that I describe—I feel that no one who speaks only from hearsay can have so full a knowledge of all the causes of these events as I; and as perhaps no one has been more severely censured by enemies, or regarded in greater error by some sincere and valued friends, I feel that not only a regard to truth and the general good, but decent regard to the opinions of others, requires me to speak.

Mr. Lovejoy having decided on his course, the friends of law and order made their arrangements for the defense of his press. Personal violence or an attempt to murder him was not expected. It was supposed that the main effort, if any were made, would be to destroy the press as it was landed. We all felt that if once deposited in Godfrey and Gilman's store it would be safe. Great difficulty was encountered in obtaining a special constable to direct the friends of law in case of an attack, under the authority of the Mayor. The Mayor himself did not refuse to act; but as it might be inconvenient to find him when most needed, it was considered important to have one of the supporters of the press appointed as special constable on any sudden emergency. Though the Mayor acceded to the proposal, it was from time to time delayed, and finally it was not carried into effect. The Mayor, however, still consented to direct their movement when called upon.

On Monday, Mr. W. S. Gilman was informed that the press was at St. Louis on board a boat which would probably arrive at Alton about evening. He immediately sent an express to the captain of the boat requesting him to delay the hour of his arrival until three o'clock at night, in order to avoid an affray with the rioters. This movement was successful. The spies of the mob watched for the arrival of boats for some time; but late in the evening seemed to give up the expectation of any arrival that night, and retired.

Meantime the supporters of the press met at Mr. Gilman's store to the number of thirty or more; and, as before stated, organized themselves into a volunteer company according to law, and spent the night in the store. At the appointed hour the boat arrived, and the press was safely landed; the Mayor being present. All arrangements had been made with such judgment, and the men were stationed at such commanding points, that an attack would have been vain. But it was not made. A horn was indeed sounded, but no one came.

Shortly after the hour fixed on for the landing of the boat, Mr. Lovejoy arose and called me to go with him to see what was the result.

The moon had set and it was still dark, but day was near; and here and there a light was glimmering from the window of some sickroom or of some early riser. The streets were empty and silent, and the sounds of our feet echoed from the walls as we passed along. Little did he dream, at that hour, of the contest which the next night would witness: that these same streets would echo with the shouts of an infuriate mob, and be stained with his own heart's blood!

We found the boat there and the press in the warehouse; aided in raising it to the third story. We were all rejoiced that no conflict had ensued and that the press was safe; and all felt that the crisis was over. We were sure that the store could not be carried by storm by so few men as had ever yet acted in a mob; and though the majority of the citizens would not aid to defend the press we had no fear that they would aid in an attack. So deep was this feeling that it was thought that a small number was sufficient to guard the press afterward; and it was agreed that the company should be divided into sections of six, and take turns on successive nights. As they had been up all night, Mr. Lovejoy and myself offered to take charge of the press till morning, and they retired.

The morning soon began to dawn; and that morning I shall never forget. I passed through the scuttle to the roof and ascended to the highest point of the wall. The sky and the river were beginning to glow with approaching day, and the busy hum of business to be heard. I looked with exultation on the scenes below. I felt that a bloodless battle had been gained for God and for the truth; and that Alton was redeemed from eternal shame. And as all around grew brighter with approaching day, I thought of that still brighter sun, even now dawning on the world, and soon to bathe it with floods of glorious light.

Brother Lovejoy, too, was happy. He did not exult: he was tranquil and composed; but his countenance indicated the state of his mind. It was a calm and tranquil joy, for he trusted in God that the point was gained: that the banner of an unfettered press would soon wave over that mighty stream.

Vain hopes! How soon to be buried in a martyr's grave. Vain! did I say? No: they are not vain. Though dead he still speaketh; and a united world can never silence his voice. Ten thousand presses, had he employed them all, could never have done what the simple tale of his death will do. Up and down the mighty streams of the West his voice will go; it will penetrate the remotest corner of our land; it will be heard to the extremities of the civilized world. From henceforth no boat will pass the spot where he fell, heedless of his name, or of his sentiments, or of the cause for which he died. And if God in his mercy shall use this event to arouse a slumbering nation to maintain the right for which he died, he will look down from the throne of his glory on the scene of his martyrdom and say, "It is enough: truth is triumphant; the victory is gained."

We returned to his house, and before my departure we united in prayer. His wife, through weakness, had not risen. In her chamber we met in the last act of worship in which we were to unite on earth. I commended him and his family to the care of God. As I left her I cheered her with the hope that her days of trial were nearly over and that more tranquil hours were at hand. Cheered by these hopes I bade them and my other friends farewell, and began my journey homeward. On my way I heard passing rumors of a meditated attack on the store, but gave them no weight. The events of a few hours proved them but too well founded.

Of the tragic catastrophe I was not a spectator; but after careful inquiry of eyewitnesses I shall proceed to narrate the leading facts.

From the statement of the Mayor it seems that an attack was apprehended; and that the matter was laid before the common council, and that they did not deem it necessary to take any action on the subject.

On account of the fatigue and watching of the preceding night, most of the defenders of the press who were in the store the night before were absent; and others took their place. The number was larger than at first intended in consequence of an increased apprehension of an attack. Their apprehensions were realized. An attack was commenced at about ten o'clock at night.

In order to render the narrative more clear, it is necessary to say a few words concerning the structure and location of the store. It consisted of two long stone buildings, side by side, in one block, extending from the landing in Water Street back to Second Street; with doors and windows at each gable end, but with no windows at the sides. Hence it can be defended at the ends from within, but not at the sides. The roofs are of wood. The lots on each side being vacant, these stores form a detached block, accessible on every side.

About ten o'clock a mob, *already armed*, came and formed a line at the end of the store in Water Street, and hailed those within. Mr. Gilman opened the end door of the third story, and asked what they wanted. They demanded the press. He, of course, refused to give it up; and earnestly entreated them to use no violence. He told them that the property was committed to his care, and that they should defend it at the risk and sacrifice of their lives. At the same time they had no ill will against them, and should deprecate doing them an injury. One of them, a leading individual among the friends of free inquiry at the late convention, replied that they would have it at the sacrifice of their lives, and presented a pistol at him: upon which he retired.

They then went to the other end of the store and commenced an attack. They demolished two or three windows with stones and fired two or three guns. As those within threw back the stones, one without was distinctly recognized and seen taking aim at one within: for it was a moonlight evening, and persons could be distinctly seen and recognized.

A few guns were then fired by individuals from within, by which Lyman Bishop, one of the mob, was killed. The story that he was a mere stranger waiting for a boat, and that Mr. Lovejoy shot him, are alike incapable of proof. He was heard during the day, by a person in whose employ he was, to express his intention to join the mob.

After this the mob retired for a few moments, and then returned with ladders which they lashed together to make them the proper length, and prepared to set fire to the roof.

About this time the Mayor, having been informed of the riot, came on to the ground; but having few to sustain him, was unable to compel the rioters to desist by force. They requested him to go into the store, and state to its defenders that they were determined to have the press, and would not desist until they had accomplished their object; and agreed to suspend operations until his return. Attended by a Justice of the Peace, he entered and delivered the message of the mob.

Suppose now it had been delivered up by its defenders and destroyed. How remarkable the narrative must have been, of a press given up to the mob to be destroyed by the agency of the Mayor and a Justice of the Peace!

However, they did not give it up. Mr. Gilman requested the Mayor to call on certain citizens to see if they could not prevent the destruction of the building. He said he could not: he had used his official authority in vain. He then asked him whether he should continue to defend the property by arms. This the Mayor, as he had previously done, authorized him to do. The Mayor and the Justice were then informed that the press would not be given up, and the decision was by them communicated to the mob. They then proceeded to fire the roof, taking care to keep on the side of the store where they were secure from the fire of those within.

It now became evident to the defenders that their means of defense, so long as they remained with, was cut off; and nothing remained but to attack the assailants without. It was a hazardous step; but they determined to take it. A select number, of whom Mr. Lovejoy was one, undertook the work. They went out at the end, turned the corner, and saw one of the incendiaries on the ladder, and a number standing at the foot. They fired and it is supposed wounded, but did not kill him; and then, after continuing their fire some minutes and dispersing the mob, returned to load their guns. When they went out again no one was near the ladder, the assailants having so secreted themselves as to be able to fire, unseen, on the defenders of the press as they came out. No assailant being in sight Mr. Lovejoy stood, and was looking round. Yet, though he saw no assailant, the eye of his murderer was on him. The object of hatred, deep, malignant, and long continued, was fully before him—and the bloody tragedy was consummated. Five balls were lodged in his body, and he soon breathed his last. Yet after his mortal wound he had strength remaining to return to the building and ascend one flight of stairs before he fell and expired. They then attempted to capitulate, but were refused with curses by the mob, who threatened to burn the store and shoot them as they came out. Mr. Roff now determined at all hazards to go out and make some terms, but he was wounded as soon as he set his foot over the threshold.

The defenders then held a consultation. They were shut up within the building, unable to resist the ferocious mode of attack now adopted, and seemed devoted to destruction. At length Mr. West came to the door, informed them that the building was actually on fire, and urged them to escape by passing down the riverbank; saying that he would stand between them and the assailants so that if they fired they must fire on him. This was done. All but two or three marched out and ran down Water Street, being fired on by the mob as they went. Two, who were wounded, were left in the building, and one, who was not, remained to take care of the body of their murdered brother. The mob then entered, destroyed the press, and retired. Among them were seen some of those leading "friends of free inquiry" who had taken an active part in the convention.

Before these tragic scenes were ended, the streets were crowded with spectators. They came out to see the winding up of the plot, but not to aid in repressing violence or maintaining the law. The vote to aid the Mayor in suppressing violence they had refused to pass, because it was their duty to aid without it; and here we see how powerful their sense of duty was. The time of the conflict was from one hour and a half to two hours. During this time the bells were rung, and a general notice given; and yet none came to the rescue. It has been said, however, in extenuation of this inactivity that it was owing to a want of concert and arrangement among the citizens or by the police. No man knew on whom he might call to aid in suppressing the riot; and some who have professed that it was their desire to do so say that they were hindered by the apprehension that they might be only rallying the mob in the attempt to quell it.

The feelings exhibited by the mob were in keeping with the deed on which they were intent. Oaths, curses, blasphemy, and malignant yells broke upon the silence of the night as they prosecuted their work of death. But even passions so malignant were not enough to give them the hardihood and recklessness needed for their work. To drench conscience, blind reason, and arouse passion to its highest fury by the intoxicating cup was needed to fit them for the consummation of their work. The leaders in this business were adepts; they knew what means were adapted to their ends, and used them without stint or treason.

Thus closes a tragedy without parallel in the history of our land. In other popular excitements, there has been an equal amount of feeling: in some, blood has been shed. But never was there an avowed effort to overthrow the foundations of human society pushed to such bloody results: and that, on principles adapted so utterly to dissolve the social system, and plunge the nation into anarchy and blood.

SUGGESTIONS FOR
FURTHER READING

The special characteristics of the *Lowell Factory* are described in H.J. Habbakkuk, *American and British Technology in the 19th Century* (Cambridge, Eng. 1962). For a survey of the rise of industrialization in America informed by economic theory, see Douglas North, *Economic Growth in the United States, 1790–1860* (New York, 1966).

The most important works on the *Southern Plantations* include: Stanley Elkins, *Slavery* (Chicago, 1968, 2d. ed.) and Kenneth Stampp, *The Peculiar Institution* (New York, 1956). For a new view that is heavily based on quantitative techniques see, Robert Fogel and Stanley Engerman, *Time on the Cross* (Boston, 1974). A remarkably thorough account of slave life, more traditional in approach, is Eugene Genovese, *Roll, Jordan, Roll* (New York, 1974).

The nature of the *Frontier Community* is analyzed from a social science point of view in the collection of essays edited by Richard Hofstadter and Seymour Lipset, *Turner and the Sociology of the Frontier* (New York, 1968). A very detailed look at life in one American frontier community, based on quantitative materials, is Merle Curti, *The Making of an American Community* (Stanford, 1959).

The quality of the American *Common School* and the motives of its founders are analyzed in Michael Katz, *The Irony of Early School Reform* (Cambridge, Mass., 1968). Like Katz, Stanley Schultz, *The Culture Factory* (New York, 1973) is also suspicious of the benevolence of the program. For similarities between schools and custodial institutions see David J. Rothman, *The Discovery of the Asylum* (Boston, 1971).

The history of the *American Art Union* in particular and American artistic productions in general is imaginatively described in Neil Harris, *The Artist in American Society* (New York, 1966). A well-illustrated volume on the subject is Oliver Larkin's *Art and Life in America* (New York, 1949).

A revisionist collection of articles treating *Abolitionist Societies* is edited by Martin Duberman, *The Anti-Slavery Vanguard* (Princeton, 1965). Richard Hofstadter and Michael Wallace, *American Violence: A Documentary History* (New York, 1970) puts anti-abolitionist violence in a broader perspective. On anti-abolitionist mobs in particular see, Leonard Richards, *Gentlemen of Property and Standing* (New York, 1970).